Manager's Guide to Employee Engagement

Other titles in the Briefcase Books series include:

Customer Relationship Management by Kristin Anderson and Carol Kerr

Communicating Effectively by Lani Arredondo

Performance Management by Robert Bacal

Manager's Guide to Performance Reviews by Robert Bacal

Manager's Guide to Crisis Management by Jonathan Bernstein

Recognizing and Rewarding Employees by R. Brayton Bowen

Sales Techniques by Bill Brooks

Motivating Employees, Second Edition by Anne Bruce

Building a High Morale Workplace by Anne Bruce

Six Sigma for Managers by Greg Brue

Design for Six Sigma by Greg Brue and Robert G. Launsby

Manager's Guide to Marketing, Advertising, and Publicity by Barry Callen

Manager's Guide to Planning by Peter J. Capezio

Leadership Skills for Managers by Marlene Caroselli

Negotiating Skills for Managers by Steven P. Cohen

Effective Coaching, Second Edition by Marshall J. Cook and Laura Poole

Manager's Guide to Mentoring by Curtis J. Crawford

Conflict Resolution by Daniel Dana

Manager's Guide to Virtual Teams by Kimball Fisher and Mareen Fisher

The Manager's Guide to Business Writing, Second Edition by Suzanne D. Sparks Fitzgerald

Manager's Guide to Strategy by Roger A. Formisano

Project Management by Gary R. Heerkens

Budgeting for Managers by Sid Kemp and Eric Dunbar

Hiring Great People by Kevin C. Klinvex, Matthew S. O'Connell, and Christopher P. Klinvex

Manager's Guide to Social Media by Scott Klososky

Time Management by Marc Mancini

Manager's Guide to Fostering Innovation and Creativity in Teams by Charles Prather

Presentation Skills for Managers by Jennifer Rotondo and Mike Rotondo Jr.

Finance for Non-Financial Managers by Gene Siciliano

Skills for New Managers by Morey Stettner

Manager's Survival Guide by Morey Stettner

The Manager's Guide to Effective Meetings by Barbara J. Streibel

Managing Multiple Projects by Michael Tobis and Irene P. Tobis

Accounting for Managers by William H. Webster

To learn more about titles in the Briefcase Books series go to
www.briefcasebooks.com

Manager's Guide to Employee Engagement

Scott Carbonara

McGraw-Hill

New York Chicago San Francisco Lisbon
London Madrid Mexico City Milan New Delhi
San Juan Seoul Singapore Sydney Toronto

The **McGraw·Hill** Companies

1 2 3 4 5 6 7 8 9 0 QFR/QFR 1 8 7 6 5 4 3 2

ISBN   978-0-07-179950-8
MHID   0-07-179950-8

e-ISBN   978-0-07-179951-5
e-MHID   0-07-179951-6

This is a CWL Publishing Enterprises book developed for McGraw-Hill by CWL Publishing Enterprises, Inc., Madison, Wisconsin, www.cwlpub.com.

McGraw-Hill books are available at special quantity discounts to use as premiums and sales promotions, or for use in corporate training programs. To contact a representative, please e-mail us at bulksales@mcgraw-hill.com.

This book is printed on acid-free paper.

Contents

Preface   ix

Acknowledgments   xiii

1. **The Case for Employee Engagement**   **1**
   Yesterday and Today   1
   Satisfaction Isn't Enough: Survival vs. "Thrival"   2
   Engagement Defined   7
   The Bruno Effect   8
   What Engages Employees?   10
   Engagement Business Case—The Hard Facts   14
   Two Employee Engagement Myths   17
   High Attrition = Low Engagement x Poor Leadership   22
   Why Engage?   24
   Manager's Checklist for Chapter 1   25

2. **Are You a Manager or a Leader? Becoming the "Best Boss Ever"**   **26**
   Would Your Employees Drive Through a Blizzard for You?   27
   Manager vs. Leader   27
   "I Knew It Was Time to Leave When ..."   29
   Two Views of Human Nature: Theory X and Theory Y   30
   Engagement Starts with "I Do"   35
   The Engagement Wheel: Awareness, Alignment, Action   36
   Becoming the "Best Boss Ever"   37
   W.H.I.P. Your Employees into Engagement   42
   Fostering Loyalty, Trust, and Hope   42
   Pay It Forward: Invest in Training   48
   The Importance of the Leader-Employee Relationship   49
   Manager's Checklist for Chapter 2   52

3. The ABCs of Engagement: Why People Do What They Do   53

People Do What They Do Because ...   54

The ABC Model   57

Antecedents: Leading the Horse to Water ...   58

The Top Engagement Antecedent:
  Defining Clear Expectations   60

What Makes Consequences Effective?   64

Two Consequences That Kill Engagement:
  Extinction and Punishment   67

When Punishment Is in Order   71

Using the ABCs Builds Trust   72

Give 'Em a Reason to Engage! Positive
  and Negative Reinforcement   74

The Discretionary Effort Advantage:
  Positive Reinforcement   78

Manager's Checklist for Chapter 3   84

4. A Positive Culture Starts Here: Positive Thinking   85

Finding Opportunity Amid Calamity   86

A Case for Positivity   88

Pragmatic vs. Positive   91

"I'm Too Smart to Believe That It Matters to the End
  Results" Why Smarter Managers Embrace Positivity   91

"I Can't Change Who I Am ... Or Can I?"   93

Look in the Mirror: Are You a Positive
  "Super Model" Leader?   96

10 Activities to Increase Your Positive Thinking   99

Safeguard Your Attitude with Boundaries   104

Thinking Your Way into an Engaged Culture   108

Manager's Checklist for Chapter 4   110

5. Empowering Employees to Act as Entrepreneurial Owners 112

What If This Were Your Company?   113

Replace Bureaucracy with Ownership   114

The Entrepreneurial Advantage   115

C.O.U.R.S.E.: The 6 Core Traits of an Entrepreneur   115

Grant Appropriate Control and Autonomy   123

What Does This Have to Do with Engagement?   124

Empower Employees to Be Owners, Not Renters   126

Ownership Is Like an "LTR"   127

Fostering a Culture of Entrepreneurial Engagement   129
Autonomy, Complexity, and an Effort-Reward Connection   130
But What If They Leave—With All Their Creative Ideas?
  Handling the Fear of Talent Abandonment   134
Manager's Checklist for Chapter 5   134

6. **Aligning Employee and Organizational Values,**
   Missions, and Goals   **136**
   What Values Are and Why They Matter to Engagement   137
   Revisit Your Values, Goals, and Mission Statements   140
   Brand Your Values   141
   Create Learning Maps to Get at the Mission   144
   Where Do Goals Fit In?   145
   Bringing the Employee into the Mission   148
   What If the Company's Mission and the Employee's
     Mission Don't Align?   150
   Aligning to Goals by Getting Employees in on the Action 151
   Engaging Through Social Service   152
   Manager's Checklist for Chapter 6   155

7. **Know Your Employees: Get PSST (Personal,**
   Strengths-Based, Social, and Targeted)   **156**
   Get PSST!   156
   Passion and On-the-Job Performance   158
   Get Personal   161
   Get Strengths-Based   167
   What a Focus on Strengths Gets You   171
   Get Social   173
   Get Targeted   177
   Manager's Checklist for Chapter 7   180

8. **Communication: The Art of Asking Others to Dance**   **181**
   What Communication Is and Isn't   181
   The Three I's of Communication   185
   Communication Is Hard: Four Roadblocks
     to Effective Communication   187
   Cost of Communication: Even Good
     Communication Isn't Cheap   193
   Engagement-Building Communication Tips   195
   Manager's Checklist for Chapter 8   205

**9. Tickling the Engagement Bone: Stimulating Happiness
   with Humor, Fun, and Exercise at Work**   **206**
   Discretionary Effort in Action   207
   The Engagement Bone   208
   People Don't Quit Jobs That Provide Well-Being—
      Promoting Happiness at Work   209
   Are You Serious? A Scientific Case for Humor   211
   Humor and the Engagement Tie   214
   When Happiness Doesn't Come Naturally—
      Using Humor and Fun as Survival Tools   217
   Strengthening Relationships Through Humor   219
   Why Managers Might Avoid Humor   222
   Ignite a Culture of Humor and Fun by Minding Your P's   225
   Tricks and Tips for Promoting Fun   226
   Exercise as a Means of Fun and Relationship Building   230
   Manager's Checklist for Chapter 9   232

10. Tackling Barriers to Engagement   **234**
   What's In It For Me (WIIFM)?   234
   The Goal: To Flourish   235
   Special Circumstance #1: My Boss Is
      a Barrier to Engagement   236
   Special Circumstance #2: Change Is Hindering
      Employee Engagement   240
   Special Circumstance #3: The Business
      Backdrop Hampers Engagement   246
   Special Circumstance #4: Engaging Remote Employees   249
   Special Circumstance #5: Engaging the Unengageable   251
   In Conclusion: Starting the Dance   258
   Manager's Checklist for Chapter 10   259

Index   **261**

Preface

Depending on how long you've been in management, you may have seen various management programs come to stay—and others go. Do you remember or still practice some of these?

- Management by Objectives (MBO)
- Matrix Management
- Management by Walking Around
- One-Minute Management
- Total Quality Management
- Theory Z
- Reengineering
- Knowledge Management
- Six Sigma

These programs were designed to find some sort of efficiency, either by fixing the things that didn't work well or maximizing the things that did. And each of these programs was designed to strengthen a company's bottom line. Some are still used heavily today, while others have been almost forgotten.

What about the concept of *employee engagement*—which has become increasingly popular over the last several years? Is employee engagement just another corporate buzzword about which in 20 years we'll laugh and say, "I can't believe that I ever believed that stuff!?"

I doubt it. The study of employee engagement is closely linked to the expanding research in a growing movement known as positive psychology. As Shawn Achor points out in *The Happiness Advantage* (Crown Business, 2010), up until the late 1990s, the field of psychology studied people with problems—the most broken, dysfunctional people—17 times for every one study that attempted to discover why people functioned and thrived at the most optimal levels.

The growing body of research suggests that employee engagement isn't a fad, nor are its strategies based on unproven theories. Rather, employee engagement research is growing rapidly. It has begun to pinpoint what drives employees to do more than show up for work to receive a paycheck. In fact, much of the employee engagement findings carry encouraging news for companies and managers: Engagement strategies can be learned, applied, and maximized to unleash the discretionary effort that employees have within their personal reservoirs.

Leader, wouldn't you love to see your employees do more than *show up* for work to give you a day's work for a day's pay? How would you like your employees to:

- Give you their hearts and minds when they come to work?
- Stick with you and your company even when they have other employment options?
- Drive through a blizzard to get to work instead of leaving you short and in a bind?
- Get excited about you, your customers, and the goals and mission of your organization?
- Give you personal and professional loyalty?
- Share their most brilliant, creative business ideas and suggestions with you?
- Treat the business like they're co-owners?
- Contribute to making your workplace culture one that flourishes?

I hope that's why you picked up this book and are reading the Preface right now. Leader, you have more control over employee engagement than you might know. You can help your employees and workplace culture flourish. It's not complicated, but it requires that you learn what engages your employees and apply it by creating an environment that unleashes the power of a passionate, engaged workforce.

The purpose of this book is to provide you with a practical employee engagement guide—a How-To of sorts. Along the way, I'll point out why engagement makes sense from a business standpoint, as well as what you personally stand to gain from it. No, I'm not asking you to put forth the effort to engage your employees without offering you something in return. So here's my guarantee: If you practice these engagement-building concepts with your employees, *you will become a more engaged and effective leader*. If you don't, you can revert to your pre-engagement practices and get all your mediocre employee engagement back. Deal?

As a final note, let me warn you that while this book contains direct improvement tips, it also includes stories. As a leader, I have a bias that says, "Lessons last longer when they are learned in story form." Yes, I'll share facts and figures. But be prepared to see stories throughout that are designed to pull you in, give you relevant examples on how things work, and reinforce key learning points.

Special Features

The idea behind the books in the Briefcase Series is to give you practical information written in a friendly, person-to-person style. The chapters deal with tactical issues and include lots of examples. They also feature numerous sidebars designed to give you different types of specific information. Here's a description of the sidebars you'll find in this book.

KEY TERM

Every subject has some jargon, including this one, dealing with engaging employees. These sidebars provide definitions of terms and concepts as they are introduced.

SMART

MANAGING

These sidebars do just what their name suggests: give you tips for using the ideas in this book to intelligently apply the strategies and tactics that will reduce costs, improve productivity, and create a positive workplace for all employees.

Tricks of the Trade sidebars give you insider how-to hints on techniques managers use to execute the practices described in this book.

It's always useful to have examples that show how the principles in the book are applied. These sidebars describe situations and companies that help you understand the benefits of employee engagement.

Caution sidebars provide warnings for where things could go wrong when implementing the practices described in this book and things you should be aware of to prevent problems.

How can you ensure you won't make a mistake when you're trying to implement the techniques the book describes? You can't completely, but these sidebars give you practical advice on how to minimize the possibility of things going wrong.

This icon identifies sidebars where you'll find specific procedures and techniques you can use to successfully implement the book's principles and practices.

Acknowledgments

Writing a book is a labor of love—with moments of hate sprinkled in for good measure. The process can be simultaneously exciting, dynamic, and thrilling as well as overwhelming, humbling, and discouraging. Purely from a philosophical standpoint, it stands to reason that without some darkness, we can never fully appreciate the light.

On that note, I owe a debt of gratitude to those who kept my world bright while writing this book; any periods of darkness were brief.

Professionally, I am grateful to John Woods of CWL Publishing Enterprises and McGraw-Hill for giving me the opportunity to write a book in the Briefcase Books series. I had read several books in the popular, successful series before John contacted me to write *Manager's Guide to Employee Engagement*. Today, I am honored to be part of this series, and John, I am grateful for the support you gave me along the way.

Another part of my professional support network is friend, author, and speaker Anne Bruce (www.annebruce.com), who first introduced me to the Briefcase Books series by asking me to contribute a few thoughts in her own books. Anne, thank you for making the introduction to the excellent team at Briefcase Books. You are the consummate role model of what it means to mentor others who are newer to the field, and I am in your debt. I look forward to working with you in the future!

Additionally, I appreciate these other friends who took turns holding the light for me as I wrote this book: engagement guru Doug McKinley (www.tmgleader.com) for sharing his insight and expertise with me over the last few years; Marlene Chism (www.marlenechism.com) for listening and helping me stay drama-free while I wrote; Craig Wortmann (www.salesengine.com) for his years of friendship, coaching, and mentoring; Ken Grant (www.ken-grant.com), for sharing stories and a few laughs with me; Linda Dulye (www.dulye.com) who consulted with me many moons ago as I began learning the connection between communication and engagement; my former boss and mentor, Ray Angeli, who served as the preeminent role model on how to unleash engagement. If this book falls short in any area, the fault lies with me and not the example Ray set for me; and finally, president, founder, and my business partner at Spiritus Communications (www.spirituscommunications.com), Jocelyn Godfrey, who provided me with critical insight and endless encouragement. Beyond your talents as a gifted entrepreneur and business expert, I'm most grateful that you agreed to become Jocelyn Carbonara during the writing process.

Finally, I want to thank every employee I've ever had the opportunity to serve throughout my career. I appreciate your patience with me as I grew from manager to leader. You were my engagement *guinea pigs*! Thank you for the lessons you taught me and the laughter you shared with me through each of my successes and failures.

Manager's Guide to Employee Engagement

The Case for Employee Engagement

Picture this. An old steam locomotive chugs and lumbers along the ravine—belching black billows of smoke from its stack. Long before the rise of the approaching mountain, the engineer bellows for the boilerman to pick up steam—increasing the train's speed by adding fuel.

To comply, the boilerman scoops shovels of coal into the firebox. Soon, the black coal turns to red embers, and soot and ash fill the smokestack. The heat from the firebox radiates outward, and several times the boilerman has to step back to catch his breath away from the extreme temperature and the heavy, acrid smoke.

But within minutes, his efforts are rewarded. The steam pressure rises to a level sufficient for the train's engineer to maintain a steady speed up the side of the mountain pass. To reward himself, the boilerman puts his shovel down, takes several sips of water from his canteen, and leans back to take a well-earned rest.

Yesterday and Today

Steam locomotives were a simple mode of transportation for travelers of yesteryear. To keep moving, the locomotive required at least two people and a fuel source. One served as an engineer, or driver. The engineer kept his eyes on the train's speed and the rise and fall of the land. And of course, the engineer controlled when the train started and stopped along the route. Think of this person as the boss on the train. The other key person was the boilerman, or fireman, whose job entailed monitoring steam and boiler pressures and, of course, feeding the firebox with fuel, usually coal.

Steam locomotives are a metaphor for corporations of yesteryear. Like steam locomotives, companies of the past traditionally had an autocratic boss, the person in charge who made all the important decisions. To keep on track, the boss needed a crew to focus more on the day-to-day tasks, so he employed managers to keep the company moving.

But neither the boss nor the managers could power the business alone. They needed fuel, not just of the literal type, but also in the form of people. In good times, the boss hired more employees to produce steam. Employees, like coal, were viewed as renewable resources, and they were added to projects by the shovelful whenever the business required more speed.

That was yesterday. Things are different today.

Think about your company and your current challenges. Many leaders in various industries have heard messages similar to these over the last couple of years:

- Your team needs to increase productivity . . .
- Your budget's getting cut again next year . . .
- We're currently evaluating various cost reduction options, and your department keeps coming up . . .
- You need to lower your headcount . . .

Regardless of how the message is framed, most leaders concede that they understand one central point: I need to do more with less!

That's today's business reality. As a leader, you have two options. You can find a way to maximize the performance of your employees, or you can step aside and let someone else do it. I'm guessing you don't view failure as an option, so that leaves you with maximizing the performance of your employees.

Satisfaction Isn't Enough: Survival vs. "Thrival"

If you want to maximize performance, you can't settle for satisfied employees. Satisfaction isn't enough. You don't want employees to merely *survive* at work. You want them to *thrive*.

The Satisfaction Conundrum

On a cold winter morning in 1975, I sat in the kitchen of my family's home with my father, my Uncle Wes, and my Uncle Wade. The talk hovered over my head most of the time as the men discussed topics like world affairs and the state of the U.S. economy. But finally the conversation hit on a topic I understood: jobs and work. Even though I was a child, I'd already held a paper route and routinely shoveled snow in the neighborhood to supplement my meager allowance of 50¢ per week.

So at least in a simplistic way, I understood the nature of work and I was gratified when Uncle Wes pulled me into the discussion.

"Scott, I'm going to tell you what I tell my own boys," he intoned solemnly. "When you find a job, go to work for a big company—one that's stable and pays a decent wage. Show up for work each day and don't give the boss a reason to yell at you. Then, maybe after 30 years, you can retire and go fishing."

"He's right," my Uncle Wade confirmed. "In another 10 years or so, we'll be fishing every day," he said with a nod to Wes.

It wasn't until I'd had a few real jobs of my own that I recognized that what my uncles described to me back in 1975 about their jobs formed a puzzle of sorts—but one that would only be assembled over time. Over the years, I connected additional pieces to this puzzle and came to this conclusion: My uncles depicted *satisfied employees* for their generation—in that they received paychecks for the jobs they did. They were *surviving* at work. They did not, however, represent *engaged employees* for our current climate—in which employees not only show up and get paid, but also feel connected, inspired, and motivated to give beyond their mere roles. My uncles were not *thriving* at work.

Why isn't it enough to create merely satisfied employees? Here are three reasons:

1. Satisfaction is situation-based—prone to change with circumstances. When things are going right with

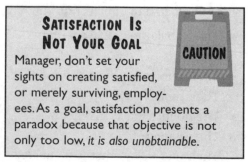

SATISFACTION IS NOT YOUR GOAL CAUTION
Manager, don't set your sights on creating satisfied, or merely surviving, employees. As a goal, satisfaction presents a paradox because that objective is not only too low, *it is also unobtainable.*

Satisfied All the online dictionaries I perused included this definition of *satisfied*: Filled with satisfaction (i.e., the fulfillment or gratification of a desire, need, or appetite); being content.

KEY TERM   Satisfaction is hygiene level, a passive state of contentment. Satisfied people aren't ambassadors or cheerleaders; rather, satisfied people are merely *not actively discontent at the moment*.

No definition of satisfied that I researched included words like loyal, devoted, dedicated, committed, passionate, or excited.

Now ask yourself: Do you really want *satisfied* employees?

the world, most people are satisfied. But when things are going poorly, people get dissatisfied.

2. Much of what dissatisfies your employees as people falls outside your direct control.

3. Satisfaction doesn't drive people to want more or give more; rather, it motivates them to maintain the status quo.

Satisfaction Isn't Sustainable

There's a long list of qualities that create satisfied or dissatisfied people. Feelings of satisfaction or dissatisfaction have a way of spreading from one part of our lives to others. At any given time, each of us juggles our desires for satisfaction.

SMART

STRIVE FOR MORE

Satisfaction is nice in a relationship. But it's situation-based, meaning it can change from interaction to interaction, from moment to moment. Satisfaction is temporary.

MANAGING

So ask yourself: *As a leader, how much power do you have to remove potential dissatisfiers associated with things taking place outside of the office?* For your employees—or even your closest friends—what kind of power do you have over their satisfaction with . . .

- The global or national economy?
- Traffic?
- Their physical appearance?
- Their monthly bills?
- The political party in office?
- The weather?
- Their marital or other personal relationship issues?

You see the point. Too many potential dissatisfiers occur in areas outside your immediate control as a manager. If your job description included "satisfy your employees," you couldn't do it thoroughly or consistently. It's simply not always within your power to create satisfaction. But as leaders, keep in mind these two important facts:

1. The attitudes your employees hold toward these uncontrollable factors come to work with them each day.

2. Leaders can greatly shape the general fulfillment levels of their employees, at least during work hours.

FULFILLMENT IS THE GOAL **SMART**

Yes, leaders, you can contribute to the satisfaction levels of employees. But don't make satisfaction your goal. Instead, **MANAGING** strive to promote fulfillment—or thriving—in the areas you can influence and control. Later in the book, we refer to this as a state of *flourishing*.

According to MetLife's *9th Annual Study of Employee Benefits Trends: A Blueprint for the New Benefits Economy* (MetLife, 2011), employee satisfaction and employee loyalty have declined over the last few years.

During the economic downturn, many companies kicked into survival mode, and the mantra for many organizations became a chant: Don't sink! To stay afloat, companies tried to cut costs. Since the biggest operating expenses are often employee pay and benefits, employees were let go.

In many cases, remaining employees were asked to put in more hours—absorbing the work done by terminated employees. Some organizations even cut employee pay and benefits; others kept pay at the same level but offered no raises or even cost-of-living adjustments—something that employees had grown to expect in a robust economy. Most incentives and extras were axed.

As a final insult, when the economic news couldn't seem to get any worse, nightly news reports repeated top stories about government bailouts as well as senior executives receiving stock options and millions of dollars in bonuses. The same news shared stories about average people losing their jobs to downsizing and their homes to foreclosure.

Many leaders shifted their focus from corporate thriving to personal survival, and spent little thought on retaining and nurturing existing employees. *But that's okay, isn't it? I mean, in a bad economy, one positive outcome is that employees can't go anywhere, right? It's not like they can quit, can they?*

Wrong.

The same MetLife study concluded that one in three employees hopes to be working somewhere else in the next 12 months. That means one of every three of your own employees is fueling up his or her escape pod at this very moment. Where are they going? Who knows. But you need to be aware that they want out of the job they are in today. And do you know what's even worse? Some of your best employees are flight risks. That's right, your employees with the most marketable, up-to-date skills—those who are sustaining your company during this downturn—are possibly the ones who are looking to leave you.

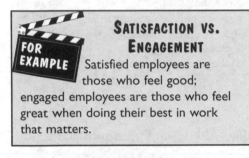

SATISFACTION VS. ENGAGEMENT

Satisfied employees are those who feel good; engaged employees are those who feel great when doing their best in work that matters.

In summary, employee satisfaction is down, and you as a manager can do little to improve it since so many of the drivers for employee satisfaction are beyond your personal control.

Satisfaction isn't enough, and it isn't sustainable. It's often out of your reach to satisfy your employees, and even if you could accomplish that goal, any resulting gain would be short lived because satisfaction is situation-based. But you can ask for and develop something even better: engaged employees.

SMART MANAGING

FIND NEW CONNECTIONS

The world has changed, and employee issues are different—and in some ways, more difficult—than they used to be. Smart leaders don't use the changes in the world, the economy, the country, the industry, or even the company as excuses for not learning new ways to connect with employees. Rather, smart leaders find new ways to address these challenges, seeing them as opportunities to dig deep and engage new skills.

Engagement Defined

Amit managed a small sales team in a manufacturing company in a western suburb of Chicago. As the company grew, Amit recognized he needed to move away from direct sales so he could focus on the bigger picture. With the approval of the company president, Amit hired two sales employees at the same time: Glenda and Jim.

Both employees earned business degrees from the University of Illinois within two years of one another. Both had experience making cold calls with large manufacturing companies as well as smaller niche firms. According to their résumés, both personally generated more than $1 million in sales over the previous year. And when they had lunch in downtown Naperville at Lou Malnati's Pizzeria, both Glenda and Jim preferred the Chicago deep-dish pizza.

That's where their similarities ended.

Glenda consistently arrived first at the office each morning. She brewed a pot of coffee, followed up on e-mails from the previous evening, updated the work plan for the day that she had drafted before leaving the night before, and started making calls to the East Coast—all before Amit got to his desk at 8 a.m.! Glenda had already reached her second quarter sales goals by the end of the first quarter. With her relatively low salary of $40,000 on top of huge sales commissions she had already earned, Amit believed that Glenda would earn almost what he made for that calendar year.

"Which is fine by me," Amit thought with admiration. "I wish I had a team of Glendas!"

Sadly, Amit didn't have a team of Glendas. He had a team of one Glenda—and one Jim.

Jim couldn't be more unlike Glenda. He arrived each morning around 9 a.m.—rarely sooner and often later. Since the office worked on flex time, Amit never cared much about when his employees arrived or left for the day. However, Jim's sales numbers were dismal. Amit knew that each salesperson needed to bring in at least $100,000 annually in sales to pay their own salaries, benefits, and office space. Jim was costing the company money instead of contributing to its success.

KEY TERM   **Engagement** Refers to the level of dedication, commitment, passion, innovation, and emotional energy a person is willing to expend. An engaged employee gives of their discretionary effort while demonstrating what subjectively might be called *happiness*. An engaged employee doesn't rely on a situation to stimulate satisfaction, but instead finds fulfillment in his or her work role.

"The two of them looked so similar on paper, but they couldn't be more different," Amit lamented. "What I wouldn't give to have a team of Glendas!"

You probably wish you had a team of Glendas, too. So what's the difference? Why are some employees like Glenda and others like Jim?

It's all about engagement.

Lord Currie, former chair of the office of communications and dean of Cass Business School in London, captured the essence of the word with this description: "You sort of smell it, don't you, that engagement of people as people. What goes on in meetings, how people talk to each other. You get the sense of energy, engagement, commitment, belief in what the organisation stands for" (David McLeod & Chris Brady, *The Extra Mile: How to Engage Your People to Win*, UK: Prentice Hall, 2008).

KEY TERM   **Discretionary effort** At its core, this is the margin between the effort someone is capable of applying to a task and the minimal effort required merely to make do.

While satisfaction describes *what people are feeling*, engagement explains *what people are doing and how they're doing it*.

The Bruno Effect

Figure 1-1 illustrates the effect of discretionary effort on any sort of behavior, such as productive work performance or engagement. The baseline portion of the graph depicts the current performance level before any intervention or change is introduced. The intervention portion shows what takes place once a consequence is delivered (such as negative or positive reinforcement, which is explained in Chapter 2). Minimal standards represents the lowest acceptable level you will tolerate before you're tempted to use punishment.

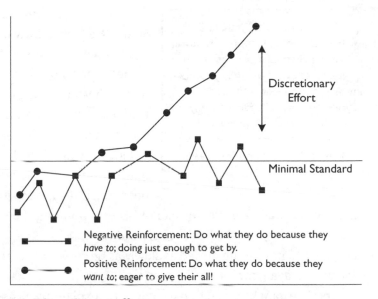

Figure 1-1. Discretionary effort

Years ago, I had a Yorkshire terrier named Bruno who loved me with all his little heart. When I'd call him, he would run as fast as his legs would carry him until he found me. Then his tail would wag and wag, and his ears would perk up—perfectly tuned to my voice. His eyes would get all shiny, and he would run and jump in front of me until I picked him up and kissed him. That's how Bruno responded when he was happy to see me. That's how Bruno acted when he *wanted to* come to me.

One time, Bruno found something nasty and he rolled in it. Without going into much detail, let me just say that a black bear had deposited something not far from my back door, and Bruno hoped that by rolling in it, he could mask his scent and thereby effectively stalk, hunt, and kill the animal that encroached on the inner sanctum of the yard.

After Bruno replaced his doggy scent with bear filth, he set off in pursuit of the interloper. Fearing that Bruno wouldn't be the winner if these two met, I intervened.

"Bruno! Stop! No!" I ordered sharply.

Bruno showed some signs of internal conflict. Instinct told him to hunt; his master told him to stop. After a few more sharp calls and one-word commands like "Come!" Bruno complied.

LOSE THE SNOOZE

Few children sleep in until noon on Christmas morning. When you're engaged in what you do, you similarly don't want a snooze button on your alarm clock. Do you rely on the snooze button every morning? If so, ask yourself if it's because you love to sleep ... or is it that you aren't excited about going to work?

But how did he comply? Slowly. He inched forward one small paw at a time. As he came, I don't think his eyes were shiny, but I can't be sure. He looked at the ground and not at me. His tail not only failed to wag, but I could hardly find a trace of it because it dropped so low between his legs it was invisible. Instead of his ears pointing the way to me, they stood plastered to the back of his head.

Bruno came to me, but he moved as slowly as he could move without risking me yelling again for him to "Come!"

For years, I've taught discretionary effort by explaining it as "The Bruno Effect"—the difference between how quickly Bruno's legs would carry him when he was happy to see me and how slowly he would move when he was simply trying to *avoid punishment*.

What Engages Employees?

Gallup interviewed employees from across the globe in virtually every industry to find out what factors contribute most to employee engagement. With the results, Gallup created a list of engagement questions they called the Q12 Index. From their research, an employee who can answer an extreme *yes* to these 12 questions is both a high performer as well as highly engaged. Review the Q12 Index in the sidebar, as I refer to the questions periodically as we introduce engagement concepts.

Many organizations use employee engagement survey firms to develop and administer employee surveys—many of which are based on the Q12—and then interpret that survey data for the company leaders. I've developed these surveys myself in the workplace and still do in my consulting practice. But even if your company doesn't use a formal survey tool, you can evaluate the engagement levels of your employees based on nothing more than observation.

Engagement occurs on a continuum—a sliding scale. In other words,

---

GALLUP'S Q12 INDEX

Read through the list below. Ask yourself, "How would my employees answer these questions?"

TOOLS

1. Do you know what's expected of you at work?
2. Do you have the materials and equipment to do your work right?
3. At work, do you have the opportunity to do what you do best every day?
4. In the last seven days, have you received recognition or praise for doing good work?
5. Does your supervisor, or someone at work, seem to care about you as a person?
6. Is there someone at work who encourages your development?
7. At work, do your opinions seem to count?
8. Does the mission/purpose of your company make you feel your job is important?
9. Are your associates (fellow employees) committed to doing quality work?
10. Do you have a best friend at work?
11. In the last six months, has someone at work talked to you about your progress?
12. In the last year, have you had opportunities to learn and grow?

Gallup.com

---

an employee can be more than simply engaged or not. You might have employees who seem fulfilled around certain tasks or parts of their work while remaining negative or downright toxic when it comes to other components of the job.

In Gallup's groundbreaking 1999 book, *First, Break All the Rules*, authors Marcus Buckingham and Curt Coffman published the results of interviews from 10 million employees in 114 countries on the topic of engagement and performance. In the United States—the country with the highest engagement scores—Gallup found interesting and disturbing results about the state of employee engagement. According to their often-cited research:

- 29 percent of employees are engaged
- 55 percent of employees are not engaged
- 16 percent of employees are actively not engaged

    Again, not everyone fits into a tidy category. On your team, expect to

AM I WATCHING SOMEONE WHO'S ENGAGED?

TOOLS

Watching an employee is one simple way to find out if he or she is engaged at work. Think of a particular employee you've worked with for some time who performs well. Next to the 11 items below, use the following scale to evaluate that employee.

1–Never; 2–Occasionally; 3–Often; 4–Consistently

The employee I'm thinking about is characterized by ...

_____ 1. Saying *yes* to new challenges and opportunities
_____ 2. Taking time to learn new skills
_____ 3. Showing up for work physically, mentally, and emotionally
_____ 4. Giving a little extra whether helping a customer or a coworker
_____ 5. Pushing hard in the face of obstacles
_____ 6. Coming in early or staying late
_____ 7. Volunteering for additional projects or assignments
_____ 8. Accomplishing more in their workweeks than average employees
_____ 9. Exhibiting a can-do attitude
_____ 10. Getting along with nearly everyone in the office
_____ 11. Representing both you and your company well
_____ Total

Total the numbers. If you come up with a total over 30, there's a good chance you're observing someone with a high engagement level.

KEY TERMS

Engaged Employees who are *engaged* give their best by demonstrating not only a zeal for the work, but also a strong affinity for their company. Years ago, engaged employees may have gone by names such as "high potentials" or "movers and shakers." Whatever name they go by, leaders know them by their can-do attitudes and their outstanding results.

Not engaged *Not engaged* employees periodically "check out" and seem to go through the motions at work by punching the clock and collecting a paycheck. They can be described as those who do what's expected of them—rarely more, sometimes less.

Actively disengaged *Actively disengaged* employees actively hurt their companies. They often appear hostile and they act miserable at work by undermining the efforts of their company, leaders, and coworkers.

---

see variants—like the employees who seem on fire one day and switched off the next. What's less important than the exact name or percentage of employees in a particular bucket is the cost associated with their engagement levels.

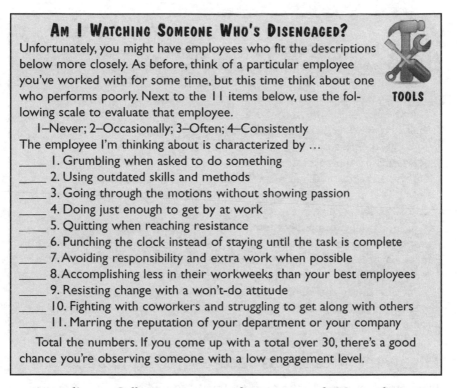

AM I WATCHING SOMEONE WHO'S DISENGAGED?

Unfortunately, you might have employees who fit the descriptions below more closely. As before, think of a particular employee you've worked with for some time, but this time think about one who performs poorly. Next to the 11 items below, use the following scale to evaluate that employee.

1–Never; 2–Occasionally; 3–Often; 4–Consistently

The employee I'm thinking about is characterized by ...

____ 1. Grumbling when asked to do something
____ 2. Using outdated skills and methods
____ 3. Going through the motions without showing passion
____ 4. Doing just enough to get by at work
____ 5. Quitting when reaching resistance
____ 6. Punching the clock instead of staying until the task is complete
____ 7. Avoiding responsibility and extra work when possible
____ 8. Accomplishing less in their workweeks than your best employees
____ 9. Resisting change with a won't-do attitude
____ 10. Fighting with coworkers and struggling to get along with others
____ 11. Marring the reputation of your department or your company

Total the numbers. If you come up with a total over 30, there's a good chance you're observing someone with a low engagement level.

According to Gallup, an average of 71 percent of U.S. employees are not actively engaged (Nikki Blacksmith & Jim Harter, "Majority of American Workers Not Engaged in Their Jobs," (Gallup.com, 2011). If you were to survey your employees, you might find that your actual number may be a little higher or a little lower. The number is not as important as these questions:

1. What percent of your employees need to be engaged for you to meet or exceed your departmental goals? Can you do it with 10 percent? How about 20 percent? Maybe 30 percent?
2. What do you think you could accomplish if you were to double that number? How about triple?

I hope I'm getting your attention. It's not a fantasy to consider doubling your engagement level. You can greatly increase it by being the right kind of leader and doing the right things.

ENGAGEMENT: YOU KNOW IT WHEN YOU SEE IT

U. S. Supreme Court Justice Potter Stewart, in the decision for *Jacobellis v. Ohio* regarding what constitutes pornography (1964), uttered these famous words: "I know it when I see it."

In that sense, when you see an engaged employee at work, you know it. They are the ones who show up for work—not only physically by placing their butts in their seats, but also mentally and emotionally.

Engaged employees aren't content to punch a clock. They invest their hearts, minds, and best efforts in their work. They see opportunities where others see obstacles. Their attitudes demonstrate *I can* instead of *I won't* or *I can't.* They tackle new assignments by saying "Yes" and "I'll take care of it," instead of "No, I can't, because …"

Do you want to identify these employees quickly? If you had to pick one employee to get things done the right way the first time when it mattered most, chances are the person you choose would be one of your engaged employees. Do you want to gauge the engagement level of your entire team? If you feel safe being out of the office for a couple of days or even weeks, it's because you have a team of engaged employees who deliver the same exceptional level of performance whether or not you're around.

Engagement Business Case—The Hard Facts

But before getting into the how-to, I want to make sure you understand what's at stake. Employee engagement is like the law of gravity. Both are natural phenomenon by which physical bodies are attracted to one another. The law of gravity describes what keeps the Earth orbiting around the Sun; employee engagement describes what keeps employees orbiting around you and your company! But I'm getting ahead of myself.

Employee engagement is not soft. If I had it within my power, I would change the use of the word *soft* so that it would stop getting added to form new words like *soft skills* or *soft training.* Used in that sense, soft connotes that what follows can't be quantified—making it sound like something is nice to have rather than business-relevant and imperative.

No, engagement is not soft. It can be both quantified and qualified. I suggest that anything capable of making or losing money for a company is business-relevant and imperative!

Consider the following facts about engaged employees:

- Engaged employees have lower turnover than disengaged employees. In other words, engaged employees demonstrate a higher degree of company loyalty and are less likely to jump ship if they get a better offer from another organization.

- Engaged employees take less sick time and have lower absenteeism than disengaged employees. Does it seem like your employees are sick a lot? Maybe they need to wash their hands more often. Or maybe they're just not engaged.

- Engaged employees increase customer loyalty. Beyond merely knowing how to satisfy customers, engaged employees become customer advocates to the point that they actually increase customer loyalty levels. If your customers are leaving, maybe your products are stale or your prices aren't competitive. Or maybe your employees aren't engaged.

- Engaged employees are more productive than disengaged employees. No, it's not your imagination. Your most engaged employees vastly outperform your lesser engaged employees (Gallup Employee Engagement Survey, 2003). It seems that happiness matters when it comes to engagement as well as job performance.

- Engaged employees recover faster when their companies go through times of change and people get caught up thinking about themselves. Corporate change can be hard on everyone. But engaged employees bounce back after organizational or structural changes more quickly than others.

- Engaged employees offer a significantly higher level of innovation. According to Gallup, 59 percent of engaged employees say they bring their most creative ideas to work, whereas only 3 percent of disengaged employees make that same claim (J. Krueger & E. Killham, "The Innovation Equation," *Gallup Management Journal*, 2007).

- Engaged employees increase the profitability of their companies. Add up the items listed above, and they amount to real money. In fact, companies conducting employee engagement surveys attribute a direct, hard-dollar amount to improved survey scores!

If that's not enough to convince you to make employee engagement a higher priority, consider these two facts about disengaged employees:

- Disengaged employees cost you money. According to Gallup, disengaged employees cost U.S. companies $350 billion each year (Curt

Coffman, "The High Cost of Disengaged Employees," (Gallup.com, 2002). That's right. Disengaged employees steal items out of corporate inventory. Even more common, though, employees steal time. At the most basic level, if you pay an employee for an eight-hour day, you should receive at least eight hours of work. Disengaged employees don't give you the full eight hours that you pay them for. In fact, they give you far less. Consider your most disengaged employee, and think about the cost of fixing his or her errors—errors caused by carelessness, indifference, or even spite.

■ Disengaged employees have an exponential voice. Most companies set aside a budget for marketing or public relations to tell the world about the company and the great products they offer. Is your budget big enough and your reach great enough to do damage control for every disengaged employee who has access to a social media platform? It's scary to think that any one of your employees might be using Facebook or Twitter or their personal blogs to badmouth you or your company right now. Even if you were to harness the talent of the best spin-doctors in the world, it's doubtful that your company could withstand the passive or overtly aggressive dissent from an insider with a grudge and a negative story to tell. One voice can be amplified exponentially until leaders, brands, and entire organizations get tarnished.

What's Being Said Behind Your Back?

I recently used the photo department inside one of the nation's largest retail chain stores. I waited for several minutes before an associate named Karl appeared to apologize that my picture wasn't printed yet.

"Sorry, but my supervisor's a joke. He sent me on break right when it got busy. I'm surprised you're still here. I would have taken off if I were you."

What are your employees saying about you when you're not around? What do these key spokespersons say about your organization when the lights go off? What kind of ambassador are they for your brand and your company? Your employees and customers are your biggest advocates, but can also spread negativity like a virus. Don't expect the words to be positive if the workplace isn't. Foster an engagement culture so that employees and customers serve as PR agents working for your business—not for your competitors.

■ If the business case for employee engagement isn't compelling enough for your boss or CEO—who may be concerned with the bottom line more than the smiles on employees' faces—share these facts we just covered about how engagement can cost or support an organization. Or if the business case for employee engagement isn't enough for you as a manager yet, mull over this reality: Engaged employees make you look good as a leader; disengaged employees make you look bad. If you want to be considered a viable candidate for a promotion or new opportunity, the team performance levels of your engaged employees will increase your chances!

Two Employee Engagement Myths

In 1999, I worked for a major health insurance company that had an attrition problem. If you're wondering why I'm discussing attrition in a book about employee engagement, smart leaders will know that attri-

---

ENGAGED EMPLOYEES CREATE LOYAL CUSTOMERS

FOR EXAMPLE

Recently, I walked into a local Italian diner. When I arrived, I saw a sign that said, "Seat yourself," so I meandered to a nearby table where an employee, Sarah, ignored me and continued wiping down tables. Eventually, she looked up and stared right into my eyes. Instead of coming over or even acknowledging me with a wave or smile, she made a face and sighed—and kept wiping off tables! "Can I get a calzone with a side of bad attitude to go, please?" I thought to myself as I stood to leave without turning back. But in the nick of time, my server, Jessica, walked up to the table, greeted me with her sweet Southern accent, and proceeded throughout the night to deliver more than expected—including talking me out of ordering extra cheese by saying, "Let me clue you in on a little secret, honey. The calzone already comes with so much cheese, you won't want to waste your money on any extra!" She was right and saved me a dollar. It may not seem like a lot, but when it was time to go, I tipped her appropriately for her service and promised I'd return to that restaurant. If I tell others about my experience, I may even create future customers for this restaurant. But if Sarah's initial attitude had been reflective of the entire crew, I wouldn't have come back. I might have even shared my negative story with the next person who crossed my path—or more likely, with the very poor rating I would have left online for that restaurant to warn potential customers! Your employees have the power to affect not only workplace morale, but also customer involvement and the bottom line.

tion often serves as a terminal sign of an employee engagement problem. Note: I reference my experiences with this company several times throughout this book, as I served in a variety of roles—from working in HR, to becoming executive director of strategic communications and change management, to eventually chief of staff of internal operations over several states. In each of these roles, I was directly involved in creating and implementing engagement strategies.

This company initially hired me because of my background in clinical psychology and my ability to apply behavioral principles in a corporate setting. My first project was in operations, where I served as the human resources liaison to the business.

LOW ATTRITION MIGHT MEAN HIGH ENGAGEMENT
Low turnover might be a sign that you have highly engaged employees. Keep in mind, however, that your least skilled employees have the fewest employment options. And in times of economic unrest, even your skilled employees may be afraid to make a quick move. If an employee stays with you, it might be loyalty. Or it might be a case of fear—or lacking the skills to go elsewhere.

In the years leading up to the attrition problem, the organization had experienced dynamic changes. The corporate structure had moved from centralized to opening several remote, regional offices. Driven by a recent merger and explosive customer growth, the company opened new offices every year. While technology and processes were readily replicable to multiple geographic locations, company culture proved harder to export. As a result, leadership practices and policies ranged from permissive to authoritarian. When it came time to do the annual budget, they found that attrition rates had reached nearly 50 percent in some offices. For one critical job family, it hovered at 38 percent. We were losing customer service representatives (CSRs). In virtual call centers, which our company relied on, CSRs are the face of the company to customers.

When I started to evaluate the situation, the department responsible for developing and monitoring all operational metrics didn't yet have a measurement in place to estimate turnover costs. Pooling knowledge from various HR disciplines, we realized that the cost of turnover went deep.

Hidden Costs of Attrition

Maybe you don't have voluntary attrition today. But imagine losing an employee on your team. Now imagine losing two, three, four. Picture losing half your team—the better half! If that doesn't raise your blood pressure, these hidden costs of attrition might:

Productivity costs. When an employee leaves your team, productivity drops. Others are asked to do more, and you have to spend your time finding a replacement. You work with HR, review piles of applicants, and conduct countless interviews. And until you get a new person hired and trained past the learning curve stage into being fully productive, your performance—and likely that of your entire team—will drop.

Customer retention costs. All positions are customer facing: They either face external customers or internal customers, such as those in other departments or functions like information technology, legal, marketing, operations, etc. When you lose an employee, consider the impact on your customers. In my organization, I found that customer retention levels (the rate at which customers stayed with us) mirrored employee retention levels (the rate at which employees stayed with us). If half your customers left, could you survive?

Replacement costs. When an employee leaves, productivity is interrupted along with continuity of customer advocacy. But what about your time and the cost to hire and train a replacement? What about the cost associated with new employee on-boarding and orientation? What about the formal training costs that take place before the employee begins working for you?

Using cost-of-turnover formulas from the Society for Human Resource Management as well as the American Society for Training and Development, we conservatively estimated our CSR

KEEP YOUR EMPLOYEES **SMART**
The cheapest way to avoid the hidden costs of attrition is to keep your employees. And the way to keep your employees **MANAGING** is to engage them.

replacement cost based on our current turnover levels at $8 million to $10 million annually.

Our company experienced an $8 million to $10 million per-year attrition problem, and we didn't even know why employees were leaving! But there were theories ...

Myth #1: Engagement Is a Generational Issue. You Can't Engage This Generation of Job-Hoppers

HR surveys of exiting employees indicated that people who left did so because of a survey code known as FNJ: Found New Job.

When I talked to local managers, they all told me similar stories:

- This new generation craves excitement, and our jobs aren't exciting enough.
- No one stays in a job for long these days.
- They're all job-hoppers. We hardly have any employees who stay longer than a year.
- It's the nature of the CSR role. It's a hard job, and people burn out. Attrition is bad across the entire industry.

Still, FNJ didn't make sense to me. I couldn't argue with the surveys that told me Found New Job was a destination for our exiting employees, but it didn't offer a cause or reason for them to leave. More than that, it failed to answer a more basic question: Why were our employees even looking for new jobs? These were lower-level, hourly employees. It's not like recruiters or head-hunters were actively seeking them—luring them with lucrative signing bonuses, new cars, or six-figure incomes.

No, if our employees were finding new jobs, it meant they were looking for new jobs.

From my background as a family therapist, I knew that things weren't always what they seemed. So instead of relying on an HR form that exiting employees completed, I decided to conduct exit interviews of my own. I gathered a list of more than 250 of our employees who had voluntarily left the company over the previous two years. Using a small team of colleagues, we started making phone calls during the evening hours.

I'm glad I did. Because it turned out that many of the exiting employees who checked off Found New Job lied. More than 65 percent of the people we interviewed admitted that they hadn't left because they found a new job. In reality, these people quit without another job lined up!

It's a myth that employees are in a constant search for better jobs. It's hard to start over—to leave a job you know in pursuit of something unknown. The fear of change keeps most employees from impulsively or casually job-hopping. You don't just wake up one morning deciding there may be something more interesting or exciting out there, and neither do your employees. When you see your employees abandoning their posts, there has to be a concrete reason.

I confirmed that employees weren't passively finding new jobs. No, that's not why they were leaving.

Myth #2: Engagement Is About the Money

Money is nice. Everyone wants more money. I've never met a person who would refuse the offer of a larger paycheck. Money might influence satisfaction. But money doesn't create engagement. And in the case of the CSR attrition problem our company faced, money didn't seem to be the bait to lure our employees away from the company.

On the HR exit form, many of the CSRs responded in the open-ended section with comments like "I'm taking a job that pays more money."

At first blush, this seems logical, right? I mean, who doesn't want more money? Why look any further for the truth? After all, the employees told us themselves that they were leaving for more money.

But these were the same employees who told us they had found new jobs. So were they being honest about leaving for more money?

No. Of the 35 percent of employees who in fact left for another position, only 8 percent of those employees actually made more money.

I worked closely with the compensation department and I knew they regularly conducted sweeping assessments of compensation trends. When we opened a new office, our goal wasn't to offer more pay and benefits. We wanted to be the best in the areas in which we did business, and that meant we offered a comprehensive, competitive package that included amenities beyond great pay and benefits. We offered employees a new office building, state-of-the-art technology, and opportunities within a large organization that enjoyed some of the highest name recognition and brand reputation of any company.

At the time, the average starting wage the company paid CSRs was $8.50 an hour. To test the power of money as a motivator, my team and I posed the following question to former employees: Would you have been willing to stay in the job if you made $___ more money per hour?

At first, we filled in that blank with $0.50. Then $1.00. $1.50. $2.00. $2.50.

Usually, between $2.00 and $2.50, the person we were interviewing interrupted us. What did we hear in response to our inquiry? "I would not have stayed for any amount of money."

We didn't hear this once or twice. When I met with each member of my HR team conducting the interviews, this theme came up repeatedly as well as loudly and clearly. People didn't leave because of money. In fact, they seemed insulted that we would ask them if they could have been bought at any price.

No, employees don't leave companies because of money. So why do they leave?

High Attrition = Low Engagement x Poor Leadership

The CSRs who left weren't completely honest when they filled out their exit surveys. They told HR they'd found new jobs making more money. Most of them admitted to me the reason they reported this when they left is that they "didn't want to burn bridges." But when they opened up to me and my team, they told us the real story behind their disengagement and eventual departure:

- It was a sweatshop with air conditioning.
- If only [managers] treated us like we were human.
- The supervisors were so mean. I would cry all the way to work and all the way home from work each day.
- When I voiced my concerns, I was told, "You can be replaced tomorrow."

Look at the comments above. Do you see any complaints about pay or benefits? Do you see any comments about the administrative, technical, or strategic deficiencies of their bosses? No. All the issues they cited dealt with people management—with the leaders' inability to connect with and engage their employees.

What was true of the employees I talked with in 1999 is true of employees today: People don't quit companies, they quit bosses. (For more on this example, see my book, *Firsthand Lessons, Secondhand Dogs*, available at www.LeadershipTherapist.com or my interview in Chapter 12 "Becoming an Engaging and Influential Leader" in Anne Bruce's 2012 revised book, *Leaders—Start to Finish*, ASTD Press, which is, incidentally, a great resource for leadership ideas). Greg Smith serves as president of a management consulting firm specializing in teaching executives how to build loyal customers by developing organizations that motivate their employees. In an article he wrote titled "Top-10 Reasons Why People Quit Their Jobs" (see www.managerwise.com/article.phtml?id=298), Smith hit the nail on the head. Instead of listing all 10 reasons why employees quit, let me tell you the first word of each of his points: management.

Employees don't walk out at the first sign of trouble. Before employees quit, they become disillusioned. They see fewer reasons to stay than to quit. Then they become disengaged.

Why do employees quit? What disengages them? While employees may learn more about the company's operations—including details they dislike—these factors don't usually send them fleeing. Brick-and-mortar companies can't love or hate people; so at the core, employees rarely have feelings of love or hate for corporate entities. No, employees reserve that level of emotion for individuals—like their supervisors or managers. Disengaged employees act like they've been hurt—as if something has been done to them personally. In fact, the leading cause of attrition and disengagement is *poor leadership*.

Think about it. Even if the culture stinks or operations are a mess, it usually boils down to a leadership issue. Employees tend to emulate the behavior, attitudes, and actions modeled for them by those leaders.

Are you ready for the good news? As a manager, you're a leader. We discuss this more in the next chapter, but for now, understand that it's within your power to create a high-engagement environment. Beyond the environment, a great manager directly fuels individual employee engagement levels. In fact, according to Accenture's internal research, 80 percent of the variation in engagement levels can be attributed to the line manager (David MacLeod & Nita Clark, *Engaging for Success: Enhancing Performance Through Employee Engagement*, Crown Publishing, 2009).

SMART

MANAGING

ENGAGEMENT IS YOUR JOB

The engagement of your employees cannot be outsourced or delegated. Your peers, your boss, and probably your human resource department can certainly help you create an engaged team. But the employee engagement "hat" sits on your head!

Why Engage?

When employees experience intense, positive levels of emotion at work, they're engaged. Managers can trust them with more and can expect great things from them. They spread happiness and excitement through the department just as the sweet scents from the perfume counter permeate the air at a cosmetics counter.

CAUTION

RESIST OTHER ENGAGEMENT MYTHS

Myth: I have no control over employee engagement.
Reality: If the meal you ordered in a restaurant tasted like dirt, you'd blame the cook, not the landscaper. Engagement is within your control. As a leader, you create the engagement environment.
Myth: I can't compete with Facebook, smartphones, and other forces that compete for my employees' attention.
Reality: You can compete with social media and technology if you understand what makes those outlets so engaging. Facebook and smartphones involve interaction, real-time feedback, and information access at their fingertips. If you engage with your employees using dynamic interaction, real-time feedback, and robust information sharing, your employees will seek your engagement. And if face-to-face communication is something you can offer instead of virtual interaction, that's a bonus!

But when employees experience an intense level of negative emotion at work, they become disengaged. And then they're likely to do one of two things:

1. They might finally tire of going through the motions at work and quit.
2. Far worse, they might stay, tearing down morale and positivity at each turn and causing you the extra burden of damage control or some sort of intervention before matters can be resolved.

Disengaged employees cost your company money whether they stay or leave. When disengaged employees leave, you'll spend a lot of time screening, interviewing, hiring, and training new employees. When disengaged employees stay, you have to put in time finding and repairing the damage these hostile employees create in your office or workplace. The negative impact on your company's brand—and your personal reputation—may never recover.

Manager, which kind of employee do you want? You have the ability to make your employees feel valued or feel rejected. When employees don't feel they matter—or worse, they feel beaten down—they act out against the source of their discontent. The source is usually you, their manager. When employees feel cared for, they give you an impressive amount of loyalty and work. Since you're reading this book, I'm guessing that you want to engage your employees. Congratulations! Now that you understand the case for engagement and the role you play as a leader, the rest of the book tells you how to engage yourself and your team.

Manager's Checklist for Chapter 1

☑ You need engaged employees to help you solve the challenge of "How do I do more with less?"

☑ Trying to create satisfied employees presents a paradox because that objective is not only too low, but it's also unobtainable.

☑ Discretionary effort is the difference between how much someone can give you and how little is required to be considered passable.

☑ Engagement refers to the level of dedication, commitment, passion, innovation, and emotional energy a person is willing to expend. A highly engaged person tends to demonstrate what subjectively might be called happiness.

☑ Engagement is a continuum, a sliding scale. In other words, it's not like an employee is either engaged or not.

☑ Employee engagement is both business-relevant and imperative since it translates into money! Engaged employees save/make you money; disengaged employees cost you money.

☑ Engagement is within your control. As a leader, you create the engagement environment.

Chapter
2

Are You a Manager or a Leader? Becoming the "Best Boss Ever"

I had the privilege of working with a woman named Patricia Hipps, who as a supervisor developed some of the most engaged employees I had the opportunity to know. A few times I served on the interview team that hired new supervisors in the office where Pat worked and, more often than not, the final candidates were former employees of Pat's. In fact, many of them told me the reason they aspired to management could be traced back to Pat's nature and character.

One winter, a blizzard hit the region of Pat's office. When employees called in that morning to see if the office would remain open, they were told the roads were bad and they could take the day off if they wanted.

Pat lived close to the office, so she decided to go in and get some things done. When she arrived, she was floored to see that almost all her employees were already hard at work! They had driven through a blizzard even though they were told they could take the day off.

Before the day ended, Pat got around to each employee, thanking each one for coming in and asking them why they'd gone to such lengths to come in even though the weather was dreadful.

One employee best summarized the sentiments of the others: "We knew you'd be here, Pat, and that there was work to be done. We didn't want to let you down!"

In summary, it all came down to leadership. Engaged employees are managed by engaging leaders like Pat. In this chapter, you'll learn what makes a leader and how to use your leadership skills to become the best boss ever.

Would Your Employees Drive Through a Blizzard for You?

How do you become the type of manager who inspires your people to risk driving through a blizzard—not for the company—but for the person who you are to them? Engaged employees give their best by demonstrating not only a zeal for the work but also a strong affinity for their companies. Engaged employees are plugged in—excited about the work itself and the people around them. That means an engaged employee rarely takes shortcuts or quits a company or his or her leader, even when things get hard.

Developing employees with this level of engagement requires that you see yourself not only as a manager, but as a leader. Consider this quote from one of the most influential leaders on management in the last century, Peter Drucker: "Management is doing things right; leadership is doing the right things." Guess what? Doing things right may have qualified you for management; but you have to *know* and *do* the right things to earn the title of leader. The word *manager* on the cover and inside this book refers to anyone who manages others *and* is somewhere along the continuum of true leadership strength.

In this chapter, I outline the traits that will help you become a leader, to become the "best boss ever."

Manager vs. Leader

In the previous chapter, I told you about my uncles, Wes and Wade, and how they exemplified *satisfied* employees for workers of their generation. What they expected from work was straightforward: a fair wage, decent working conditions, and some level of security.

Management looked different then than it does today. For example, my uncles worked in a factory at a time when the U.S. economy was based largely on unionized manufacturing jobs. What gender were their bosses? Male. Why? The work was "hard" and "dangerous," and working

BACK IN THE DAY

FOR EXAMPLE

In 1943, L. H. Sanders wrote an article in *Mass Transportation* magazine called "Eleven Tips on Getting More Efficiency Out of Women Employees." Here are a handful of "tips" he offered men who had the task of selecting "the most efficient women available and how to use them to the best advantage."

1. If you can get them, pick young married women. They have ... more of a sense of responsibility than do their unmarried sisters; they're less likely to be flirtatious; ... they still have the pep and interest to work hard and to deal with the public efficiently.

2. While there are exceptions, of course, to this rule, general experience indicates that "husky" girls—those who are just a little on the heavy side—are likely to be more even-tempered and efficient than their underweight sisters.

3. Give every girl an adequate number of rest periods during the day ... A girl has more confidence and consequently is more efficient if she can keep her hair tidied, apply fresh lipstick, and wash her hands several times a day.

4. Be tactful in issuing instructions or in making criticisms. Women are often sensitive; they can't shrug off harsh words the way that men do. Never ridicule a woman—it breaks her spirit and cuts her efficiency.

5. Be reasonably considerate about using strong language around women. Even though a girl's husband or father may swear vociferously, she'll grow to dislike a place of business where she hears too much of this.

Yes, times have certainly changed! And aren't you glad?

conditions weren't deemed suitable for women. None were in management, and few were even on the factory floor. Where did the factory foremen get their management education? Not Yale or Harvard or Chicago Booth. No, most the leaders were educated on battlefields overseas. And many of them brought home that same sense of urgency and directive management style. But instead of overseeing missions involving life and death, they oversaw employees manufacturing washers and dryers.

Many jobs of yesteryear required management—the art of doing things right. It mattered less how management got results than that people performed. But that's not enough today. Leaders understand that how results are obtained matters as much as the actual results.

THEN AND NOW	
Yesterday, many managers ...	**Today, real leaders ...**
Said, "Here's what I need you to do."	Ask, "What can I do to help you?"
Expected obedience.	Expect innovation and discernment.
Threatened employees to motivate them.	Win cooperation through collaboration.
Noticed employees only when they made mistakes.	Catch employees when they perform well and provide positive reinforcement.
Corrected employees publicly and often loudly.	Coach employees to bring out the best in them.
Expected that the paycheck was enough.	Understand that employees have several needs, the paycheck being only one of them.

"I Knew It Was Time to Leave When ..."

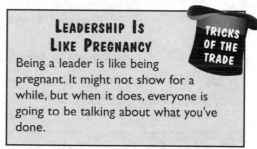

LEADERSHIP IS LIKE PREGNANCY

TRICKS OF THE TRADE

Being a leader is like being pregnant. It might not show for a while, but when it does, everyone is going to be talking about what you've done.

I've mentioned that people leave because of bad bosses, but I want to be more specific here so you can see exactly what constitutes a bad boss. While conducting some research in 2009, I polled and interviewed hundreds of people about one aspect of employee engagement: What does it take to make you give up? I used the research I gathered to produce a series of blogs on the subject. The lesson learned serves as a caution for what leaders can do well to head off disengagement before it starts.

Here's how I set up the question: "One way to measure the strength of a work relationship is to determine what it takes to end it. I'd love to hear about a job you left; specifically, I'm interested in that moment when you knew that relationship was over."

Here are some of the answers I received.

Finish this statement: I knew it was time to leave when ...

- My boss threw a pile of unorganized papers all over my desk and said, "I'm too busy. Clean this up." —Emily
- A high-ranking manager shouted at me and a fellow coworker for a choice that we both made—in front of customers and other employees. —Cheryl
- The ethics of HR went out the window—with no regard for professionalism, public humiliation of employees, and termination with no basis. When you question ethics, it's time to go, or better yet—*run*. —Lisa
- My boss told me that she didn't like me. —Grace
- I came up against an obstacle that I've bumped into before—and I felt too tired to challenge or find a way around it. —G. B.
- Senior executives got huge bonuses, and it took me five months to get a computer that wouldn't crash every time the wind was blowing. —Nicholas
- My leaders were no longer listening to me. I knew it was time to leave. —Betsy
- My boss contacted me for the first time in over a month! —Terry

Do you notice a trend? All these employees had issues with their boss. What kind of issues? People issues!

Two Views of Human Nature: Theory X and Theory Y

CAUTION

THE THEORY X–THEORY Y CONTINUUM

Don't view Theory X and Theory Y management in absolute terms. As you review these concepts, keep in mind that they occur on a sliding scale—a continuum. Most managers use both Theory X and Theory Y components in leading others. Instead of viewing these two extreme positions in absolute terms, use them as guidelines for evaluating your own natural tendencies as a leader.

When it comes to deepening your understanding of how you lead others, I want to highlight the 1960 work of social psychologist Douglas McGregor. He wrote *The Human Side of Enterprise* (McGraw-Hill, 1960), in which he conceived widely used

Theory X managers They are autocratic administrators, responsible for overseeing all parts of production, people, and profitability. Theory X managers view employees as lazy, so they must police and control employees.

KEY TERMS

Theory Y managers They are participative leaders, responsible for overseeing all parts of production, people, and profitability. Theory Y managers view employees as willing participants in achieving business success, so the manager coaches and cheerleads employees by aligning them with the strategy of the organization.

concepts known as Theory X and Theory Y. These theories outline the two basic approaches managers take in viewing and treating their employees.

YOU MIGHT BE A THEORY X BOSS IF ...

Fill in your response on the line provided next to each statement by writing Yes or No. Don't overanalyze or think too hard about the questions. Answer honestly from your gut level as you read the statements.

TOOLS

I'm inclined to think most of my employees ...
____ Dislike work
____ Avoid work and responsibility
____ Lack ambition
____ Are lazy
____ Value job security above everything else
____ Work best when I push them hard
____ Need to be monitored closely to be certain they'll do the right things

Yes answers indicate the ways you lean toward a Theory X style of management.

Theory X managers tend to be authoritarian—kind of like the old-school factory foremen I mentioned earlier. If you were to ask a Theory X boss if a glass was half empty or half full, he or she would say half empty. And then might add a comment like, "I'll bet one of my employees stole the other half!" In other words, Theory X leaders hold a negative view of human nature and, well, humans.

I'm not going to dance around this point: Theory X managers have a harder time engaging their employees than Theory Y managers. Take a look

y X management traits listed below. Then ask yourself: Would I
give more and care more for a boss who acted this way?

Theory X Management Traits

- Is short-tempered, emotionally volatile, prone to raised voice
- Issues demands, threats, ultimatums, and deadlines in one-way decrees
- Is intolerant of mistakes, assigns blames, seeks culprits
- Micromanages, is given to looking over shoulders and second-guessing
- Appears aloof and unapproachable, as if he or she is better than the "little people" (aka, employees)
- Takes criticism and suggestions poorly, especially from employees
- Is title conscious, often spending time trying to curry favor with those of higher rank
- Takes credit for successes, but shifts accountability for failures
- Withholds praise and rewards
- Seems generally unhappy, others steer clear of him or her

I'm guessing that reading this list didn't give you a warm and fuzzy feeling inside. Theory X managers get what they expect to see: bad people behaving badly if not for management intervention.

If you lean to the Theory X side, don't despair. Holding Theory X *beliefs* is not a death sentence; Theory X *actions*, however, most certainly don't endear you to your employees.

I'm not getting into the how-to just yet, but let me assure you that you can become a more effective, engaging leader—one capable of obtaining better business results and stronger followers—by expanding your current beliefs about people and practicing key engagement behaviors. Be assured that no one is going to ask you to do a group hug to make this happen. You only have to be willing to adjust your answer to this question: Why do people do what they do?

For now, let's look at the other side of McGregor's concepts of human nature, Theory Y.

Theory Y managers use a participative leadership approach with their employees. Instead of playing the role of the traditional boss, these

> ### You Might Be a Theory Y Boss If ...
>
> Fill in your response on the line provided next to each statement by writing Yes or No. Don't overanalyze or think too hard about the questions. Answer honestly from your gut level as you read the statements.
>
> **TOOLS**
>
> I'm inclined to think most of my employees ...
>
> ____ Like work
>
> ____ Treat work like they do play (e.g., They have fun!)
>
> ____ Want to succeed
>
> ____ Are responsible and do the right things
>
> ____ See achievement at work as part of the reward
>
> ____ Enjoy being part of the team and sharing in goals
>
> ____ Have limitless capability to solve organizational challenges
>
> Yes answers indicate the ways you lean toward the Theory Y style of management. Yes answers make it likely that you naturally engage your employees as colleagues and collaborators in departmental and corporate successes.

leaders function more as the "first among equals"—much like team leaders. Theory Y managers believe in the goodness of their employees.

Theory Y managers hold very different assumptions and beliefs than their Theory X counterparts and, not surprisingly, this leads them to act differently.

Traits Shared by Many Theory Y Managers

Theory Y managers ...

- Invite the opinions, suggestions, and feedback of others
- View failure as a learning opportunity
- Share context and vision, delegate authority with responsibility
- Provide direction, remove barriers, advocate for group solutions
- Think and act like a team member
- Put people in positions where they excel
- Offer generous praise, encouragement, and rewards
- Seem happy, others gravitate to him or her

Both Theory X and Theory Y leaders get results. Both are capable of achieving deadlines, goals, objectives, and deliverables for the good of the organization. But, of course, they approach their work differently because they hold opposite philosophies of human nature.

WHICH IS BETTER?

The answer is: It depends. Different situations may call for different approaches.

TOOLS   When an important, unpopular decision must be made quickly, Theory X managers generally decide more rapidly than their more participative counterparts.

When it comes to engagement, Theory Y managers create the most eager followers.

Since Theory X managers tend to view people in a negative light, these managers project an attitude that says, "I could get a lot more done around here if I didn't have all these employees!" In the Theory X world view, employees are obstacles to overcome—potential slackers who need threats of punishment to motivate them. Theory X managers get results through people in the same way a karate expert puts his hand through a stack of bricks!

Theory Y managers get results, too, but they accomplish things with people. They think their people are amazing and that they achieve amazing things—similar to how most parents believe everything their child does is above average. At work, Theory Y managers are the kind of leaders who are often seen laughing with their employees, grabbing a cup of coffee or having lunch with them, or giving a warm, friendly greeting to each employee when he or she arrives in the morning.

But let's look at the real differences between these approaches to managing people. Theory X managers spend their energies installing policies to keep their people in line; Theory Y managers spend their energies igniting passions to get their people inspired! In other words, Theory X managers rely on *rules*; Theory Y managers rely on *relationships*.

Before moving on, answer the following questions:

1. Do you lean toward Theory X or Theory Y?
2. Would you prefer to be led by a Theory X or Theory Y manager?

From an engagement standpoint, I want you to be aware of this reality: What you believe about employees comes out in how you treat them. And how you treat them ultimately determines how effectively you engage them.

Engagement Starts with "I Do"

Imagine walking down the aisle to get married while saying to yourself, "This is stupid. I don't even like the person I'm marrying. It's just a matter of time before we lose interest in each other and end up hating each other!"

Likewise, few employees say, "I do" to a new job while thinking to themselves, "This is stupid. I don't even like this kind of work. It's just a matter of time before I lose interest in this job and end up hating it!"

Managers, the best time to engage your employees is when they're new! When they're new, your "engagement bank" is neutral. In other words, you haven't done anything to breach their engagement level.

Hiring for Engagement

While you likely inherited much of the team you work with, know what to look for in new hires. As you deepen your understanding of what qualities feed engagement, spotting an employee who is likely to engage becomes more second nature. For now, recognize that a prospect who comes to you with a positive mental attitude and willingness to learn is more apt to remain engaged than an employee who is simply all about the skills or job description. Look for signs of positivity while interviewing—both through the attitude a prospect displays and through the past experience an employee demonstrates with delivering discretionary effort.

Ask yourself if the employee is applying discretionary effort in the interview by:

- Asking questions that go beyond the job description, things that required research on their part
- Showing interest in what they can give and not just what they stand to get
- Demonstrating a thirst to know the company's goals and business direction, and not only the salary and benefits of the job

If you don't see discretionary effort in the interview, don't expect to see much if you hire that person. When hiring, keep the old adage in mind: Hire for attitude, train for skill. Some things are ingrained and not as easily trained. You can train a warm, outgoing person how to use a computer, but you can't train a computer to be warm and outgoing.

The Engagement Wheel: Awareness, Alignment, Action

While writing the training program "Go Positive: Lead to Engage" (Pfeiffer, 2012) with my coauthors Doug McKinley, PsyD and Sam Glenn, we developed what we called The Engagement Wheel, consisting of the Three A's of engagement: Awareness, Alignment, Action (see Figure 2-1). McKinley, who also owns a consulting and training company, www.TMGLeader.com, and I have trained on this principle, which involves helping leaders:

1. Become "aware" of their own attitudes and engagement level, and that of their team members
2. Become "aligned" with the organization's goals, and each person's role within the bigger picture
3. "Act" to achieve engagement

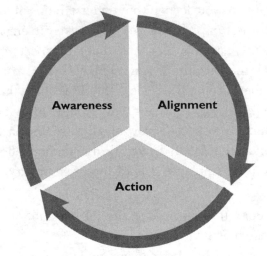

Figure 2-1. The engagement wheel

These elements of engagement operate like a wheel. That is, in order to progress, all three must operate simultaneously. Sometimes leaders must focus more on one element than another, but the elements work together to drive an organization forward. And as we illustrate in our training, before we can engage our employees, we must first focus on ourselves as leaders—to ensure that our own engagement is optimized in a way that models and motivates.

Becoming the "Best Boss Ever"

Employees expect more than a paycheck. They want an engaging environment, one managed by the Best Boss Ever. That's where you come in.

Wouldn't it be great if everyone on your team found you to be results-oriented as well as caring, compassionate, and well, likable? I was fortunate to work for such a boss, named Ray. See how you compare to him. Take special note of what you can add to or change in your current approach to promote positivity in the workplace on your journey to becoming the Best Boss Ever.

Best Boss Ever Tip #1: Empower Them

Terms like *empowerment* and *earned autonomy* are just buzzwords when spouted by a boss who micromanages. My boss believed "the best executive is one who has sense enough to pick good people to do what he wants done and self-restraint enough to keep from meddling with them while they do it." A great boss hires talented people and then gets out of their way. Former chief executive of the Leadership Centre in the UK, Stephen Taylor, reminds us that most employees come to work determined to do their best. But, he laments, "Too often, organizations seem to do their best to stop them" (David MacLeod & Nita Clarke, *Engaging for Success: Enhancing Performance Through Employee Engagement*). We talk more about this crucial concept of empowering employees to become like entrepreneurs in Chapter 5.

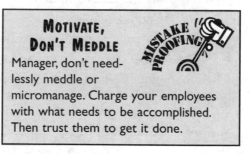

MOTIVATE, DON'T MEDDLE

Manager, don't needlessly meddle or micromanage. Charge your employees with what needs to be accomplished. Then trust them to get it done.

Best Boss Ever Tip #2: Talk About Them Behind Their Backs

"Rhetoric is a poor substitute for action ... [W]e must not merely talk; we must act big." During the 10-plus years I worked with Ray, he not only praised me to my face, he also talked about me behind my back! Do you know what he said? "Go to Scott. He's the expert on this." Or, "I might not always understand Scott's process, but I love his results."

DON'T GOSSIP

Don't make the rookie mistake of bad-mouthing your employees. Pretend your phone is tapped, your emails censored, and your personal thoughts read!

According to one recent study, confidence in leaders and managers is disturbingly low, especially when it relates to the interpersonal shortcomings of a leader (*The Shape of the Emerging "Deal": Insights from Towers Watson's 2010 Global Workforce Study*, www.towerswatson.com/global-workforce-study, 2010). Talking negatively about an employee behind his back is a prime example of an interpersonal shortcoming. Managers, do what the best leaders do. Be known for spreading praise, not manure.

Best Boss Ever Tip #3: Correct with Love

A great boss accepts that "the only person who never makes a mistake is the person who never does anything." Making mistakes is inevitable, but the best boss knows that when using correction, the end result should be to make us thirsty to learn from our errors so we can be successful the next time. My boss did just that. When I screwed up, instead of rubbing my nose in it, he would ask, "What did you learn from that?" He helped me confront my mistakes and fix them. Then he'd say, "Okay. Now that you know, don't do it again."

The late Professor Sumantra Ghoshal, formerly of the London Business School, suggested that an engaging leader be "both tough and tender" (enablinggreatperformance.blogspot.com/2011/01/engaging-with-engagement.html).

TRICKS OF THE TRADE

BE KIND

When you need to correct an employee, do so in such a way that keeps the relationship intact. Make certain your words and actions convey care and kindness.

Manager, take a look at your tolerance for imperfection. If you're known to expect nothing except perfection, your employees will be certain that they show you perfection. That also means they'll be encouraged to hide their failures from you! You can't teach employees how to improve if you don't know where they're struggling.

Best Boss Ever Tip #4: Accept Responsibility; Expect Them to Do the Same

How many of us have done something amazing only to have another jump in to claim responsibility? Everyone wants to take credit for a success, but no one wants to be close to a failure. My boss understood that "if you could kick the person in the pants responsible for most of your trouble, you wouldn't sit for a month." A boss willing to accept responsibility when things go awry fosters an environment where others accept responsibility, too.

GIVE CREDIT   SMART

If you want to create cheerful followers who bring their best to work each day, be known as a leader who gives away   MANAGING credit for their accomplishments and carries some of the responsibility for their errors.

Best Boss Ever Tip #5: Demonstrate Care

Marriage coaches suggest that couples plan a "date night" to keep communication flowing. At work, a great boss knows that spending time with employees is one of the best ways to show care. The reality is that "nobody cares how much you know, until they know how much you care." Imagine trying to grow a relationship without committing time to it. The relationship would atrophy, drift, and eventually dry up. In the workplace, meeting with your employees and taking time to know them as individuals shows care.

According to ColeySmith Consulting's Strategic Communication Forum research, "Findings of Top 6 Engagers," one of the top drivers of employee engagement is a leader who demonstrates a genuine commitment to employee well-being. The employer-employee relationship works like a marital relationship: Neither remains strong without care. When you are known as a leader who's the first to find successes and achievements, your employees will give you more successes and achievements!

Best Boss Ever Tip #6: Recognize, Reward, and Reinforce Them

Some companies have splashy rewards programs where employees can earn money, gift certificates, or prizes for stellar performance. But you don't need things to truly reinforce positive behavior and instill loyalty. In my years of conducting exit interviews, I never heard an employee say, "I would have stayed if my boss had given me a fancy mouse pad." A great leader understands that what drives most work behavior is the reward of being trusted with even more. "Big jobs usually go to [those] who prove their ability to outgrow small ones."

How important is recognition to employee engagement? It's important enough to be one of the top drivers Gallup identified in the Q12 Index. In Chapter 3, we discuss why people do what they do and how to reward them through reinforcement.

SMART

BE PRESENT FOR THE GAME

MANAGING

Manager, you can't stay in your office 90 percent of the time and expect to create world-class engagement. Can you imagine a winning sports coach staying in the locker room instead of showing up on the court or playing field during practice and games? You have to be in the game, where the action takes place, and able to give your thumbs up when you see something you want to see again.

Best Boss Ever Tip #7: Role Model

If everyone at work behaved exactly like you, would it make for a better workplace or would someone have to call in the National Guard? A great boss knows there's little value in words except when they're backed up with consistent actions.

According to a Towers Perrin Global Workforce Study, one of the top employee engagement drivers is having an effective and engaged leader (*Closing the Engagement Gap: A Road Map for Driving Superior Business Performance* 2007–2008). That's the power of being a role model. Monkey see, monkey do? I don't know. I haven't spent time with many monkeys. But I do know that employees mirror the engagement levels of their boss.

SMART

BE A MODEL

MANAGING

Manager, pretend that your employees are watching you. Because they are. Now imagine that they copy your own engagement level. What kind of office would you see?

Best Boss Ever Tip #8: Remain a Student

Can you say that you're "part of everything that [you] have read"? When you keep the mindset of a learner, you won't be accused of arrogance, nor will you run out of novel ideas to try when you're facing new situations.

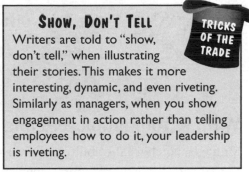

Show, Don't Tell

Writers are told to "show, don't tell," when illustrating their stories. This makes it more interesting, dynamic, and even riveting. Similarly as managers, when you show engagement in action rather than telling employees how to do it, your leadership is riveting.

Managers, imagine the power you could tap into if everything you heard and read went through this filter: How can I use this information to become a better leader? For example, look at the quotes I used in this section. These were all sayings you would likely come across by reading a biography of the 26th President of the United States, Theodore Roosevelt.

Be the Light

Managers, employee engagement requires the basics, Leadership 101. Don't try to be the best boss ever in the traditional sense of the word *boss*, because that connotes an old-fashioned dictator-in-charge method of riding people hard to get results. Being a boss means you hire and fire, sign paychecks, conduct performance reviews, approve time off, etc. Who would want to become an expert in that aspect of the management role?

Set your sights on becoming the most engaging leader ever. I liken a good leader to the sun. A houseplant doesn't have to be taught to seek the light streaming in through the window; it does so automatically. Similarly, if you're a great leader, your employees will seek your leadership in much the same way: automatically.

How do you become the light? I mentioned the importance of modeling engagement. As the leader, you set the tone for others to follow. What would happen to employee engagement levels if everyone in the office thought and behaved like you?

To model engagement, you must "control the controllables"—a concept I teach in my consulting. This means you do what you can with what you have. For that, I've developed a tool called W.H.I.P.

 **You Can't Give What You Don't Have**
If you aren't engaged, it's going to be hard for you to foster engagement in your employees, in the same way that a dead car battery can't offer a jump to another car. You must first be engaged before you can engage others.

W.H.I.P. Your Employees into Engagement

Manager, you have the ability to deliver meaningful engagement regardless of your budget or resources by using this acronym: W.H.I.P. (What you Have In your Possession)!

What things do you have in your possession? Regardless of your budget, you always have the opportunity to model engagement by providing

- A smile
- Your kind word
- A nod
- Encouragement
- A pat on the back (of the nonsexual harassment variety)
- Praise
- A raised thumb
- Opportunities like "Would you be willing to share what you learned with the rest of the team?"

These tools are within your control, and they are with you at all times.

Did you notice a theme in the W.H.I.P. how-tos? They are all positive actions. I discuss positivity much more in Chapter 4, but I want to mention here that if positivity doesn't come naturally for you, start practicing. You don't have to be positive to manage computer programs, but you have to be positive to lead people.

Fostering Loyalty, Trust, and Hope

As a side benefit, positive leaders are more optimistic—which means they are more apt to see options rather than dead ends, opportunities instead of disasters.

Optimistic leaders demonstrate and communicate:

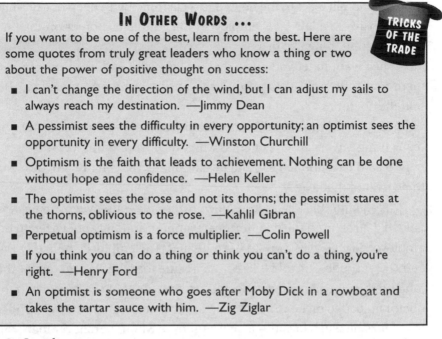

In Other Words ...

TRICKS OF THE TRADE

If you want to be one of the best, learn from the best. Here are some quotes from truly great leaders who know a thing or two about the power of positive thought on success:

- I can't change the direction of the wind, but I can adjust my sails to always reach my destination. —Jimmy Dean
- A pessimist sees the difficulty in every opportunity; an optimist sees the opportunity in every difficulty. —Winston Churchill
- Optimism is the faith that leads to achievement. Nothing can be done without hope and confidence. —Helen Keller
- The optimist sees the rose and not its thorns; the pessimist stares at the thorns, oblivious to the rose. —Kahlil Gibran
- Perpetual optimism is a force multiplier. —Colin Powell
- If you think you can do a thing or think you can't do a thing, you're right. —Henry Ford
- An optimist is someone who goes after Moby Dick in a rowboat and takes the tartar sauce with him. —Zig Ziglar

1. Loyalty
2. Trust
3. Hope

Leader: Loyalty Starts with You

At a recent keynote speech I delivered on employee engagement, I stressed that leaders must offer loyalty if they want to receive loyalty in return. After I finished speaking, an audience member named Bill introduced himself to me and told me his story about building employee loyalty.

Bill worked as a senior partner for a firm specializing in helping medical doctors with their financial investments. Most doctors he served had multiple medical degrees and deep financial resources; however, a couple came up short when it came to people skills. One particular client with a reputation for his foul mouth became verbally abusive over the phone when speaking to a low-level employee working for Bill's firm from a remote office. The call had been recorded for quality assurance. After the employee's manager reviewed the call, the manager called Bill at the headquarters to report the situation.

How did Bill react to the news that a customer with deep pockets had been abusive to a low-level employee? Bill got the customer on the line, and said something like this:

"I just want to let you know that we will work with your new investment firm to transfer your accounts to ensure a smooth transition," Bill told the doctor.

"Are you firing me, Bill?" the doctor asked incredulously. "Are you really firing me because I got cross with one of your employees?"

"Yes," Bill responded without hesitation. "No one in my firm deserves to be treated that way."

Weeks later, Bill visited the office where the employee worked who fielded the call from the now-former customer, and Bill apologized to the employee for the way she had been treated. The employee blinked away tears of gratitude. She told Bill she wasn't sure that she was cut out for this job and that she had already decided to find another position when the doctor unloaded on her. She went on to say that after the way Bill stepped in to show her such loyalty—a new employee whom he'd never met—she decided to stay on and become the best account manager the company had ever seen.

According to Bill, that employee is well on her way to achieving that goal. But something else began to happen, too. When the other employees saw how Bill and the organization stood behind one of their own, a team environment started to replace the "lone ranger" attitude held by many of the other account managers. Bill suggested that his actions and the emergence of the team environment might be entirely coincidental. I don't think so. I think it more likely that the team emerged when each member understood that if senior leadership stood behind them, they could more readily stand behind senior leadership.

Managers, if you want your employees to be loyal to you and your organization, demonstrate loyalty to them first.

Fostering Trust

If engagement involves an employee voluntarily giving you his or her loyalty and best efforts, you'd better believe that the bedrock of engagement is trust. What would make an employee care more and give more? Trust. And that's not trust in the corporation. Remember that a brick-and-mortar establishment is unlikely to produce strong, intense emotions for employees. In most cases, extreme emotions are reserved for other people.

As a manager, you represent your company. If your employees have positive experiences with you, they will vicariously ascribe positive thoughts and feelings to the organization; however, if your employees have negative experiences with you, they will transfer those thoughts and feelings to blanket organizations, even industries.

In New York, a movement started in 2011 called Occupy Wall Street that soon spread across the United States. Protesters gathered on courthouse steps of many cities to speak out against the broken U.S. economy. The largest target for the negative energy of these protesters was big business.

An offshoot of the Occupy Wall Street group cropped up called "We are the 99%." Here's a short portion of their "Allow Us to Introduce Ourselves" statement from their website, wearethe99percent.com:

> They are the 1 percent. They are the banks, the mortgage industry, the insurance industry. They are the important ones. They need help and get bailed out and are praised as job creators. We need help and get nothing and are called entitled. We live in a society made for them, not for us. It's their world, not ours. If we're lucky, they'll let us work in it so long as we don't question the extent of their charity.

There's a common theme to the comments that frustrated American citizens shared on this website: Corporations are greedy, granting their executives huge stock options and salaries while taking taxpayer bailout money and treating the "little people" like dirt. Corporations can't be trusted!

Even amid such extreme cases where employees are totally disgusted with your corporation, fostering trust will help, especially during times of change. I built trust with my employees about the future of their jobs even while our company went through a major merger.

As a leader, here are some simple tips for fostering trust:

- Make small promises, then follow through. Remember the words of Tom Peters: "Under promise, over deliver." Promise only what's in your power to deliver, and follow through.
- Keep your eyes on business results. Why? It communicates that when it comes to performance, it's "business as usual." Many things will change in companies over time, but I've never seen a company take

its eyes off the business for long and survive. Keeping people focused on things that are within their control offers stability, and it channels their energy away from less productive activities like speculation and gossip.

- Communicate your doors off (much more on this later)! If you claim to have an open-door policy, leave your *door open*! Nothing gets the rumor mill rumbling like continuous closed-door meetings during times of uncertainty.

Feeding Hope

Perhaps in no other area do the nuances of leadership play out more strongly than in politics. Some politicians run negative campaigns— sponsoring TV commercials discussing what's wrong with the world and, even more pointedly, what's wrong with the other candidate. Negative campaigning is so prevalent that most politicians feel they have to use it or risk being clobbered by one-sided gobs of muck from the other person's mudslinging.

I spent a fair amount of time studying rhetoric and public speaking in college, so I'm one of those unusual individuals who tunes into political debates less interested in the ideology of the speakers than in what they say and how they say it. (Please keep that point in mind in the event that I use an example of a politician who rubs you the wrong way—because I'm sure I will.)

For the purpose of this book—which has less to do with politics than it does with management—realize that what works to engage the voting masses isn't so different than what works to engage your employees.

The most successful politicians and business leaders understand that the most important commodity they offer is a product called Hope. For example, former U.S. President Ronald Reagan ran a campaign and won two elections by promoting hope. Here's a recap of what was happening in the world in 1979 when Ronald Reagan first ran for president:

- The economy was gripped by double-digit inflation.
- Gasoline shortages made long lines at gas pumps a regular sight.
- Fifty-two American hostages were held in Iran in what was referred to as the Iran Hostage Crisis.

- The United States boycotted the Summer Olympics to protest the then–Soviet Union's invasion of Afghanistan.

How did Reagan galvanize voters in such an unprecedentedly difficult time in U.S. history? He offered *hope*. As he stated, "Whatever else history may say about me when I'm gone, I hope it will record that I appealed to your best hopes, not your worst fears; to your confidence rather than your doubts."

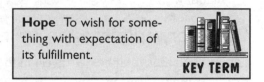

Hope To wish for something with expectation of its fulfillment.

KEY TERM

Another president who capitalized on the concept of hope is former President Bill Clinton. He was featured in a short film unveiled at the 1992 Democratic National Convention. The film was called *Man from Hope*—a play on his birthplace of Hope, Arkansas. More than an homage to his birthplace, hope became the commodity he offered the nation if elected president. Bill Clinton was elected—twice. He understood the importance of selling hope. In fact, he said in his speech at the Democratic National Convention in 1996, "I still believe in a place called Hope, a place called America."

President Barack Obama similarly delivered a speech at the 2004 Democratic National Convention titled "The Audacity of Hope," which propelled the relative newcomer, a U.S. senator from Illinois, into the national spotlight. Obama used the same name for the title of his second book published in 2006 (Random House). In 2009, Barack Obama was inaugurated as the 44th President of the United States.

You might be asking yourself why I'm spending time talking about the concept of hope in a book on employee engagement. Here's why: An inexperienced manager often thinks that his or her role is to offer employees pragmatic, fact-based, Theory X tell-it-like-it-is realities as a way to inspire them. Telling the truth is essential for engagement (as discussed in the earlier section on trust). Every good leader I've known could be counted on to tell the truth. But every outstanding leader I've known balanced even the most dismal truths with hope! Managers, if you want to engage your employees, offer them hope that:

- You'll always keep them in the know about important issues.

- You'll do what you can to care for them.
- You're committed to your organization's growth and improvement.
- There's always a future worth striving for, and it starts with investing in today.

Pay It Forward: Invest in Training

I mentioned that great bosses invest in their own learning. They also pay this learning forward by training their employees on an ongoing basis. Research of both Gallup and Towers Perrin concludes that employee growth and development are key employee engagement drivers.

Why is learning an engagement driver? Think about how many children you've taught to tie their own shoes. I'm going to guess that the number is the same as the number of children you have, plus maybe the number of younger siblings you have. Why? Teaching that skill takes time and patience—and a level of personal commitment to see the child past the frustration of failure and through the rabbit hole to success. You don't usually make that kind of investment in a child you don't love or have responsibility for.

Similarly, when you care about your employees, you want to see them be successful. So you train them, which is an investment—a demonstration that you care for them and want to do whatever it takes to make them a success.

Great organizations like the American Society of Training and Development can help you grow your employees, but if you're not yet a member, don't fear. Here are some no- and low-cost ideas for making employee learning a priority.

Do-It-Yourself Training

When I first started in management, I didn't have a training budget, but I did have a team of people who had specialized expertise of their own. So I held internal training sessions, asking employees to share their specialized knowledge and skills for the betterment of the entire team.

Use Internal Experts as Educators

You can ask cross-department or cross-divisional leaders and professionals to educate your employees on a different part of the business.

When I worked in the training and organizational development department within human resources, we would hold cross-department meetings so we could learn from each other. It served as an additional benefit to our customers and the company because each employee broadened his or her HR knowledge.

Tap into Internal Training

A couple years ago, I talked to a manager who lamented that his company didn't offer more training. I asked him to find and talk to a manager in his training and development department. Turns out, the company offered multiple, free training classes to its employees. This manager was excited when describing the LMS and all the training that was at his fingertips. Don't know what an LMS (Learning Management System) is or how it relates to training? Neither did he at first. Manager, make it your business to research what your company has to offer regarding training and encourage your employees to take more than just the required workshops.

Budget for Employee Learning

Many companies use training as a reward for outstanding performance. If your company permits this, allow any employee with satisfactory performance to attend free workshops; but offer to your top-performing employees the opportunity to go off-site, perhaps to a nice resort as a perk. And if your policies allow you to spend training dollars as an incentive, take the advice I offered my own managers: Use every penny!

Create Your Own Learning Library

If your company is small, you can still promote learning by starting your own learning library. Years ago, I worked for a small company with an equally small training budget. The department received two business and industry publications each month. They got routed around to each employee to read.

The Importance of the Leader-Employee Relationship

In all the work you do to promote engagement, think of it as a relationship. Foster your employees as you would family members or loved ones whom you want to succeed. When you see yourself in relationship to your employees, they're no longer drones only there to get the job done, rather, they are part of a living entity that includes you as a key component.

Create a Spectator-Free Workplace

Engaged leaders don't simply watch employees act. They actively promote the right behavior. Dulye and Company (www.dulye.com) offers services to create a "spectator-free workplace"—work environments fueled by engaged employees.

Dulye explains that spectator-free workplaces don't lead themselves—not at first, anyway. They require leaders who are committed to creating and sustaining momentum in the engagement levels of their employees. Dulye suggests five tips for engaged leaders to follow to jumpstart employee engagement:

Tip #1: Get invested. How do you demonstrate your investment? It's where you spend your time. If something is important to you, you probably block it off on your calendar. Why? We schedule the things that matter most. If engagement matters to you, show it. Build in time every day to check in with employees—face-to-face or over the phone if you work virtually.

Tip #2: Get immersed. What's going to get you soaked: standing in a fine mist or jumping into a pool of water? To get soaked, you have to immerse yourself. Get out of your office and experience the full dynamics of your workplace instead of only a sampling of those immediately outside your office. Go where your employees can be found: to the cafeteria, around the coffee shop or water cooler, and at their workstations.

Tip #3: Get interested. Think about meeting someone you find attractive and might like to date. How do you start a conversation with that person? One way would be to tell that person everything about yourself. Do that, and you'll likely be seen as a bore. A better way is to ask questions to demonstrate you're interested. The same applies with engaging your employees. Tell less, ask more. Ask open-ended questions—ones that don't generate a yes or no response.

Tip #4: Get interactive. How do you go beyond showing interest? Become interactive when you talk with your employees. Instead of saying to a suggestion your employee makes, "Great idea. I'm going to have to remember that!" write down that idea and say, "I want to make sure I remember that great idea of yours!" Practice less monologue and more dialogue.

Tip #5: Get better. Doing the first four items will jumpstart your employee engagement efforts, but to get better, longer-lasting results, get more feedback on your efforts. Have a trusted colleague shadow you to evaluate your interactions. Did you check your watch the whole time? Come across as really interested? Another approach is to circle back with a few trusted employees, and ask them to openly canvas feedback from their colleagues to share with you.

The Engagement Dance

Engagement is like a dance. Once you arrive, you scan the dance floor. Eventually, you approach a potential partner asking something like, "May I have this dance?"

The other person decides if this is agreeable. Most of the time, the two of you come together, but it's not for a set amount of time. Maybe it's until the song ends, or perhaps when the discotheque closes for the night. In rare cases, two people find themselves destined to be together and they marry after having met on the dance floor!

But you know, that question, "May I have this dance?" isn't a lifetime commitment. It's just a dance. Either party can end the dance at any time. Both parties remain together voluntarily and both parties have nearly identical power.

Neither is that question "May I have this dance?" a collective question—not something you ask a group of people. It's personal. You might want to dance with every person you see at the dance. But you don't use a loudspeaker. You approach each person one-on-one.

Engagement is like a dance, in which you invite each employee to participate with you individually.

Throughout the rest of the book, I refer to the dance metaphor as a way to remind you how to set the stage and create the kind of environment where something magical can occur at any time. And, like a real dance, it will help you set reasonable engagement expectations, value small progress along the way, and encourage you to keep dancing, even when you feel like you have two left feet! By the time you're done, you'll be inviting others to join the dance and making the experience pleasant, positive, and productive for all parties involved.

TRICKS OF THE TRADE

How to Know When You're Dancing

Recently my friend Laurence met with her boss, Scott. Following their meeting, she sent me an e-mail because she was excited to share what her boss said to her.

1. You learn quickly.
2. You demonstrate a high degree of accuracy and productivity.
3. You practice the art of active listening.
4. You act as a role model.
5. You seek and incorporate input from others.
6. You greet work challenges with enthusiasm.

Her boss ended their meeting saying this: "[You're] the glue that holds the group together."

Scott took the opportunity to reinforce Laurence's behaviors. What did Scott get in return? An employee who was so excited and so loyal to her boss that she went out of her way to talk about her boss—*in a good way!*

Manager's Checklist for Chapter 2

☑ Your *beliefs* about human nature drive how you *behave* toward your employees.

☑ Theory X managers rely on *rules*; Theory Y managers rely on *relationships*.

☑ As a leader, one of the most important commodities you offer is hope.

☑ Before employees engage with you, they must trust you.

☑ Become the Best Boss Ever by being a leader, one who instills positive, engagement-building practices in the workplace.

☑ Engagement is like a dance, in which you invite each employee to participate with you individually.

The ABCs of Engagement: Why People Do What They Do

Even at a young age, I watched people around me, wondering what made them tick. I set out to answer one seemingly simple question: Why do people do what they do?

In the course of my studies, I took every class that might help me answer that question, psychology classes like abnormal, behavioral, organizational, clinical, developmental, adolescent, counseling, environmental, experimental, social, etc.

After exhausting every course in the psychology department, I had more questions than answers. So I broadened my field of study from psychology to include theology and philosophy. I found that every field of study had its own school of thought. From psychology, I gleaned that people were mentally ill; theology taught me that people were sinners; philosophy indicated that truth resided in pursuing knowledge more than in attaining knowledge. The more I learned, the less confidence I had that an answer existed!

After finishing school, I appeared briefly in the business world before plunging into my passion for helping others. I took a position as a social worker in a residential group home for juvenile delinquents in Michigan's Upper Peninsula. After a few years in that role, I moved into true crisis intervention counseling where I worked with some of the toughest, most "hopeless" families in the state.

The organization I worked for was called Teaching-Family Homes of Upper Michigan, and they provided me with regular, ongoing training in behavioral science. On top of that, they contracted with excellent organizations such as Boys Town to conduct classroom and on-the-job training, evaluations, and formal feedback. (For more on my experiences in the group home, see my book *Don't Throw Underwear on the Table & Other Lessons Learned at Work* available at www.LeadershipTherapist.com.)

My curiosity continued unabated—whether in the classroom or on the job. I never stopped trying to answer that simple question: Why do people do what they do?

What does this question have to do with engagement? As a manager, understanding why people behave as they do will provide you with the keys to engage them.

People Do What They Do Because …

While working in a juvenile group home, many of the children I served hated me at first. These kids had been removed from their homes by authorities due to parental neglect or abuse, and most of the kids had juvenile records that made their futures in a lock-up facility seem likely. Who could blame them for not automatically liking me, given that they were yanked out of their homes, schools, and towns to be placed into a home with me!

Many of the families I conducted crisis intervention counseling with hated me at first, too. (For more on my experiences as a crisis intervention counselor, see my book *Paint Won't Cover That Stain* available at www.LeadershipTherapist.com.) The authorities told these families something like this: "Either you work with Scott, or you're going to lose your child/children." Can you blame them for disliking me? I represented the slightly lesser of two evils.

While the kids I served didn't immediately want to engage with me, I have to admit I felt the same way about many of them. More than once, a child in my care got violent with me—throwing punches, kicks, and sometimes household objects—heavy ones! One child held a knife to my throat while seething, "I can cut you!"

I found it hard to get close to some of the adults I served, too. In some cases, these "caregivers" didn't act as if they cared for their children. In fact, some used their children as human punching bags. Others pretended their kids were little adults, and left them to fend for themselves. Often, these people would lie to me or try to "play along" just to get me out of their lives.

At times, I had a front-row seat to horrific, unspeakable acts of cruelty and insanity. More than once, my thoughts became extremely Theory X, and I believed that *these people were hopeless, and without my help they'd all be in prison where they belong!*

And yet, other clients of mine acted with kindness and dearness—as people who had lost their way. Some of them found themselves in situations they didn't know how to resolve and they willingly accepted my help. Over time, these clients became as close as family, and more than once I would share a meal with them.

All told, the majority of both children and adults—even those who started off disliking and distrusting me—ended up engaged with me as a person and engaging with what I had to offer. And this is because I first tried to engage them as people. I saw beyond the task at hand to notice their complexities, needs, and most important, what would inspire them to change. In short, I tried to determine what they wanted and to motivate them based on these drivers.

So here's an answer to the question I posed at the beginning of this section: Why do people do what they do? Do they act the way they do because they're rotten, lazy, and more than a little crazy? Or do they do what they do because they're good and kind, and have a touch of the divine?

People do what they do because they get what they want when they do it. Period.

To engage your employees, you must first understand what they want and how to give it to them. Here are some key points to digest while setting the stage for your engagement efforts:

Key Point #1: Your Employees Are Not Lazy or Flawed. When we use labels and blanket statements, we tend to believe them over time (more on this later). Employees simply act in ways to get more of what they want. This combats Theory X management and other judgmental beliefs.

SMART MANAGING

CHALLENGE YOUR THINKING

Expand your current thinking by challenging your assumptions. When you observe an employee doing something at work, ask yourself: What does the employee get out of that?

When someone shows up for work on time, ask "Why?" When someone shows up late, ask "Why?" When someone gives you more than you asked for, ask "Why?" When someone fails to deliver what you asked for, ask "Why?"

The answer to all those questions is the same: because they get what they want when they do it. So ask yourself, "What do they want?"

Key Point #2: Your Beliefs About People Don't Need to Go from One Extreme to the Other Overnight for You to Become More Engaging. You only need to move to a place of neutrality—an openness to consider that while perhaps people are driven to avoid unpleasantness, they are also driven to obtain rewards.

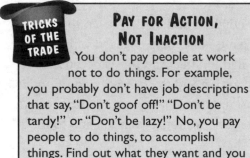

TRICKS OF THE TRADE

PAY FOR ACTION, NOT INACTION

You don't pay people at work not to do things. For example, you probably don't have job descriptions that say, "Don't goof off!" "Don't be tardy!" or "Don't be lazy!" No, you pay people to do things, to accomplish things. Find out what they want and you can motivate them to act.

Key Point #3: If You Know What Your Employees Want, You Can Help Them Get It. At the most basic level, people expend efforts for one of two reasons:

1. To obtain pleasure

or

2. To avoid discomfort

Look at the following examples from events you may see every day at work:

- An employee completes a project early in hopes of getting recognition or even more responsibility (receives pleasure) or because he hates the pressure of working under time pressures (avoids stress)
- An employee offers to mentor others because she loves teaching and helping (receives pleasure) or because she no longer finds her "day job" challenging or rewarding (avoids boredom)
- An employee networks and collaborates with others on the team because she finds that yields the best outcomes (receives pleasure) or because she loves socializing and talking with people (avoids loneliness)

■ An employee keeps double-checking with you because he craves your approval and recognition (receives pleasure) or because he's afraid you'll yell at him if he messes up (avoids a reprimand)

When you look at this list, you might notice that in some cases an employee may receive pleasure and avoid discomfort simultaneously. Pretty smart, don't you think?

If you need additional proof about the soundness of this principle of human behavior, ask yourself this question: Why are you reading this book?

Maybe you're doing it for what you can receive—like new techniques and tips to improve the engagement level of your employees. Perhaps you want to help your team become more productive and passionate. It could be that you want to impress your boss, who keeps talking about employee engagement.

On the other hand, maybe you're doing it because of what you're afraid you might lose—like your key employees, your performance edge, the confidence of your boss. Or, if you list increasing employee engagement as a goal, perhaps you're concerned you could lose your job if you don't improve things.

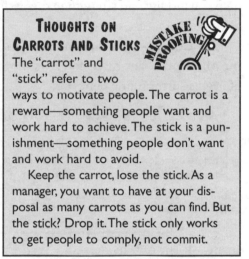

THOUGHTS ON CARROTS AND STICKS The "carrot" and "stick" refer to two ways to motivate people. The carrot is a reward—something people want and work hard to achieve. The stick is a punishment—something people don't want and work hard to avoid.

Keep the carrot, lose the stick. As a manager, you want to have at your disposal as many carrots as you can find. But the stick? Drop it. The stick only works to get people to comply, not commit.

People do what they do because they get what they want when they do it. Take that to the bank. And hold on. Because that's just the first piece of information you need to ignite the engagement of your employees!

The ABC Model

Knowing why employees do what they do is the first piece of critical information you need to know as a leader. The second thing you need to know is how to get the most from your employees. To answer that, we have to delve into what behaviorists refer to as behavior modification.

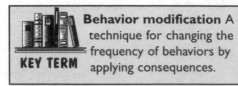

Behavior modification A technique for changing the frequency of behaviors by applying consequences.

KEY TERM

You've probably heard the names of famous behavioral scientists like Ivan Pavlov and his work with dogs, John B. Watson and his work with rats, and B. F. Skinner and his work with pigeons.

"Wait!" you might be thinking. "Are you suggesting that I can increase the engagement of my employees by treating them like dogs, rats, and pigeons?"

Yes, sort of. The same behavioral principles used with animals can help you modify and strengthen the performance and engagement levels of your employees.

The easiest way to explain the basics of behavior modification is with the ABC Model. The ABC Model, as shown in Figure 3-1, charts the chain of events surrounding behavior:

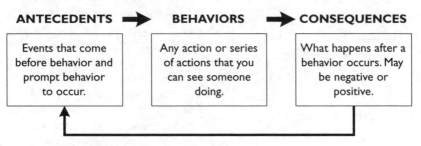

ANTECEDENTS ➡ **BEHAVIORS** ➡ **CONSEQUENCES**

| Events that come before behavior and prompt behavior to occur. | Any action or series of actions that you can see someone doing. | What happens after a behavior occurs. May be negative or positive. |

Figure 3-1. The ABC model

The ABC Model provides leaders with powerful insights about employee engagement because the model supplies a deeper understanding about why people do what they do.

"ABC" stands for:

A = Antecedent

B = Behavior

C = Consequence

Antecedents: Leading the Horse to Water

It's 5:30 a.m. Your alarm clock goes off with a loud *brrrinnng*! That terrible sound is an antecedent prompting you to do something: get out of bed.

> **A = Antecedent** An archaic-sounding word that means trigger, prompt, or cue.
>
> **B = Behavior** Any observable action or series of actions that a person performs. If you or someone else can watch something occur, what you're watching is a behavior.
>
> **KEY TERMS**
>
> **C = Consequence** Follows behaviors and is the byproduct of behavior. A consequence, much more than an antecedent, transforms and changes behaviors.

In reality, the noise might just as easily prompt you to curse, put a pillow over your head, or hit the snooze button. What you do when the alarm sounds is up to you, but that noise calls you to take action.

Our lives are a series of antecedents, and they may be so abundant that you don't think of them as such. Take a look at the list below to find some common antecedents you encounter at work:

- A coworker sends you an invite for a meeting to be held in two months.
- Your telephone rings.
- The server crashes ... and you're the manager responsible for servers.
- The fire alarm sounds.
- Your boss IMs asking you to meet with her.
- A customer asks to speak to you.
- An employee comes into your office crying.
- Your performance review is two weeks away.

Antecedents abound. When our eyes and ears are open, we're pounded with antecedents prompting us to respond in a specific manner.

Did you know that TV commercials are antecedents? The marketing copy, pictures, and sounds are all designed to prompt you to purchase a particular product.

As a leader, you constantly use antecedents to prompt your people to follow a desired course of action. That's why you give employees manuals and user guides, provide targeted performance coaching, perform regular feedback sessions, and conduct formal performance appraisals.

The Top Engagement Antecedent: Defining Clear Expectations

The first Gallup Q12 question asked: "Do you know what's expected of you at work?" According to W. Edward Deming, the management guru most closely associated with the concept of quality improvement, "Eighty percent of American managers cannot answer with any measure of confidence these seemingly simple questions: What is my job? What in it really counts? How well am I doing?"

If you can't answer these questions for yourself as the leader, how much more unlikely is it that your employees can answer them with certainty when it comes to their own jobs? Do your employees know what's expected of them?

Matthew and Mark

Years ago, I heard about Marge and her 7-year-old twin boys, Matthew and Mark, whose irreverent old Uncle Ollie came to stay for two weeks. Once Ollie left, Marge found herself dealing with the sassy and profane way of speaking her boys had picked up from their great-uncle.

Matthew showed up first in the kitchen the morning after Uncle Ollie departed.

"What would you like for breakfast, Hon?" Matthew's mother asked.

"Just make me some damn oatmeal," the boy shrugged, unaware of his mother's resolve to stop the profane language.

Determined to nip the problem in the bud, Marge silently swatted the boy's behind with her hand. Shocked, Matthew's face puffed up with tears and he ran past his brother who had entered the kitchen in time to watch this scene unfold.

Still breathing hard, Marge turned her attention to Mark.

"Well, let's see if you can do a little better," she said, placing her hands on her hips. "What do you want for breakfast?"

Mark looked solemnly at his mother. Then he looked in the direction where he could hear his brother Matthew crying in their room. Finally, he answered his mother slowly and calmly, "I don't care, Mom, but it sure as hell ain't going to be oatmeal!"

Marge shouldn't be too surprised that she didn't receive some sort of magical compliance since she never specified her new expectation for her boys.

And likewise, if your employees don't know what you expect, you shouldn't be surprised when they don't consistently deliver for you. In fact, that's a recipe for setting up your employees for failure.

Leaders, the first step to engaging your employees is to make certain that each knows what you expect. Why? If you outline what needs to be done (antecedent), they have a much better chance of delivering for you (behavior), and that gives you an opportunity to reward them (consequences).

Why Is It So Important to Clarify Your Expectations with Your Employees?

It allows for a dialogue, not just a monologue. Do you know why it's often possible to fall asleep in church or during a classroom lecture? It's because those are passive, one-sided conversations. Your participation isn't expected, and won't be missed. Discussions around expectations, though, require dialogue between you and your employee. Don't miss the opportunity to have an interactive discussion about what needs to be accomplished.

It allows you to test their understanding. Often we think we're being perfectly clear when we're not. I've used a simple way of demonstrating this in training classes for several years. I provide new mousetraps to participants—the old-fashioned variety with a spring and a bait station. I ask each participant to write instructions for how to properly set the trap. Then, I partner participants up, have them exchange instructions, and ask each to try to set the trap by using their partner's written instructions. My last instructions before letting them start are: "No talking. Just follow what's written down." Then I ask them to stop working if they come to a part of the instructions that's either unclear or unsafe to follow. In my years of doing this, I've seen this done correctly and safely fewer than five times. Why? It's rare that those written instructions include labels for the parts of the trap. If you've never before handled a mousetrap, you have no experience or common language to help you. The exercise demonstrates how we often assume, "Well, they'll know what I mean!" As a leader, it's your job to test for understanding, not assume that it's a given.

It reduces your frustration ... and theirs. Recently, I found myself frustrated at bedtime. My two youngest daughters popped out of bed several times because, as Sascha said at the time, "I just remembered what I forgot!" By the last "Goodnight!" we were all a little frustrated with each other. But while on a run the next morning, I started thinking about this simple concept, and it dawned on me that I'm never too old to make a rookie mistake. When I got back home, I made a bedtime checklist for the girls. It included things like this:

- I brushed my teeth.
- I got a drink of water.
- I applied lip balm and hand lotion.
- I shared three positive things that happened to me today.
- I used the restroom.
- I got another drink of water.

The girls loved it! They thanked me and then asked for a morning checklist, too. Why? They felt frustrated the night before, too, because they didn't know what I expected and they didn't know how they could be successful. Once the expectations were clear, we went from frustrated to successful, and even empowered. In fact, Sascha now wakes herself up each morning and quickly proceeds through her list, with a smile on her face to boot. She sounds like an engaged employee, doesn't she?

It allows you to provide praise. Yes, you provide an antecedent so you'll later have the opportunity to provide a consequence, such as a reward. Just as with the bedtime and morning checklist for my girls, clear expectations gave me a chance to tell them, "Awesome job!" once they did what I wanted them to do. I felt good with their behavior, and it felt great for them to receive so much encouragement and praise.

It allows increased opportunity for feedback. According to the Watson Wyatt 2008–2009 Work Survey Report, *Continuous Engagement: The Key to Unlocking the Value of Your People During Tough Times*, 43 percent of engaged employees receive weekly feedback compared to 18 percent for disengaged employees. One simple way to increase the amount of feedback—and more important, positive feedback—is to have ongoing discussions that come full circle: Here's what's expected, and here's how you're doing.

Antecedents Aren't Enough

At work, you as a manager pay people for one thing: to behave a certain way.

Wouldn't it be nice if you could just tell your employees to behave in an engaged way? Sadly, it doesn't work that way. Remember that telling people what to do is a Theory X practice. Think back to the picture of engagement as a dance. You won't likely attract many excited, eager dance partners by snapping your fingers, pointing at a group of people, and saying "Let's dance!" No, they have to be asked, and they need a reason to join you—a consequence related to the behavior.

STOP SIGN

While antecedents prompt behaviors, they can't ensure compliance. Have you ever run a stop sign, maybe on a country road in the middle of nowhere when no one was around? The sign may prompt you to stop, but you could choose if you wish to ignore it or not. Maybe you slowed down and looked both ways for the signs of traffic or a parked police car. The sign clearly told you to stop. But antecedents alone don't change behaviors.

Keep in mind this oft-used proverb: You can lead a horse to water but you can't make it drink.

Telling people what to do is just another antecedent. Antecedents don't necessarily change behaviors. Engagement requires that you as a leader maximize the *right* employee behaviors by providing positive or negative consequences. Think about that as I've defined it: Consequences follow behaviors and are the byproduct of behaviors.

How many consequences do you experience each day? Literally thousands!

- You turn on the faucet. What happens? Water comes out. *Consequence.*
- You meet an important deadline. What happens? Your boss thanks you or your customers smile. *Consequence.*
- You call your spouse with a question and quickly receive an answer. *Consequence.*
- You forgot to pay your credit card bill and now you've been hit with a late fee as well as an interest charge. *Consequence.*

- You invite your team to a staff meeting, and everyone shows up on time. *Consequence.*
- You exceed your goals two years in a row. Your boss asks you if you're ready to assume more responsibility. *Consequence.*

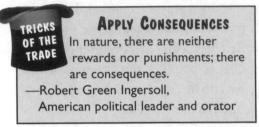

TRICKS OF THE TRADE

APPLY CONSEQUENCES

In nature, there are neither rewards nor punishments; there are consequences.
—Robert Green Ingersoll, American political leader and orator

Every behavior creates a consequence.

Consequences, more than antecedents, transform and change behaviors. If you want to gain an exponential advantage in building engagement, understand this: Consequences for current or past behavior have the strongest influence on future behaviors.

For example, you've learned in the past that the act of flipping on a light switch creates the consequence of lighting a dark room. Therefore, in the future, you'll look for and turn on light switches when you enter a dark room.

You want to create such consequences for employees—so they see the connection between what they do and what they get.

What Makes Consequences Effective?

Not all consequences are weighted equally, nor do they serve the same function and purpose.

When Antecedents Meet Consequences

Look at the following list of antecedents. Put in rank order those antecedents that would most likely get your attention and change your behavior. For ranking, use 1 as most effective to 10 as least effective.

1. ____ Red light at a busy intersection
2. ____ Instructions on changing your printer cartridges
3. ____ Annual performance objectives 10 months before your next review
4. ____ Suggestion box
5. ____ Angry phone call from your boss about an immediate problem
6. ____ A book on parenting tips

7. ____ Emergency Exit sign at a restaurant

8. ____ TV commercial suggesting you purchase a new car

9. ____ Nutrition information on a bag of chips when you're hungry

10. ____ Safety rules posted on the walls

I've conducted this exercise for years, and here are some trends. Coming in at the 1 and 2 spots are usually #1 and #5. The *red light at a busy intersection* and an *angry phone call from your boss about an immediate problem* seem to generate excitement every time I conduct a workshop using them as examples.

What do they have in common? The antecedents promise consequences—like what might happen if you ignore the red light at a busy intersection or a phone call from your boss who is angry about an immediate problem. And those consequences are harsh! Both antecedents imply strong and negative consequences if you don't respond quickly and in the right way.

At the bottom of the list are #4 and #8. Walking past a suggestion box won't make you stop in your tracks each time unless you have an idea burning inside or the hope of earning a cash award if your idea is selected. Likewise, a TV commercial about a new car will fall on deaf ears unless you happen to be in the market for a new car in the near future.

As this exercise demonstrates, not all antecedents and consequences are created equal. You know this intuitively, but what factors do our minds process in a nanosecond when faced with responding to an antecedent?

Applying Consequences with Intensity, Immediacy, and Certainty

While variables such as mood and experience have something to do with our response, there are three main factors that help us process our actions:

1. Intensity
2. Immediacy
3. Certainty

Intensity. Intensity refers to the amount of positive return or negative costs associated with a behavior. Consequences grab our attention when they have an intense positive return or negative cost. What happens if you ignore a suggestion box? Nothing. Without promise of a return for our actions or a price for our inactions, the suggestion box rarely even comes into your focus.

Immediacy. Immediacy specifies when the impact of a particular consequence will occur: either immediately or at some time in the future. For that reason, when you see directions for changing the printer cartridges sitting on your desk as you're leaving town for vacation, it's unlikely that you'd be prompted to bring it along to read. Why? The information in the book won't help you today. The information in the manual won't even be relevant until some point in the future, if ever.

Certainty. Certainty relates to your confidence that an event will occur. Something is considered certain if we believe that an event will occur six out of 10 times. If an event is certain to occur, we pay attention; if an event will likely not take place, it's easy to ignore.

What happens if you ignore the red light at the intersection? You may receive an intense, negative consequence: serious injury or death. If you were to sustain an injury or get killed from going through the intersection, when would that occur—immediately or in the future? BOOM! It would happen immediately. I mean, it's not like you'd be in bed the following week and suddenly be jolted by the impact of a car slamming into you! No, the consequence would hit you the moment you went through the intersection. Finally, in that situation, how likely is it that you would be in an accident? Very likely. Busy intersections have regular cross-traffic. If you go through a red light, six times out of 10 you'll either get into an accident or, at the very least, cause one.

How can this information help you as a leader in building engagement? You can foster powerful engagement by delivering *intense, immediate,* and *certain* consequences to your employees.

The Power of Consequences

The consequences you deliver as a leader are more powerful than you know. By delivering the right kind of consequences, you can:

- Build employee trust
- Reinforce expectations

- Improve employee performance
- Increase employee engagement

Do you see why that paycheck you give your employees has its limits as a consequence? While the paycheck may be certain, a paycheck is not:

- Intense. It's part of the employee–employer contract. You pay your employees what you promised to pay them, no more, no less.
- Immediate. In most companies, you get paid for the time you put in weeks ago.

Two Consequences That Kill Engagement: Extinction and Punishment

Engaging your employees involves delivering consequences for their behaviors at work—but not just any consequences. In this section, I cover the two behavioral consequences that you should never get good at delivering. I share these engagement-killing consequences along with examples to help you steer clear of them.

Consequences fall into two categories: those that increase and those that decrease the frequency of behaviors they follow. First, I want to focus on those that decrease behaviors:

- Extinction (abbreviated as E)
and
- Punishment (abbreviated as P).

Extinction and punishment are effective tools to make people stop doing things (see Figure 3-2). But since you employ people to do things, these consequences do nothing to promote action and, therefore, engagement. In fact, these two consequences actually serve to decrease engagement!

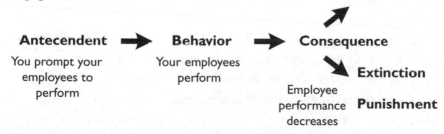

Antecedent ➡ **Behavior** ➡ **Consequence**

You prompt your employees to perform

Your employees perform

Extinction

Employee performance decreases **Punishment**

Figure 3-2. Extinction and punishment decrease performance

KEY TERM

Extinction Under this, a performer gets nothing as a result of his or her behavior.

Extinction happens in two ways: intentionally (active) or unintentionally (passive).

Active extinction is a technique that many parents use when they choose to ignore a child's undesirable behavior. By giving the problem behavior no attention, it often goes away over time.

Passive extinction occurs when you unintentionally fail to recognize the behavior of others. Often this happens at work when a good performer gets less attention than the "squeaky wheel."

Extinction happens at work all the time, but it's usually unintentional, as shown in Table 3-1.

Antecedent	Behavior	Consequence of Extinction	Future Effect
You invite your team to a 9 a.m. meeting.	You show up 15 minutes late to your own meeting while many of your employees arrive early to be certain they're on time.	Those who were on time got nothing for their efforts.	Employees may watch you and leave when you go for future meetings. You've decreased the frequency of their on-time behavior while simultaneously lowering their trust in you.
You ask an employee to complete a project ahead of schedule.	Your employee delivers, but you are too busy to express appreciation or even notice.	Your employee gets nothing, not a thank you or even a nod.	You've decreased the likelihood that your employee will make great efforts to deliver next time.

Table 3-1. Extinction scenarios

Do either of these examples sound familiar?

Whenever an employee does something that you like and want to see again, you have an opportunity to deliver an intense, immediate, and certain consequence. Extinction fails because it lacks all three elements of a good consequence!

Extinction includes acts like ignoring employees, providing no response to employee requests or questions, or not paying attention or expressing interest in what your employees are doing.

Those management behaviors aren't exactly a recipe for unleashing an engaged workforce, are they? And yet they occur all the time, not because managers are bad people, but because they're busy and distracted people and sometimes unaware of the consequences they're delivering.

Extinction Causes Frustration

Pretend that we live in pre-Internet times. A particular musical group is performing a concert in town, and you've waited years to see them live. You know that tickets are hard to come by, but you get in line in hopes of securing a coveted ticket. When the ticket office opens, you queue up, patiently awaiting your opportunity to hold a ticket in your hand! The line snakes slowly to the window. You shift your feet back and forth while moving forward a little at a time. Finally, you're the next person in line! Your persistence paid off … or so you hoped. But before you take that final step to the counter, the ticket window slides shut and the person behind the glass tapes up a sign that says SOLD OUT.

That emotion you're feeling is likely frustration. You failed to get what you wanted. You practiced all the "right behaviors" to secure a ticket, but you got nothing for your efforts.

Consequences for past or current behavior have the strongest influence on our future behaviors. If you waited in line for 10 consecutive days for 10 must-see concerts only to be turned away as you approached your goal, what would you do when the 11th concert comes to town? You'd probably do nothing. Why? You've learned over time that no matter what you do, no matter how long you wait in line, you won't get what you want. This phenomenon is known as *learned helplessness*.

Keep that feeling in mind when one of your employees puts in extra effort to deliver an

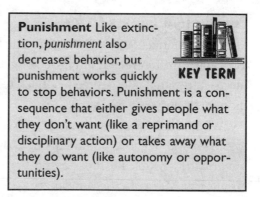

Punishment Like extinction, *punishment* also decreases behavior, but punishment works quickly **KEY TERM** to stop behaviors. Punishment is a consequence that either gives people what they don't want (like a reprimand or disciplinary action) or takes away what they do want (like autonomy or opportunities).

outstanding result. If you frustrate your employees too often with your extinction, they'll stop putting forth the effort.

How often as a leader do you use punishment? Take a look at the following list, and ask yourself if you rely on these behaviors to get your employees to perform:

Giving your employees:

■ Criticism, threats, or promises of future punishment
■ Verbal or written warnings, reprimands
■ Embarrassment or humiliation
■ Extra assignments or stress

Taking away your employees':

■ Privileges like flex time or work-from-home options
■ Autonomy and decision making
■ Growth and learning opportunities, training

> **ELIMINATE THREATS**
> **CAUTION** Strong leaders never stoop to using threats. Where weak leaders threaten in an attempt to manipulate, strong leaders rely on praise, motivation, and positive influence.

As a leader, your role is to increase productivity, morale, and engagement. Keep in mind that punishment takes away freedoms that contribute to an engagement environment. Punishment also delivers discomfort—creating active hostility and disengagement. Since punishment only decreases or stops behaviors instead of starts them, punishment is not an employee engagement–building tool.

Punishment Causes Anger

Mary Ann managed the training function in a midsized company. Due to low scores from a recent employee engagement survey, her boss asked her to undergo a 360-degree feedback tool to discover what employees thought of her leadership skills.

When she reviewed the results with her boss, Mary Ann was crushed to see several negative comments and low scores under the category of integrity. But when her boss asked her to discuss the results with her employees, Mary Ann became angry.

During the meeting with her direct reports, she looked around the room while waving her report in the air. Finally she read from the paper in her hand: "Mary Ann exhibits no personal or professional integrity." She paused, scanning the faces in the room. "Do you know what that means? That means that some of you in this room don't even understand what the word *integrity* means!"

Later, I spoke with one of Mary Ann's employees who sat in on that meeting, who told me something like this: "I won't be filling out any other surveys that come across my desk." What does punishment do? It decreases the likelihood that a behavior will recur. And guess what? Mary Ann's punishment decreased the likelihood that her employees would fill out another survey in the future.

You can create a more engaging culture by reducing the elements of pain in your environment. But that's not enough. The absence of pain isn't the same as the presence of pleasure.

IF YOU LEARN JUST ONE THING ...

SMART

MANAGING

At times, managers deliver consequences that stifle the development of an engagement culture. If you learn one thing from this book, let it be this: Engagement doesn't flourish in an environment of punishment and extinction! If you want to improve your engagement levels with your employees, eliminate punishment and extinction from your management style. Even if you don't embrace more positive engagement tools, cutting out your behavior that creates angry or frustrated employees will lift employee engagement much in the same way that reducing the weight of a bicycle makes a rider race faster! Lose the friction, increase the engagement!

When Punishment Is in Order

I've dedicated many words to warning you away from using punishment and extinction as management tools, especially when your goal is to create an engagement culture. Now, let me tell you the one exception to that rule: You may have no choice but to apply punishment or extinction as your last resort in dealing with an employee's behavior that's so poor that it jeopardizes the engagement of others, harms customer relationships, or hurts the reputation of the company.

As a manager, you have a responsibility to develop solid corporate citizens—employees who adhere to the code of conduct of your organization and at least the minimal standard of performance within your team. If you have an employee who can't perform within those acceptable parameters, he or she is a liability that must be dealt with. And as a leader, you might need to cut your losses and encourage that employee out the door. We discuss more specifics on how to handle the problem employee in Chapter 10.

Using the ABCs Builds Trust

We talked in Chapter 2 about the importance of building trust as a leader. The ABC Model offers you a powerful tool for building trust: Trust is the faithful pairing of antecedents with consequences. In other words, *what you say* is the same as *what you do*.

To understand the connection between antecedents and consequences as they relate to trust, look at the following examples:

Example: Rhianna and Steve

Antecedent. Rhianna, manager of the project manager office, pulled her employee, Steve, into her office to talk.

"Steve," Rhianna said to her employee, "the project you have on your desk is critical to this department. I can't make any promises to you, but if you can get this done ahead of schedule and under budget, I'll do everything in my power to make it worth your while."

Behavior. Steve got to work feeling excited. He had only worked for Rhianna for a few weeks and he was thrilled to think that she trusted his work enough to give him such an important project.

Steve jumped into the project, attending to every detail, big and small. For weeks, he came in early and stayed late, making sure the project moved swiftly and smoothly.

By the time Steve e-mailed the end product to Rhianna, his work had come in below budget and well ahead of all expectations.

Consequence: Nothing (extinction). After a week, Rhianna finally responded to Steve's work by sending him a short e-mail: "Steve, Nice work on the project. I haven't looked at it yet, but I'm sure it's fine. Thanks!"

Impact on trust. As a new employee, Steve eagerly set about to build a reputation for delivering outstanding results. But Rhianna's late and lackluster response to his efforts created a breach of trust for Steve. Steve didn't expect much, but he felt used and angry that his efforts netted him a short, vague thank you via e-mail—and it came a week after he delivered! Steve thought his efforts at least merited a face-to-face thank you.

Imagine what would have happened had Rhianna used this as an opportunity to build trust with Steve. Take the same antecedent and behavior, but change the consequence:

Consequence: Praise. Later in the day after sending Rhianna the final product, Rhianna shows up at Steve's desk.

"Steve," Rhianna says with awe, "I have no idea how you did this, but I am extremely impressed! You've been with us a relatively short time, but I can tell already that you're a keeper. Can we set up a time to talk for an hour later this week? I want to know more about how you managed to get all this done and I want to pick your brain on a few things. In fact, I have another project in mind for you that can expose you to some of the key people in our organization. I'll tell you about that when we meet!"

Impact on trust. Steve beams at having been acknowledged and valued because of the quality of his work. He hoped to build a reputation for delivering outstanding results, and he feels like he's off to a good start. Rhianna's personal acknowledgment and desire to meet with him reinforced for Steve that he made the right decision by taking the job in this department with Rhianna!

Steve continues to do his best. He loves his work. More important, he trusts his manager, Rhianna.

In both scenarios, Steve performed well. He took the challenge to do his best. He applied himself and he delivered.

What changed is that Rhianna built trust with Steve because she delivered on her antecedent, or promise of "I will do everything in my power to make it worth your while." What did she deliver to Steve? More money? A promotion? A corner office with a view of the city along with a key to the executive bathroom? No! She delivered positive reinforcement in the form of simple praise and acknowledgment. And what is she now promising Steve? Exposure!

Right now, we can't say that Steve will go on to become a highly engaged employee. But we can say that Steve is currently engaged, he's delivering, and he's excited.

Give 'Em a Reason to Engage! Positive and Negative Reinforcement

Let's look at what builds an environment of pleasure, a culture of engagement.

Remember how I answered the question, Why do people do what they do? Because they get what they want when they do it. And what do they want? At the simplest level, people want to obtain pleasure or avoid discomfort. There are two consequences that give people more of what they want:

Positive reinforcement (R+) allows people to obtain pleasure.

Negative reinforcement (R–) allows people to avoid discomfort.

Positive reinforcement and negative reinforcement both increase performance.

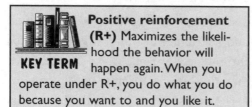 **Positive reinforcement (R+)** Maximizes the likelihood the behavior will **KEY TERM** happen again. When you operate under R+, you do what you do because you want to and you like it.

The most powerful consequences are intense, immediate, and certain. R+ and R– contain every element needed to get employees' attention and shape their engagement behaviors.

Consequences follow behaviors. If you see someone doing something you like and you want to see it again, the time to deliver positive reinforcement is right at that moment.

C.O.A.C.H. Guidelines of Positive Reinforcement

Effective positive reinforcement includes five principles that I call C.O.A.C.H. Guidelines.

Contingent. Provide R+ for behaviors you want to see an employee do again. You can't provide meaningful reinforcement based on intentions or on things an employee does *not* do, like not complaining, not making errors, not wasting time. But you can certainly find a reason and a way to reward employees who make positive, encouraging comments at work, produce high quality, and use their time effectively to get things done. Make sure your R+ is linked to specific employee behaviors that you like to see and want to see again.

Objective. Employees call *foul* when a manager has different standards for different employees. If you want to avoid being charged with playing favorites, make sure you provide positive reinforcement on employee behaviors that can be observed objectively and confirmed by others.

Action-oriented. We live in a virtual world, but that doesn't mean our positive reinforcement should be conducted virtually. As a leader, think in terms of personally meaningful things you can do for each employee. I share more on this later. For now, keep in mind that while it's easier, you should avoid one-size-fits-all positive reinforcement.

Consistent. Avoid making the "but" error in your positive reinforcement. One manager told me that he used to say something like this when he hand-delivered commission checks to his salespeople: "This is pretty good. But if you had sold 10 percent more business, you'd have earned $XX more money!" The manager meant this as encouragement. Can you see why it failed? In many circles, this feedback approach is called a s__t sandwich, trying to lessen the nastiness of feedback by putting a couple of pleasant things around it. Yes, that might make you feel more comfortable, but don't do it. It's confusing. Let your positive reinforcement stand alone and not be used as a way to ask for even more.

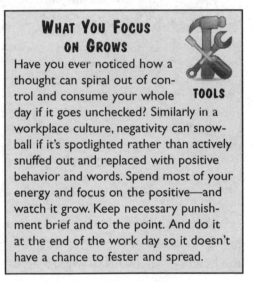

WHAT YOU FOCUS ON GROWS

Have you ever noticed how a thought can spiral out of control and consume your whole day if it goes unchecked? Similarly in a workplace culture, negativity can snowball if it's spotlighted rather than actively snuffed out and replaced with positive behavior and words. Spend most of your energy and focus on the positive—and watch it grow. Keep necessary punishment brief and to the point. And do it at the end of the work day so it doesn't have a chance to fester and spread.

TOOLS

And when you have to use correction, don't equivocate by making it sound as if everything is perfect. Reserve praise for things you want to see again; use correction when you want to see incremental improvement.

Habitual. As a manager, you want to find a way to make positive accomplishments self-rewarding and self-reinforcing. That requires you to turn positive accomplishments into habits employees want to develop. You want to develop employee habits that exhibit and exude high performance and engagement. The other habit you need to develop is your own routine of looking for positive behaviors in your employees. Condition your mind to look for behaviors that demonstrate engagement. Make it a habit to provide positive reinforcement as freely as air throughout the day in the office. If you want to make employee engagement a habit, make positive reinforcement your practice.

The entire next chapter is about creating a positive reinforcement culture. For now, know that positive reinforcement is your most important tool in creating an environment that ignites employee engagement.

Before moving on, I said earlier that two consequences increase the frequency of behaviors. Like positive reinforcement (R+), negative reinforcement (R–) also increases the frequency of behavior.

KEY TERM **Negative reinforcement (R–)** This occurs when someone avoids or escapes discomfort. People will work hardest to get what they want, but they will work hard, too, to avoid discomfort. Negative reinforcement allows people to avoid bad things. Under R–, people are motivated out of a sense of obligation. It's as if they feel like "I have to" do this, instead of "I want to" do this.

Do you ever have a day at work when you don't feel much internal motivation to give your all? You don't quit and go home, do you? No. You stay. And if you're like most people, you find some positive self-talk to drive you back into the zone. Maybe your self-talk isn't "I'm going to change the world," but I'll bet you remind yourself that by jumping in and getting back to work, at least you'll avoid discomforts like:

- Criticism
- An escalating crisis
- Needing to work late to catch up
- A poor performance review
- Letting your boss or team down
- Embarrassment
- Failure
- Termination

Before you start thinking that you want to instill a little more negative reinforcement practices into your management approach, realize some

EXAMPLES OF NEGATIVE REINFORCEMENT

Many of our behaviors fall under negative reinforcement. Don't let the word *negative* confuse you. Whereas negative in arithmetic means subtract or to take away, negative in the sense of negative reinforcement serves the purpose of increasing a behavior. Review the following list:

Why do people go to the dentist? Because they enjoy pain? No. People go to the dentist regularly to avoid more serious pain, like a root canal or other health problems.

Why do people come in early and stay late right before a vacation or a holiday? Because they love work? Maybe. But it's more likely they want to avoid taking work with them or having their minds fixated on work while trying to enjoy some downtime.

Why do you pay your credit card bill on time? Because it feels good to pay bills? No. You pay it on time to avoid late fees or interest charges.

features make it a less-than-ideal practice in engaging your workforce.

First, negative reinforcement increases behavior, but only to a point. Negative reinforcement gets you moving forward, but only positive reinforcement maximizes your efforts. If you were being chased by a wild animal while walking in the woods, how long would you run? Would this be the catalyst you need to sign up for marathons and Ironman events? Likely not. You would run just hard and long enough to remove the threat. Likewise, trying to inspire your employees to action by offering a way to avoid punishment won't generate much excitement or engagement.

Second, negative reinforcement is the consequence that follows punishment. For example, what happens after you get a speeding ticket? You slow down. How much do you slow down? You drive the speed limit. Once you've received a punishment, you want to avoid future punishment—not plan to get involved in a public awareness campaign for safe driving. That means by association, negative reinforcement feels like a threat or something you have to do. It's hard to operate freely and with enthusiasm when you feel coerced. Instead, you just get by.

Negative reinforcement gets people moving in the right direction, but as a management tool, it doesn't offer a quick, permanent, or direct path to an engaged employee.

The Discretionary Effort Advantage: Positive Reinforcement

You have four consequences at your disposal as a leader. Two of those consequences make people angry or frustrated—wonderful traits, I suppose, if you want to incite a mob to overthrow a government. However, punishment and extinction do nothing to promote the engagement environment.

And I illustrate how employees might be motivated through negative reinforcement to show up and do their job.

The rest of this chapter outlines what you can do as a leader to bring more positive reinforcement into your current environment. And that's important.

In Chapter 1, I mentioned the concept of discretionary effort. Nowhere is the advantage of discretionary effort more evident than when you compare the results of positive reinforcement versus negative reinforcement. Positive reinforcement provides employees with a reward for their behavior. Engaged employees don't operate in a world dominated by the urge to avoid. Rather, engaged employees jump in with excitement.

As a manager, don't underestimate the value of positive reinforcement. Stay on the lookout for behavior you can reinforce as well as novel ways to deliver positive reinforcement.

The Losada Line

When I worked as a residential counselor for juvenile delinquents, my goal was to deliver a four-to-one positive-to-negative ratio of feedback

---

TRICKS OF THE TRADE

THE LOSADA LINE

Research done by psychologist Marcial Losada demonstrates the value of positive reinforcement at work. Losada researched the differences in positivity/negativity in work teams, and he found that individuals receiving at or above a 2.9013-to-1 positive-to-negative ratio performed at a higher level. The number 2.9013 is today known as the *Losada Line*—the lowest number of positive reinforcements needed for every negative interaction in order to create an environment that flourishes. Use this in your management to reinforce the behavior you want to see (Losada Line, Wikipedia.com).

to the children in my care. Anything less than that, and the children were prone to feel picked on and become defensive. I have to tell you, it wasn't always easy to find four positives for every one negative when I was dealing with a hormonally charged teenager who had convinced himself that I was the sworn enemy of puberty!

You have two types of positive reinforcement you can use: *tangible* and *social.*

At work, social reinforcement is simply celebrating work outcomes with positive social interaction. An example would be taking your team out to lunch to celebrate an outstanding work achievement. We will explore this subject more in Chapter 7.

Tangible Reinforcements

Tangible reinforcements involve things that you can hold and touch. These have some financial or symbolic value, like cash bonuses or paid trips, movie passes or gift certificates, or even a coffee mug or a pen with the company logo.

Not every company encourages the use of tangible rewards. And that's not a bad thing from my perspective. In all my years of conducting employee interviews to find the root cause of low morale or engagement, I never heard "lack of trinkets" as a top complaint.

COMMON TANGIBLE REINFORCEMENTS

TRICKS OF THE TRADE

I worked for one company that had a storeroom full of tangible reinforcers for employees. Here are some of the more common ones that serve the dual purpose of providing small gifts for the employees while also doing a little free marketing by emblazoning the company logo on:

- Pens or pencils
- Notepads
- Mouse pads
- Calendars
- Coffee mugs
- Water bottles
- T-shirts/sweatshirts
- Desktop toys like magnets, squishy balls, blocks, puzzles, etc.

Caution on Relying on Tangible Reinforcements

You've heard the phrase "No good deed goes unpunished." While the concept of offering tangible items to employees seems like a good idea, it has drawbacks.

Caution # 1: Some managers use company trinkets as a substitute for providing meaningful, personal, positive reinforcement. Just as a paycheck is insufficient to engage employees, coffee mugs fall short, too. Managers need to be more involved in delivering personal reinforcement.

A friend complained to me about her former employer who used tangible reinforcements as the sole way of rewarding his employees. Here is the essence of her complaint:

> I worked long hours on a project, putting in extra time at work instead of with my family. My boss gave me a couple of movie passes and a coffee mug. I can buy my own movie tickets, and I have no shortage of coffee mugs. I appreciated the gesture, but my effort cost me something personally, his effort cost him little.

Sure, movie tickets and coffee mugs are nice; but her point was that it would have been even nicer if her boss provided her with some sincere, personal gesture that demonstrated his appreciation for her efforts and results.

Caution #2: Some employees associate the cost of the item with the value of their contribution. If an employee saves the company $250,000, what kind of trinket says Thank You loud enough? It won't be an MP3 player or a backpack! Short of giving the employee some prize of equal cash value, there is no way to compete in an exchange of some corporate crap for cash. So avoid it. Trinkets don't make people feel valued; only people expressing genuine appreciation can accomplish that.

Caution #3: Some managers give what they themselves like, not what the employee would like. I heard an example of an employee who saved her company over $1 million. As a thank you, the employee and her husband were invited to have dinner in a nice restaurant with the president of the company. The boss probably thought he'd given his employee a nice treat, but that's not how it was received. Why? The woman had to purchase an outfit suitable for a fancy restaurant, spending money on something she would normally never buy for herself and would likely not wear again. Her husband worked in a blue-collar profession and he felt awkward having dinner with "big, successful, Wall Street types." I call this Giving Chocolate to a Diabetic. Just because you like and enjoy something, don't assume it's something that others will value and appreciate.

Caution #4: Some employees tend to expect some form of tangible reinforcement for every work effort they achieve. That clearly misses the point. You don't want your work environment to turn out like each episode of *Scooby Doo* where employees want to know how many Scooby snacks they can earn for each task! And it happens. I heard from a supervisor in one organization that one of her employees asked her, "Can I get a sweatshirt if I do XYZ?" in response to a work assignment. Once a tangible reward is expected, people stop developing internal motivation.

Caution #5: Over time, tangible reinforcements lose their effectiveness. In psychology, the term is *satiation*. If you give someone the same reinforcer over and over, it loses its meaningfulness and value. When I was a family therapist, I helped a harried mother work with her son by using M&Ms as a reward when her son put away his toys. Apparently, I didn't explain the concept well. The mother ended up giving the boy a handful of M&Ms each time he put a toy away. The boy grew tired of M&Ms, and they lost their appeal. And sadly, once the boy was full, his toys stayed on the floor. Gone was his desire to put away his toys.

Positive Reinforcement Checklist

Table 3-2 shows some common examples of positive reinforcement. In the space in the right column, list a specific way you can deliver positive reinforcement at work.

PAIRING TANGIBLE AND SOCIAL REINFORCEMENT

SMART

MANAGING

The most powerful kind of reinforcement you can offer as a leader combines the tangible with an opportunity for social recognition. The Stanley Cup is the highest trophy in professional hockey in the United States. Each year, the winning players, coaches, management, and club staff get their names engraved on it. But unlike the trophies awarded for other major North American sports, the team doesn't keep the cup. Instead, they hold it until the end of the next season when the new winner earns it. Winning the Stanley Cup is not about the tangible value of the chalice itself. It's about the social value in having bragging rights, retelling the story of your team's victory, and leaving a legacy that future winners will share.

General R+	Specific R+ You Can Deliver
Recognition	I can recognize my employees by _____.
Special opportunity	Some opportunities that I can offer my employees include _____.
Tangible gifts	In my organization, I can give employees _____.
Praise	As a leader, I can praise my employees in writing by _____ ; face-to-face by _____ ; other ways by _____.
Freedom	I can reward my employees with extra freedoms like [flex time, work-from-home options, etc., for companies that allow it] _____.
Autonomy	For the employees who have earned my trust, I can give them autonomy to do _____.
Additional development	I can encourage even more outstanding employee behavior if I give my employees development opportunities like _____.

Table 3-2. Positive reinforcement checklist

As a leader, it's improbable that you'll ever risk providing too much positive reinforcement at work. Do you remember the Losada Line I mentioned earlier with the lower end of flourishing hovering at a level of 2.9013 positives for each negative? The Losada Line does actually have an upper limit. According to Losada's research, the upper limit is 11.6345-to-1 of constructive positive reinforcement-to-negative correction. At the extreme rate of delivering positive reinforcement 11.6345 times more than negative feedback, team members experienced a loss of positive benefits, sort of like the law of diminishing returns.

But let's be honest. You're not at risk of using too much positive reinforcement at work. And just so you remember why I'm taking the time to write about positive reinforcement in a book on employee engagement, positive reinforcement fosters an environment of engagement. Positive reinforcement not only develops a culture of engagement, it also has a side benefit of improving performance.

Wherever I travel, I gather many creative ideas for positive reinforcement. Here are two simple examples I like to share that show the power of positive reinforcement:

1. **The Jelly Bean Jar.** In one office, whenever an employee reached a certain performance goal, he or she got to submit a guess for how many jelly beans were held in a large container that sat on the front desk. The jar was visible to everyone. At the end of the day, if an employee stood at the front desk, it meant one thing: "I hit my goal." This allowed employees to brag ... without bragging! It also created more buzz and excitement. The more employees who stood at the desk, the more others wanted the opportunity to be included.

2. **Mr. Potato Head.** Another office sent their supervisors to my coaching workshop in pairs. Within a month, performance in one department rose significantly while the other rose only a slight amount. What was different between the two areas? The supervisor who obtained outstanding improvement came up with the idea of using Mr. Potato Head stickers to track performance. Each member of the Potato Head team received a bald potato head sticker on his or her cubicle wall. Each day that a team member reached the quality goal, he or she got to pick a sticker to place on his or her potato head. Sounds juvenile, right? Are you thinking that your employees are too sophisticated to buy in to something as silly as that? You're wrong. At the end of the month, the team using the Mr. Potato Head stickers outperformed the other department by 27 percent!

When you lead using positive reinforcement as your main management tool, you see positive results. An engagement environment built on positive reinforcement is self-sustaining, collaborative, inclusive, and inviting. When people operate under your positive reinforcement, they're happy. Happiness doesn't coexist with active disengagement! It can't. You can't sneeze with your eyes open, and you can't complain when you're happy.

Positive reinforcement maximizes performance and sets the stage for engagement to occur—or for the dance to begin. When you apply R+, people get what they want and it becomes more likely they'll engage in the behaviors you just reinforced.

Managers, you don't control the economy or the direction that your company takes. But you do control the environment in which your employees perform. You have the key to make that culture one that fosters engagement.

PRAISE IS THE NORTH STAR SMART

Just like the North Star guides sailors at night, praise guides performance at work by making people feel valued and happy. Praise tells employees that what we're doing is working, and it has a way of keeping people on course.

MANAGING

To maximize the drive and motivation of your people, you have to know why they do what they do. People do what they do because they get what they want. People are motivated to obtain pleasure or avoid discomfort. As a leader, you have the power to deliver this pleasure—or positivity—to your employees.

Manager's Checklist for Chapter 3

☑ People do what they do because that gets them what they want.

☑ People expend efforts for one of two reasons: to obtain pleasure or to avoid discomfort.

☑ Clarifying expectations for your employees is a powerful antecedent for engagement.

☑ Consequences change behaviors.

☑ Effective consequences are intense, immediate, and certain, and they increase employee engagement.

☑ Extinction results when someone gets nothing for his or her efforts, and it creates a feeling of frustration.

☑ Punishment is taking away what someone wants—like freedom or opportunities—or giving someone what he or she doesn't want—like criticism or extra work. When people are punished, they experience anger—an emotion likely to create actively disengaged employees.

☑ Negative reinforcement makes people give a little more, to a point; but really it encourages people to give you just enough to get by.

☑ Positive reinforcement maximizes behavior, unleashes discretionary efforts, and fosters an environment that creates engagement.

A Positive Culture Starts Here: Positive Thinking

Whenever I return to Chicago, I try to visit the third best pizzeria in Chicago—a place called Gino's East. How do I know it's the third best? My last name is Carbonara—which obviously means that I'm Irish. No! I'm Italian, and I'm more experienced than most when it comes to knowing a thing or two about pizza.

Gino's East is famous for two things: its deep-dish, Chicago-style pizza and the customer-contributed iconic graffiti that covers everything from floor to ceiling and in between. One time while waiting for the pizza to arrive at my table, I asked my waitress about the origins of the graffiti covering the walls. I'm not sure if what she told me is based on fact or revisionist history, but I've retold it countless times. In short, here's what she told me:

Gino's East was opened in 1966 by two pizza-loving taxi drivers and their friend. As sometimes happens when starting a new business, the owners experienced delay after delay in opening the restaurant. Finally, they locked in the date of the grand opening, and they worked feverishly to get the establishment ready for business.

The grand opening was a success. People loved the food. Patrons were complimentary and promised to return: wonderful news to the new restaurateurs. But after closing that day, the owners were sickened by something they saw on the walls: peeling paint.

Apparently, in their haste to open, they had not allowed the 48 hours necessary for the paint to cure. The paint wasn't wet enough to stain customers' clothes, but it remained tacky enough to peel up wherever it was touched.

The owners worked through the night repainting the spots where the paint had peeled from the walls. By the time the storefront opened the next day, most of the signs of the opening day blemishes were covered.

But at closing time, to the owners' dismay, the places they had retouched the previous night were blemished and peeled up. And in one booth, it looked as though someone had intentionally picked at the paint. On closer scrutiny, they confirmed that a patron named "Bob Rules" wanted future guests to know that he sat at this particular table.

Let's stop the story here for a moment. Be honest. Were you trying to figure out a way to solve the paint problem? If the paint takes 48 hours to dry and the restaurant is open every day of the year except Christmas and Easter, how would you fix it? I'll admit that even while the waitress recounted this story to me back in 2004, in the back of my mind I was trying to solve the problem by asking myself questions like:

- Why didn't they look for faster-drying paint?
- Couldn't they close early and use heaters and fans to accelerate the drying over night?
- Why not close one section of the restaurant at a time while the paint cured?

If while reading this story, you started searching for a solution, don't feel bad. That's what managers do. They solve problems. But do you know what the best leaders do? They see the same limitations that the rest of us see, but they find the opportunities! In this chapter, we show you why positivity matters, and how to implement it. And learning about positivity sets the stage for creating happiness at work—a subject we delve into in depth in future chapters, particularly Chapter 9.

Finding Opportunity Amid Calamity

According to legend, the owners of Gino's East decided to take advantage of the idea some patron named Bob offered them. Instead of repainting, closing the restaurant or even a section of it, or prompting the wait staff to be on the lookout for a customer who looked like he could be named "Bob," the partners took matters into their own hands—literally. They took markers and wrote on the walls themselves. They wrote things like:

- AMY LOVES JJ
- The Beatles!
- Kilroy was here!
- Best pizza ever!

The next day, they brought a box of markers to work and instructed the wait staff to make sure each table received a couple markers along with menus. No one needed to tell patrons what to do with the markers and the "blank canvas" before them. By the end of the night, the walls looked like a New York subway!

Imagine the energy the owners could have expended had they had focused on trying to get people not to write on the walls. And in the process of fixing the problem, how do you think the owners would have treated their employees—the cooks, wait staff, bartenders, dishwashers, janitors—before coming up with a solution? What if the owners turned every employee into the Wall Police? Who would be focused on cooking and serving food, preparing the environment, or creating a positive customer experience?

The owners of Gino's East in this perhaps-apocryphal tale demonstrated elite leadership skills when they adjusted their priorities from detecting problems to discovering positives. Whereas many leaders condition their minds to see problems so they can fix them, these three partners opened up their minds to the possibility that their problem was an unanticipated gift. And in testament to the staying power of finding the positive, Gino's East is still in business today, nearly five decades later—serving the same great pizza in an environment that keeps alive the tradition of encouraging customers to write on their walls.

SHARED TRAITS OF POSITIVE AND NEGATIVE THINKING

1. Both are contagious.
2. Both are learned patterns that become habits over time.
3. Both can be sensed and felt by other people.
4. Both influence our moods, which in turn shape our behavior.

A Case for Positivity

Before going further, let me ask a question: Is it possible for an employee to generate outstanding results and offer engagement while working in a negative environment—or even an environment that simply offers little positivity? Certainly. It happens all the time. The question really shouldn't be, Is it possible? but rather, Is it likely?

Perhaps you were one such individual contributor in the past—one who delivered amazing results despite a less-than-ideal work environment. But today, as we've established, you're not only a manager, but a leader. As a leader, you're no longer paid to be the smartest doer-bee, the subject-matter expert, or the go-to problem solver. You exist to maximize the performance and engagement of your employees. And the reality is that most employees perform better and offer more engagement when they're planted in an environment of positivity.

At the same time, as a leader, you're often hired to pay attention to the pragmatic details. Is the sales department meeting its quotas? Does operations have systems in place to reduce errors? Is the IT department equipped with the latest software options? Often, amid all the 1s and 0s, we as leaders forget how important it is to "smell the roses" as we go—or, to put it in manager-speak—to be a positive leader. Or sometimes, we simply become discouraged, making it hard to stay positive.

Why bother with all this positivity stuff? Research illustrates that positivity pays off. These studies, along with anecdotal experience, suggest that great leaders are both pragmatic—paying attention to the bottom line and keeping the facts in a row—while also being positive.

As I clearly suggested in the previous chapter, one of the best ways to engage employees is through positive reinforcement. Now, I'm going to take this concept a step further and state that it's not enough to simply provide positive reinforcement for individual behaviors. Instead, you need to foster an overall culture of positivity.

Remember the dance metaphor? Recently, I attended a daddy-daughter dance at my teenage daughter Alana's high school. The dance was held in the school's large gymnasium. But do you know what? I don't remember seeing basketball hoops, scoreboards, bleachers, or wrestling mats in the gym that night. They were still there. However, the cheerleaders serving on the dance committee transformed the Naperville North High School gym into a dance hall with appropriate lighting, decorations, music, and even a disco ball!

Manager, when you look around your office, don't see cubicles, file cabinets, computers, and sticky notes. See the possibilities instead. And know that you're not a guest of the dance: You're the entire dance committee to your team! It's up to you to transform your environment into a dance hall!

Creating a Positive Engagement Culture

As a leader, you must model the behavior you want to see in others. The same goes with positivity. You influence the direction of your company's culture by demonstrating it firsthand. You can't create an engagement culture simply by pointing the way for others and saying "Go ahead. I'll catch up!" No, you lead the way by practicing and modeling the attributes you want others to follow. If you're modeling negative ideas, thoughts, and behaviors, why would you expect otherwise from your employees?

To assess your attitude as a leader, let me ask you a few questions:

- How much time do you spend each day focusing on what's wrong compared to celebrating what's right?
- Can you think of a time when you've become so obsessed with finding a solution to a challenge that you became unaware of how you treated those who were trying to help you?
- How pleasant are you to be around when your workplace experiences a setback or loss?

I'm not suggesting you should ignore problems when they must be addressed. What I'm suggesting is that you strive to focus more on the positive, so that you're feeding the culture you want to grow. Ironically, you'll learn that solutions are more apt to present themselves in a positive culture.

The level of positivity within a corporate culture affects bottom-line results, and you can become a more positive leader regardless of your title, level of education, or industry. By practicing a few tips I provide, you can increase the positivity in your workplace culture to foster engagement.

The Case for Fostering Positive Thinking in the Workplace Culture

Does positive thinking sound a little mystical, squishy, or soft to you? It might if you believe that mere pragmatism yields better engagement results, and that adding a dose of positivity into your words and actions doesn't make a lick of difference to performance or outcome.

When I shared Theory X and Theory Y management approaches earlier, I told you that if you leaned more to the Theory X style, you need to get to a position of neutrality—an acknowledgment that considering and experimenting with a new way of thinking and behaving might reap rewards.

> **KEY TERM** **Positive Thinking (aka Positive Mental Attitude)** This suggests that if we expect to see positive things like happiness, health, and success, we'll find them. Positive thinking goes beyond telling yourself that you can achieve what you want. It entails telling yourself *and believing* you'll experience a positive end result. Many athletes and public speakers harness positive thinking to visualize the outcome of events before they start. Top sales leaders are also known for uttering positive self-affirmations before making calls.

Let's start with the case against positive thinking. Through the years, I've heard several refutations of positive thinking. Would it surprise you that many of these leaders leaned to the Theory X side of things? Here are the most common objections I heard. Do any of these apply to you?

I'm Too Smart to Believe That It Matters to the End Results

One person I coached challenged, "Pollyanna people don't live in the real world."

I Can't Change Who I Am

Other variants of this response are "I'm just not that way," "Some people are born positive, but I'm not one of them," or "You can't teach an old dog new tricks."

I Won't Fake It

I've heard some say it this way, "I hate phonies, and I won't be one of them."

I want to address those concerns one at a time.

Pragmatic vs. Positive

As I've stated, good leaders are pragmatic; excellent leaders are pragmatic, yet positive.

It's funny how many leaders have told me in so many words that they don't ever want to be labeled as Pollyanna!

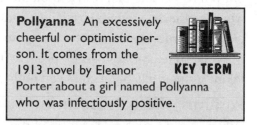

Pollyanna An excessively cheerful or optimistic person. It comes from the 1913 novel by Eleanor Porter about a girl named Pollyanna who was infectiously positive.

KEY TERM

Before you rule out positivity as something for sissies or delusional types, consider the research. The 2001 Harvard Center for Society and Health and the U.S. Department of Veterans Affairs found that older men possessing a positive outlook on life had a lower risk of heart disease (*Harvard School of Public Health's Annual Report 2002*). Similarly, a University of Pittsburgh study found that optimistic women build up less plaque on the walls of their carotid arteries. Dr. Peter Norvid, a geriatric specialist, told *The Chicago Tribune*: "Optimistic people live longer, have closer personal relationships and are able to deal with the negative things that happen to them" (chicagotribune.com/classified/realestate/chi-primetime-pma-022611,0,137010.story).

If being Pollyanna causes those things to happen, sign me up!

"I'm Too Smart to Believe That It Matters to the End Results." Why Smarter Managers Embrace Positivity

Okay, if living longer doesn't excite you, how about sticking with the matter of how positive thinking improves performance and engagement?

Science has long understood the purpose of negative emotions, such as fear, from an evolutionary standpoint. Those negative emotions release cortisol—an adrenaline-like chemical that triggers what's commonly called the Fight-Flight Reflex. In other words, fear releases a chemical that allowed early humans to fight the saber-toothed tiger, or run from it.

But science had no understanding of the purpose of positive emotions except for ... well, they felt good. That changed thanks in part to research conducted by Barbara Fredrickson, psychology professor at UNC-Chapel Hill and author of *Positivity* (Crown Publishers, 2009), who developed the Broaden and Build Theory to explain what happens when our minds operate on positive thoughts instead of negative ones. Here's what Fredrickson found: Positivity broadens the number of possibilities our mind processes and it builds our intelligence!

Are you really too smart for positive thinking? Positive thinking is like taking a smart pill, but it costs you nothing and can't be taken from you.

Positivity Affects Productivity

Other researchers have found additional benefits to being primed for positive thinking:

Doctors who were primed to think positive thoughts before making a diagnosis demonstrated three times more intelligence and creativity than doctors in the control group. Additionally, those doctors primed with positivity arrived at an accurate diagnosis nearly 20 percent faster (C. R. Snyder & Shane Lopez, *Handbook of Positive Psychology*, New York: Oxford University Press, 2005).

Salespeople demonstrating positive thinking outsold their negative-thinking colleagues by 56 percent (Shawn Achor, *The Happiness Advantage*, New York: Crown Business, 2010, p. 15).

University of Toronto researchers found that positive thoughts actually change the way the visual cortex, the part of the brain responsible for vision, processes information. Test subjects primed with positive thoughts actually saw more than those in the control group (University of Toronto, "People Who Wear Rose-Colored Glasses See More, Study Shows." *ScienceDaily*, June 3, 2009).

A successful business owner I recently spoke with noted that 10 out of the 10 top salespeople in his company were also regular borrowers from the "learning library" he stocks with materials for building a positive attitude.

Positivity affects productivity and the bottom line! What Napoleon Hill, author and motivational lecturer, suggests seems accurate: "Successful men become successful only because they acquire the habit of thinking in terms of success."

Now, leaders, let me make a rational appeal to you on the matter of the benefits of practicing positive thinking regularly as part of your management exercise regime: Even if all the research on the power of positive thinking is false, can you risk missing out on its potential to improve the performance results of your employees?

"I Can't Change Who I Am" ... Or Can I?

Are positive people born that way, or created through some blend of environment and experiences? The same question has been asked about leaders, athletes, and musicians. Any time a person exhibits outstanding achievement in one area, the world wants to know how such excellence came about.

Let's consider the flip side by examining those who engage in negative thinking as part of their job descriptions. Editors and auditors come to mind as professions based on finding and eliminating errors. But I want to focus on attorneys, an elite group of professionals who are perhaps the most highly trained in fault finding.

Shawn Achor points out in *The Happiness Advantage* that even though lawyers are more educated, earn more, and enjoy greater social status than most in American culture, they also experience 3.6 times more depressive episodes than the non-attorney population. In fact, according to a report compiled on www.lawyerswithdepression.com/depressionstatistics.asp, attorneys experience higher incidences of substance abuse and higher job dissatisfaction and are more likely to die from suicide than any other profession. Why? Were they born this way, born thinking, "Gee, I feel suicidal. I guess I'll go be a lawyer"? Of course not!

Achor suggests that from the very first law class attorneys are trained to be critical instead of accepting, and they are taught to find flaws in the logic and arguments around them. Isn't it likely, then, that after years of this kind of training and after being promoted largely based on their ability to be the most critically minded in finding faults, that this becomes a habit that goes with them from the courtroom to the breakfast table?

I'm not suggesting that all attorneys are bundles of depression waiting to snap, nor do I advocate that lawyers should quit their jobs and practice yoga (although the latter suggestion wouldn't hurt). What I am suggesting is that we may take on the personality traits inherent in the tasks we practice regularly. And that offers good news, because it means we can change those traits by changing the nature of our surroundings and tasks. But it also means that, regardless of the demands of our profession, we are obligated to pay attention to our attitude, lest it demonstrate itself as our personality.

Today in the field of positive psychology, much is being published about options we have to influence our moods and perhaps even our neurochemistry—by changing our habits. The words of Aristotle thus apply as much today as they did thousands of years ago: "We are what we repeatedly do. Excellence then, is not an act, but a habit." Likewise, negativity is not only an act; it's a habit people practice, feed, and master.

SMART MANAGING

HAPPINESS AS A HABIT

Positive people may be born with a sunny disposition gene. More likely though, they repeatedly practice positive thinking until it's a habit that becomes second nature.

"I Won't Fake It." Making Positivity Part of Who You Are

I grant you that faking it is an act of inauthenticity, and it might seem akin to lying to yourself and others.

So let me ask you this: Are you faking it if you say you're a leader the day you first get promoted to the ranks of management? No, it's an accurate statement. Even if on the day you're promoted into management you have zero leadership skills, you're somewhere on the continuum of becoming a true leader. You're only guilty of committing a lie or falsehood when you try to make others believe you're something that you aren't. But when you're striving to learn and apply new skills to become the most effective manager possible, you're doing what every great, responsible leader does: learning on the job. If you still think assuming positive thinking is faking it because you don't feel it, there's a scientific basis for the phrase "Fake it until you make it." It's called self-fulfilling prophesy—a phenomenon that occurs when people tell themselves something and then it comes true. In a study conducted at Wake Forest University, scientists challenged a group of test subjects to act like extroverts for 15 minutes, regardless of whether they tended toward introversion or extroversion. What did the research conclude? "The more assertive and energetic the students acted, the happier they were" (Jane Meredith Adams, "How You Too Can Be an Optimist," *Prevention*, December 2006).

I recently spoke to my friend Marlene Chism, who's a popular speaker and coach as well as the author of *Stop Workplace Drama* (Hoboken, NJ: Wiley & Sons, 2011). She shared with me her practice of journaling and its role in her success. In her journaling process, she subtly reframes her thoughts and then the words she writes so that she begins scripting the outcome that she wants to see. She concluded by telling me that this precise scripting helps her transform events *as they are* into events *as she wishes them to be*. Marlene's scripting is not faking it; she's simply plotting the route to success that she'll take before she starts her journey. She's able to harness positive thoughts until they become positive outcomes.

Want to be a more positive leader? Practice more positivity. And if you don't want to fake positive thinking, make it real. Build positive thinking until it becomes a habit and regular practice. If you aren't sure where to begin, start small—making short-term goals to change your behavior. We discuss specific tips later in this chapter.

THE MARATHON MARGIN

If the idea of changing the workplace culture overnight sounds daunting, consider committing to a training program of sorts that involves making a series of small changes in the right direction. Jocelyn Godfrey, my partner at Spiritus Communications, a consulting firm for entrepreneurial leaders—www.SpiritusCommuni **TOOLS** cations.com—came up with a progress principle we train leaders on known as The Marathon Margin. Marathon runners aren't born able to run 26.2 miles. Instead, they learn, condition themselves, and develop their endurance over time. If they don't ever go the distance to condition, they won't build the endurance or distance to meet their goals. But if they start out too strong—training too hard or too fast—they burn out, get defeated, give up, and fail to meet their goals. *The Marathon Margin is the optimum range wherein endurance is increased without burnout.* Similarly, this progress principle applies to the workplace by introducing the optimal range of performance wherein skills advance and goals draw closer—but wherein overexertion is averted. Put simply, it involves taking baby steps toward goals. As the famous quote uttered by Mac Anderson and others states, "Inch by inch, life's a cinch; yard by yard, life is hard." Apply The Marathon Margin to your engagement efforts to ensure continual growth and progress.

When Bluntness Doesn't Work

When my daughter Alana was 3 years old, I worked from home one day because I didn't feel well. When Alana woke up that morning, she was confused to see me at home.

"I'm sick," I said by way of explanation.

This answer didn't set well with Alana. She crawled up on my lap, placed her chunky hands on either side of my face, and looked deeply at me: "Are you going to die, Daddy?"

The pragmatic, no-nonsense leader in me responded: "Yes, Alana, I am going to die. You see, the moment we're born sets in motion the process of death. Every day we live brings us one step closer to our inevitable end. The cells in our body regenerate to a point. But life has an outer limit. At some point, usually around 75 for men of my generation, the cells regenerate more slowly until one day," I snapped my fingers, "I will die."

No, that's not what I said! But it's what I could have said if my goal were to be factual only.

Many leaders would answer an employee question of "Do you think downsizing is likely as a result of this merger?" with a response of "Hell, yeah! Of course downsizing is on the table. Companies don't merge to spend more money; they merge to leverage platforms and cut costs. And people are a huge cost! We'll probably all be looking for work once the merger is complete!"

Purely pragmatic leaders answer questions with a heavy dose of vinegar and not a trace of honey. But the best leaders understand that hope (sound familiar?) and positivity are essential to engagement.

Look in the Mirror: Are You a Positive "Super Model" Leader?

Our mood shapes our behavior. A *behavior* is any observable action or series of actions that a person performs. If you or someone else can watch something occur, what you're watching is a behavior. That means when your employees watch you at work, they interpret what they see. And even if you're unaware of it, you're sending either positive or negative messages all the time!

> ## A MODEL DANCER
> **SMART**
>
> Think back to the engagement dance. You're transforming the environment so that it's conducive to excitement, fun, and dancing. But beyond your role in setting the stage, you have to model what you want others to do. Manager, you have to learn **MANAGING** to dance. And I don't mean going through the motions of 1-2-3-dip. It's one thing to dance—to put your feet inside the little foot stickers that show you where to step. It's another to dance with passion and grace. Passion and grace mean lessons and practice time. Over time, your form will become more fluent, your movements more fluid. And then instead of telling your employees to dance, you can ask them to come join you with confidence. Become the engagement model you want your employees to follow—and a credible one.

Years ago I got a little dose of reality when I caught an employee of mine named Tara doing an impromptu and hilarious impersonation of me. At first, I didn't recognize what she was doing. I just thought Tara seemed angry and perhaps a little ill! But once I encouraged her to do it again while studying her more carefully, I couldn't deny that the stiff, determined way that I stood and walked across the room coupled with the furrowed brow and downturned lips indeed made me seem more than a little unapproachable and even angry.

And do you know what? I don't consider myself either of those things! What Tara saw and impersonated for me was my behavior when I was lost in thought and wrapped in urgency. And what I saw Tara reflect of me was undeniable: I closed myself off and crawled inside my head when stressed. And that stress was translated as negativity.

How your employees perceive you has a huge impact on how they perform and engage. In a recent experiment at Yale School of Management and highlighted by Achor in *The Happiness Advantage*, student volunteers were put into four work groups to see which team could earn the most money for a fictitious company. The manager, played by an actor, interacted with the teams while they were working. The actor spoke in one of four ways to the different teams: cheerful enthusiasm, serene warmth, depressed sluggishness, or hostile irritability.

Guess which of the four teams came up with the best ideas and earned the most money? Yes, the team that was addressed in a tone that conveyed cheerful enthusiasm.

SMART MANAGING

MIRROR, MIRROR ...
If you want to know what others see, put a mirror in a place that lets you see your face when you interact with others. When you're in deep concentration, you might be making a face that others interpret as frustrated or even angry. Watch your face, and make sure the message it conveys is the message you want to project.

Manager, what's your normal demeanor? Of the four personas the actor played in the case study above, which do you believe most accurately reflects you? And perhaps more important, which do you think your people would say best describes you?

A Tool: How Do They See You?

Take a look at the following questions and circle the response that most closely describes you. Don't overthink any of the questions. If you feel comfortable, you can ask someone close to you to respond to these questions about you.

When I experience an unexpected setback, my first response is to:

1. Get mad and blow off steam
2. Shut down for a while until I recover
3. Talk over my disappointment with someone close to me
4. Tell my employees what I experienced and what I'm learning from it

When someone brings me a problem, my first inclination is to:

1. Interrupt them and solve their problem as soon as I have the answer
2. Tell them to come back later or set up a meeting to discuss it
3. Listen long enough to know to whom to refer them
4. Listen until they're done speaking, then ask them for their ideas on solving the matter

When the stress level at work gets to a high point, my response is to:

1. Insist that people stop talking and get back to work
2. Avoid people in an attempt to avoid extra stress
3. Make some jokes to lighten the mood
4. Point out the things you see that are going well

In times of change and fear at work, I usually:

1. Shake my head and say something like "It figures!"
2. Isolate while I process
3. Ask employees what they're hearing
4. Make a point to get around to each employee to pass on what I know and am free to share

Look at your responses:

- **1s** indicate that you may behave in an outwardly negative way at work when you're under stress. Your employees will see and interpret your behaviors as negative, and that may foster an environment of fear, frustration, anger, or insecurity.
- **2s** should serve as a caution that your reserved behavior may be translated by others as a byproduct of negative thinking and feeling on your part.
- **3s** or **4s** suggest that even in difficult times, you try to maintain your own positive outlook and attempt to share that with your employees.

How we feel shapes how we act, and how we act shapes how we feel. Practice positive thinking as a way to keep your mind and actions aligned toward engaging others.

10 Activities to Increase Your Positive Thinking

Studies show that optimistic people have better performance, experience less depression, suffer fewer health problems, and have better relationships. And the best news is that the same research proves optimism and positive thinking can be learned (University of Pennsylvania site's Positive Psychology Center, www.ppc.sas.upenn.edu/faqs.htm).

So, manager, think about it this way: Even if practicing positive thinking doesn't greatly increase the performance and engagement levels of your employees, isn't it worth it for the positive benefits available to you?

Positive thinking is a habit, like any other routine in your life. The more you practice it, the stronger the habit grows. Here are some positivity-building activities for you to practice to increase your positive thinking habit.

Activity #1: Practice Gratitude

- The father of positive psychology, Martin Seligman, suggests ending each day reflecting on three happy, positive events that occurred that day. This primes the mind to focus on positive thoughts before bed and may have a subconscious effect on what your mind thinks about while you sleep.

■ At work, start each meeting by asking your team "What's something fantastic that we've accomplished today or this week?" Imagine the kind of performance you'd experience if every individual could find one thing that went great!

Activity #2: Make Your First Thoughts and Words Positive Each Day

■ Before getting out of bed, think about something positive, perhaps even some happy experience from your past. Spend a minute letting that memory fill your mind before getting up.

■ At work, make your first words to each person you meet positive and nurturing. Pretend that your words will be the first ones your employees will have heard that day. Make your words count.

Activity #3: Visualize Success

■ When anticipating an event, don't wait to get there to start picturing the outcome. Picture each step of the process going smoothly, what Chism refers to as *scripting*.

■ At work, prime the positive thoughts of your employees by sending a team e-mail saying, "Take a minute and breathe while thinking of the coolest vacation spot you've ever visited. And if you like, send me a note and tell me a little about it. I'm always looking for new places to visit." This not only opens employees up for sharing more personal information at work, but also primes them to focus on creating positive thoughts.

Activity #4: Get Moving

■ Exercise releases endorphins, a natural chemical known to create a feeling of well-being. You don't have to run a marathon. Even a short, brisk walk can give you an edge.

■ At work, encourage your team to make fitness a regular part of their work routine. I had one team at work that sponsored "The Biggest Loser" within the department—a voluntary, honor-system program for those interested in shedding a few pounds. Another time, my boss challenged the entire division to a walking contest. We issued pedometers to all employees, created a database for employees to track their steps, and celebrated winners across the organization. Win-win!

Activity #5: Look Forward to Something!

- Do you remember how excited you were as a child when a special holiday such as your birthday approached? You might have even counted down the days. My son, Jack, used to keep me posted of his upcoming special day by saying things like "Only 363 shopping days until my birthday!" (Yes, the year seemed to last longer that way.) Do the same thing for yourself. Have a personal or professional enticement you can think about when you're stressed or you need a positive focus.

- At work, ask your employees things like, "Do you have anything exciting planned this weekend?" I had a boss, Kasey, who during the week would ask each employee about any special plans. This primed people to look ahead and share some joy.

Activity #6: Have a Sense of Humor

- What makes you laugh? If that's too ambitious, what makes you smile? Take time every day to smile or laugh, and do it as often as you can. Humor reduces stress, strengthens the heart, releases endorphins, and encourages positive thinking (more on this topic in Chapter 9).

- At work, don't be afraid to get your employees laughing. You don't need to be a standup comedian. Listen to what makes people laugh, and laugh with them. Keep humor pure and fun, and encourage people to take laughter breaks often.

Activity #7: Surround Yourself with Positive People

- You've heard "You are known by the company you keep." Be known for spending time with positive cheerleaders. My friend Craig Wortmann is the happiest person I know. He teaches an award-winning graduate class at Chicago Booth, authored a bestselling book, *What's Your Story?* (Kaplan Publishing, 2006), managed and sold two highly successful learning organizations, and serves as CEO of SalesEngine.com. He's happy and he's successful, in that order. Craig's happiness and positive outlook create success wherever he goes. Guess who I want to talk to as often as possible? Craig Wortmann. Find those people in your life, and make it a point to meet with them or talk with them as often as possible.

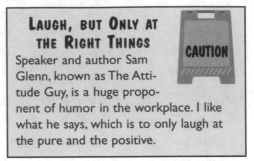

LAUGH, BUT ONLY AT THE RIGHT THINGS
Speaker and author Sam Glenn, known as The Attitude Guy, is a huge proponent of humor in the workplace. I like what he says, which is to only laugh at the pure and the positive.

CAUTION

- At work, give special opportunities to your most outspokenly positive employees. Let their enthusiasm and positivity spread to others. As a side benefit, when other people see what kind of attitudes and behaviors get reinforced, they'll want to do the same things that get positive attention.

Activity #8: Use Can-Do Words

- Replace phrases like "I'm going to try to ..." with "Here's what I'm going to accomplish. And it's going to be awesome!"
- At work, develop a signature phrase or gesture to use with your employees that demonstrates your confidence in them and the outcomes they'll achieve. I used to make this silly hand gesture with an accompanying head sway that was meant to convey "I think you're pretty neat." I never explained it nor did I need to. Employees picked up on the intention behind it, and it made them smile and reciprocate.

Activity #9: Create a Mantra or Affirmation for Yourself

- "We are as we repeatedly do." Just like you have a morning routine that likely involves a shower, getting dressed, and drinking coffee, add in there somewhere a little positive self-talk like "I am calm, and my thinking is clear." Sound hokey? A friend of mine is a hypnotist. He told me that the same concept of suggestion that allows him to hypnotize others can be used by laymen on themselves! Tell yourself what you believe and what you'll achieve. Then watch yourself get there!
- At work, ask each of your employees to create a saying that reflects how fantastic they are at getting things done. Fictitious character Stuart Smalley brilliantly played on TV by Al Franken on *Saturday*

Night Live used to say, "I'm good enough, I'm smart enough. And doggone it, people like me!" I had one employee who liked to say "I am superwoman; watch me soar," a nice take on the line from the Helen Reddy song *I Am Woman; Hear Me Roar*.

MARK IT ON THE MIRROR

TRICKS OF THE TRADE

Whenever I travel to speak, I bring markers designed to write on glass. On the bathroom mirror before going to bed, I scribble positive affirmations to myself, such as "Knock 'em dead!" "Be awesome!" "Someone needs what you have!" "Leave 'em wanting more!" and "Have fun!" This turns my mind to positive thoughts as I go to sleep, and it's the first thing I see in the morning. And I get a secret joy wondering what the housekeeper thinks when she or he walks in the bathroom after I've checked out!

As a bonus, I use these same markers at home to exchange love notes with my wife and kids. It's fun and easy, and it works! We look forward to going to the bathroom to check the mirrors!

Activity #10: Challenge Negative Thoughts; Avoid Negativity

- Don't entertain thoughts like "I can't do this!" or "This isn't going to end well!" Be ready with a plan to attack these positive energy-suckers. Know what triggered them and counter them quickly by saying and believing "I can and will be successful." When I quit smoking, I had to fight the urge to smoke one second at a time. Whenever the desire to smoke would hit me and I was tempted to fall into the false, negative promise of how wonderful my life would be if I only caved in and lit just one more cigarette, I would say loudly, "Not now!" I didn't try to banish the nicotine withdrawals forever in one second. Rather, I told myself that I could hold out for another moment. I said it, I believed it, and it worked.

- At work, counter negative comments and statements like "We can't get that done on time" or "This isn't possible" with lighthearted statements like "Ten bucks says we can" or "That's what they told the Wright Brothers. Let's prove those negative forecasts wrong." Challenging negativity won't necessarily bring your employees into a more positive way of thinking. But at least it won't reinforce their complaining.

Safeguard Your Attitude with Boundaries

We've already discussed the importance of surrounding yourself with positive people and situations. This can mean cutting out negative people and influences. Here are a few things to consider limiting or eliminating if you find yourself easily slipping into negative territory:

- **Negative TV and music.** I love psychological thrillers and horror movies, and I've been known to watch an entire season of *Dexter* in one long viewing session. I have an extensive and eclectic music collection that includes artists like Black Sabbath, Nine Inch Nails, and Rage Against the Machine. Those genres of entertainment have their place, but they can't become part of your steady diet if you want to feed yourself positivity, relaxation, and creativity. To stay in the positive zone, replace *American Horror Story* with *American Idol;* swap Black Sabbath for some Beethoven.

- **Sarcasm.** Sarcasm comes from an ancient Greek word that literally means "to tear flesh." "Now that's just the sort of thing you need more of to build engagement and positivity," I say sarcastically. Sarcasm has its place among close friends and those who know you well. But when you as a leader use it with your employees, you can put people on edge. Avoid it at work.

- **Complaining.** Venting frustration can be a cathartic release—to a point. But something happens when you complain frequently: It becomes a habit. For many people, venting as a way of release ends up growing more negative thoughts instead of releasing them.

- **Friends who aren't positive.** Do you know the proverb that goes "Just like iron sharpens iron, one man sharpens another"? That only works if you're rubbing them together the right way! Otherwise, you'll end up with two dull blades instead of one. Staying in the company of negative people for too long will suck you of your positivity. Know your limits, and don't be in the company of joy-sappers for longer than you must.

- **News updates that focus on catastrophes or the uncontrollable.** Let's face it, the evening headlines rarely start off saying "All nations of the world are at peace, and celebrations have been planned on each continent." If you find yourself feeling down after watching or reading the news, limit your time dwelling on it. Cleanse your mental palate by finding positive, uplifting news stories.

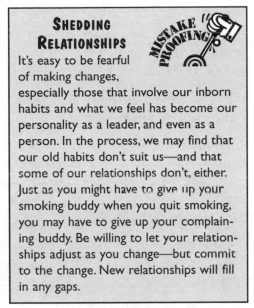

SHEDDING RELATIONSHIPS

It's easy to be fearful of making changes, especially those that involve our inborn habits and what we feel has become our personality as a leader, and even as a person. In the process, we may find that our old habits don't suit us—and that some of our relationships don't, either. Just as you might have to give up your smoking buddy when you quit smoking, you may have to give up your complaining buddy. Be willing to let your relationships adjust as you change—but commit to the change. New relationships will fill in any gaps.

- **Mementos that remind you of unhappy times.** Just as a bad dream can start your day going down a dark road, stumbling across macabre trophies of past defeats and losses can send you into a tailspin of negativity. While you're working on doing some cognitive conditioning to make positive thoughts more of your first response, do some literal housekeeping to purge from your sight things that take you to sad places.

Replace those negatives with positives. Anne Bruce, speaker and bestselling author of books such as *Discover True North*, suggests having an Inner Circle of Influencers. She suggests making such declarations as "The company I keep will be made up of individuals who are fiercely loyal, faithful and trustworthy, tolerant of people's differences, generous with their ideas and innovations, secure about themselves and where they are going, positive and focused, intelligent and accomplished, family oriented" (McGraw Hill, 2004).

In fact, from the speaker's platform, Bruce often refers to the inner circle of influencers in one's life, also an invaluable "Life Board of Directors," where each person chooses with whom to engage, draw ideas, and glean innovative business strategies. A Life Board of Directors usually is made up of a dozen or so people among us today and even historical figures. Bruce cites Einstein (who sits on her Life Board) for innovation and Winston Churchill for survival strategies. In her bestselling book, *Solving Employee Performance Problems* (New York: McGraw-Hill, 2011), Bruce illustrates the power of using a "Life Balance Wheel," where individuals can appoint

Life Board members to specifically represent various areas of their lives, such as health, career, finance, friends and family, and the popular "life expander" role. Creating such a clearly defined circle of influence will help you create positivity from the inside out.

What to Do When Fight-or-Flight Kicks In— Calming the Amygdala

There's a small, almond-shaped region located deep within the medial temporal lobes of our brains called the *amygdala*. Do you remember my earlier reference to the fight-flight response? The amygdala chemically triggers that response, which is useful when your life is in danger. Even though most jobs don't involve life and death, the same chemicals flood our bodies whether we're in mortal danger or just under extreme pressure, deadlines, or day-to-day emergencies. This condition has been called *flooding* or *amygdala hijacking*. Those same chemicals that are designed to help you act decisively and with strength come with a high price: greatly diminished problem-solving and reasoning skills.

What can you do to keep your amygdala from being hijacked? First, to stay positive as leaders, know your triggers and keep your emotional outbursts at bay. Don't give them space to take over your reasoning. Think of a toddler who has a temper tantrum. What do you do? Do you coddle him—letting him scream and then giving him what he wants? Maybe, but if you do, you aren't teaching him the emotional maturity necessary to progress toward solutions. More likely you send him to his room or a safe place to calm down until he can think more reasonably, and then you talk through whatever issue it was if it still remains. As adults, we aren't much different than the toddler. We still get overwhelmed at times and want to blow up. When our amygdala is overloaded, we're in fight-or-flight mode and we do things as if our survival depends on it—when in reality, it usually doesn't. Often, we act irrationally.

The second thing you can do when your amygdala gets triggered is to S.T.O.P. In my coaching, I teach a method called S.T.O.P. to help people master their emotions, to calm down, and to pause before reacting. It consists of:

- **Start breathing deeply.** Our first response to fear and stress often leads us to breathe in shallow gulps, depriving our brains of the oxygen we need to work properly. Take several deep breaths, letting them out slowly.

- **Tell yourself how you want the scene to play out.** When you get a call from your boss who wants to see you immediately, don't allow your mind to project the worst-case scenario for the ending: "Oh no! I'm going to be fired!" Instead, tell yourself what you want to happen when you meet, things like receiving kudos for a job well done or being asked to help him or her brainstorm a challenge.

- **Open your mind to other truths.** This might sound a little mystical, but it works. I used to hate flying. Well, actually, I don't mind flying, but I'm less than thrilled with the thought of crashing! Once during a time of bad turbulence, I started taking shallow breaths. Then I told myself, *"We are so going down!"* My wife reminded me to *start* breathing deeply and to *tell* myself it will be fine. She then suggested that I close my eyes and forget the airplane. "Imagine instead," she whispered, "that you're at the amusement park on a ride that you've waited your whole life to ride. The bouncing is part of the experience and the thrill." When I changed the context of my thoughts, I actually could enjoy the ride. The fear got tucked away, and the turbulence became less terrifying.

- **Proceed rationally.** How do you help your children combat the monsters hiding in their closets or under their beds? You empathize with their emotions (fear). You turn on the lights and show them what there is to see: a monster-free room. When your own emotions threaten to blow, don't give yourself permission to act until you've considered multiple alternatives and have the clarity required to proceed with intentional rationality.

If you find yourself about to blow your top, practice S.T.O.P. behavior before you spread negativity to others. Similarly, train your employees to do the same by reasoning with them only when they display proper emotional control.

Who Holds Your Mirror?

Sometimes, if we've endured a lifetime of negativity, it exists in our minds—reminding us of all the ways we've failed and paralyzing us.

Maybe it came in the form of a parent, or maybe it still comes in the form of a boss who doesn't see us for who we are.

I have a keynote speech titled "Who Holds Your Mirror?" that focuses on this. If the person holding your mirror doesn't reflect back whom you want to see, take back your mirror. Don't give your mirror to anyone who sees you as broken, useless, or "bad." Instead, set a boundary. Feed yourself positive words and surround yourself with as many positive people and influences as possible until you feel solid in your esteem. It's difficult to see yourself as a great leader if you can't see yourself as a great person. If you see the same struggles in your employees, encourage their esteem by increasing their positive reinforcement—and in particular, praise them.

SMART MANAGING

POSITIVITY GLUE

Praise is like cement; it sticks in our minds and makes us want to do a repeat performance of what we just did to receive commendations.

Thinking Your Way into an Engaged Culture

So far in this chapter, I've challenged you to fuel yourself with positive thoughts as a way to make more positive things happen. Perhaps you translated some of what I said as this: Positive thinking might not change our circumstances, but it can change the way we view our circumstances. I've avoided saying that until now, but it's possible that you interpreted my words as a way to motivate you to think and act more positively and less negatively.

Now I want to take it a little further. Positive thoughts do more than frame how we view reality; *positive thoughts change reality.*

Remember when I posed the question, Wouldn't it be nice if you had a whole team of employees you could count on to make things happen and get things done? Manager, you have the power to make that a reality.

Researchers Robert Rosenthal and Lenore Jacobson suggest that leaders can improve employee performance and even engagement levels by thinking it into being. Known as the Pygmalion Effect, this self-fulfilling prophecy is something you can harness to improve your results.

Researchers conducted IQ tests in an elementary school, and after-

---

11 Quick Ways to Promote the Positive

1. Post positive quotes in a visible location.
2. Promote exercise in the workplace through lunchtime sports or walks, or after-work classes in activities like yoga, boxing, or some new and intriguing sport. The endorphins cannot be beat! **TOOLS**
3. Encourage people to bring photos of family members and favorite activities to work and post them on a board in the break room.
4. Create a lending library of positive materials.
5. Hire a humorous or motivational speaker, or watch DVDs or inspirational clips on YouTube.
6. Create a Facebook page where your employees can post creative and positive material at appropriate times throughout the week.
7. Host an after-work "dog party" at a local dog park where employees bring their pets.
8. Initiate a book club or favorite book exchange at work.
9. Change your written and verbal communications to be worded positively whenever possible, and encourage the same in others.
10. Host a roasting party for employees with you as the subject.
11. Have silly contests and sillier rewards.

---

ward they debriefed teachers in each grade by telling them something about a few of their students. They'd say something like "Jamie, Lauren, and David have all of the markings of brilliance we'd expect to see from top academic achievers and those with the most growth potential."

Before leaving, the experimenters cautioned the teachers not to say anything to the students or spend extra time with them. In fact, teachers were told that they would be watched to make sure they didn't let anything slip.

At the end of the school year, all the students were retested, and not surprisingly, Jamie, Lauren, and David scored like the intellectual giants they were.

Except for one thing. Jamie, Lauren, and David weren't the brainiest kids in their class. Nor had those children scored at the top of the first test. In fact, the only reason that Jamie, Lauren, and David were named to the teachers is because they were average and ordinary.

So what happened between the first test when the children were average and second test when the children were at top performance? Two things. First, the teacher's belief in these students' potential got shared with the students indirectly, nonverbally, and accidentally. Second, the students picked up on the positive beliefs their teachers held for them, and the students performed to the level they were expected to achieve (Pygmalion Effect, Wikipedia.com).

Positive thoughts can change reality. What does this mean to you as a leader? It means you can create better, more engaged performers just by believing in the potential of your employees!

Pygmalion at Work

SMART MANAGING

Challenge yourself with these questions: What would happen at work if . . .

1. I laid out a vision and let my people decide how to proceed?
2. I believed that each team member brought excellence to his or her role and wanted to do his or her best at work?
3. I let go of negative beliefs or perceptions I held about any team member and, instead, trusted that each wanted to be a superstar?
4. I acted toward my employees like they were the best people in the world?

What would happen? First, you would create willing, passionate followers. Second, people would give you their discretionary effort because they wanted to. Third, your employees would believe that they were superstars and they would then act like superstars. Finally, you would see a team of engaged individuals dedicated to making a difference, doing their best, and reciprocating your actions.

Manager's Checklist for Chapter 4

☑ The way you think and act sets the tone for all others at work.

☑ One of the most prominent characteristics that engaging leaders and individuals possess is a positive mental attitude.

☑ Positivity is a habit that can be learned, practiced, and grown—and something that must be protected with boundaries in order to thrive.

☑ How your employees perceive you has a huge impact on how they perform and engage.

☑ Practicing positivity not only increases performance and engagement levels of your employees, it also benefits the leader as a person.

☑ Positive thoughts do more than frame how we view reality; positive thoughts can change reality.

Empowering Employees to Act as Entrepreneurial Owners

W hat would you do if you owned a Mexican restaurant and on the busiest day of the year, Cinco de Mayo, your computer system went down? For many restaurant owners, this would be a recipe to panic! This unfortunate situation is exactly what happened to Britt Guyer, owner of Estela's Mexican Restaurant in St. Petersburg, Florida, who recently pulled up a chair to chat while I ate at his restaurant.

"When something like that happens, you look to your most engaged employees for answers. I'm just the owner. My employees are the ones who have the real day-to-day understanding of how to get things done."

Guyer credited Alex—one of his most experienced, engaged employees who knows every job in the restaurant—for coming to the rescue when his system crashed.

"Alex immediately jumped in to take care of the situation. She handed me an old-fashioned 'knuckle-buster' to manually swipe credit cards and she rallied the wait staff—telling them about the new process we'd be using while the computer was off-line," Guyer told me.

What was at risk for Guyer and his restaurant? Some customers take advantage of confusion and chaos to walk out without paying their bills. Estela's stood to lose a lot of money since Cinco de Mayo customers usually have a drink or two with their meals. Alex's quick response allowed

Guyer to get around to the tables and make sure that the behind-the-scenes chaos stayed behind the scenes! In fact, most customers were unaware of any problem until informed of it when they paid their bills.

Leaders, you need an Alex. But imagine what you could do with a team of Alexes offering calm, creative solutions when you need them most! What's one way to build a team of that kind of employee? You create entrepreneurial employees who are able to take ownership in your organization—thinking and acting creatively on their feet. Like owners of a small business, entrepreneurial employees like Alex are willing to give of their discretionary effort to ensure success.

What If This Were Your Company?

In my consulting practice, I've conferred with many leaders who feel constricted or blocked around certain looming business decisions. In many cases, these leaders don't lack clarity around the needs of the business or the consequences of their decisions. But they remain afraid to choose a course of action, even when they believe they have the right answer.

To get these managers talking when they seem paralyzed, I ask this simple question: What would you do if this were your company?

Invariably, the leaders answer immediately and fluently spell out what decision should be made and why. In a matter of a minute, the leaders could articulate a full, well-thought-out business case, cost-benefit analysis, and resource requirements. During that minute, the leaders' eyes shine, and I believe that if leaders were equipped with tails like dogs, those tails would be wagging from side to side with passion and excitement.

But in many cases, the leaders will end the minute of insight by saying one or two words that seem to trump common sense, strategic objectives, and even profitability: *politics* or *bureaucracy*. Not surprisingly, those two items are top employee dissatisfiers, serving as a leading cause for disengagement.

Do bureaucracy or office politics prevent you from being the most effective leader possible? Does it prevent your employees from being engaged as entrepreneurs in your organization?

Replace Bureaucracy with Ownership

As part of debriefing with clients on the best path to take when politics or bureaucracies seem to prevent positive action, here's a coaching point that I make regardless of how the leaders end up choosing their answer: Remember how awful you feel right now, and make sure your employees never feel stifled because you put roadblocks in their way!

Corporate or **office politics** This can be described as what happens when an individual manipulates a working relationship or expends time and other business resources for personal gain, even when it comes at the expense of the team or company. **KEY TERMS** Often, individuals who play corporate politics withhold information that others need so they can either look good themselves or exert some sense of power over others.

Bureaucracy Often characterized as a nameless, faceless organizational entity made up of low-paying, power-hungry beings who oversee rules, policies, procedures, and functions within their organization. The two words most often associated with bureaucracy are *red* and *tape*. The real purpose of these employees seems to be to prevent others from getting things done.

FOR EXAMPLE

YOU MIGHT WORK IN A BUREAUCRACY IF ...

Someone I interviewed last year shared this part of her story with me: "My computer broke, so I had to work from my home until it was replaced. It took me three months of paperwork and digging through red tape to requisition a new one. Ironically, I worked for an electronics superstore. For goodness sake, *we sold computers!*" —Kathryn B.

What do bureaucracy and politics have to do with entrepreneurship? What allows small businesses to be nimble and quick when it comes to jumping on opportunities is that they aren't constrained with the bureaucratic elements that many larger corporations have in place. As a leader wanting to grow an engaged workforce, learn from entrepreneurs: Create a team with the mindset of successful, small business owners who act as if they own the company. Even if politics holds you back in some areas, you can empower your employees to make certain decisions as an entrepreneur would.

The Entreprencurial Advantage

You'll become a more engaging leader by learning what entrepreneurs do differently. After all, entrepreneurs give their discretionary efforts. Why? Entrepreneurs feel a connection between their efforts and their potential rewards. A positive relationship between efforts and rewards is a top engagement enabler, according to bestselling author Malcolm Gladwell in his book *Outliers: The Story of Success* (Little, Brown and Company, 2008).

Entrepreneur A business owner who makes money through risk and initiative.

KEY TERM

BUT I WORK IN A BIG COMPANY!
When you're an entrepreneur inside a large organization, you are called an *intrapreneur*. The same principles apply to intrapreneurs as entrepreneurs, and intrapreneurs can reap the same benefits in engagement and performance by following entrepreneurial practices.

How do you create a culture of entrepreneurship that ignites engagement or, as Chouinard describes it, drives "employees who … work like demons to produce something of the highest possible quality"? Start by following the C.O.U.R.S.E. that entrepreneurs take. If you can follow and master this C.O.U.R.S.E., you'll achieve entrepreneurial engagement! Entrepreneurs are:

- Creative
- Optimistic
- Unwavering in their pursuit
- Realistic
- Sales-minded
- Empowered by an Internal Locus of Control

C.O.U.R.S.E.: The Six Core Traits of an Entrepreneur

Managers, empower your employees to think and act as entrepreneurs by fostering the six core traits of entrepreneurship.

Trait #1: Entrepreneurs Are Creative

Most of what's taught in school and business requires convergent think-

WHAT WE WANT

FOR EXAMPLE

In his own words published in his book, *Let My People Go Surfing* (New York: Penguin Press, 2005), Yvon Chouinard, founder of Patagonia, Inc. states: "[At Patagonia, w]e don't want drones who will simply follow directions. We want the kind of employees who will question the wisdom of something they regard as a bad decision but, once they buy into something, will work like demons to produce something of the highest possible quality." What Chouinard describes is the essence of entrepreneurialism.

ing—the type of thinking measured by traditional IQ tests. *Convergent thinking* occurs when you sort through a long list of possibilities before converging on *the only one correct answer* to a *very specific problem.* Convergent thinking builds on what's already known and seeks to apply it to new, similar situations. For that reason, long division requires that a student know addition, subtraction, and multiplication to converge on the correct answer.

How would that kind of thinking apply to someone left shipwrecked on a deserted island with nothing but the clothes he's wearing, his wits, and the resources of the island to survive? A shipwreck isn't a case study that most students research in class, and it's unlikely that a four-step formula exists to solving it. As a problem, it's broad and multifaceted.

An entrepreneur wouldn't rely on convergent thinking to survive a shipwreck, regardless of how great his or her convergent thinking skills might be. Rather, the entrepreneur quickly understands that divergent thinking known as *creativity* is required to survive. *Divergent thinking* is what allows a bored child to think of a hundred fun things to do with a rock and string. Likewise, if the entrepreneur were stranded on an island, any pointy stick would look like a spear for fishing, and the sea would resemble a ripe field

ALL THINGS ARE POSSIBLE

TRICKS OF THE TRADE

If you're going to be ignorant about something, be ignorant of the meaning of *impossible*.

free for harvesting. Why? Entrepreneurs use their creativity as a third eye to see possibilities where others see none.

Here are a few ways to foster creativity in the workplace:

As a leader, encourage your employees to take creative risks by providing them with the means to experiment with new ways to accomplish tasks. Without creative thinking, instead of building an automobile, inventors would have spent all their time trying to engineer a faster horse!

If possible, give your employees flex time at work to explore interests, even if they may seem unrelated to their tasks. Companies like Google provide this, and it seems to be paying off in that they've fostered an incredibly creative and engaged workforce—and solid, bottom-line results.

Bring employees into projects even when the work may seem above their skill level or area of expertise, so they have a chance to expand their minds and offer solutions. If you wait until an employee is 100 percent ready to assume a broader role, that employee may never be ready in your eyes.

The Japanese Soap Company

One of Japan's biggest cosmetics companies received a complaint from a customer, who purchased a box of soap and found upon opening it that the box was empty. Management sprang into action, quickly discovering that the problem began on the assembly line. Then top convergent thinkers in the company were brought in to make sure that the problem never happened again. Eventually, engineers devised a solution that involved the use of an X-ray machine watched by two employees to make sure each box contained soap.

A frontline employee in the factory with no engineering experience or education looked at the situation differently and came up with a solution that didn't involve X-rays or additional employees. Instead, the factory worker pointed an industrial-sized electric fan at the assembly line. Boxes with soap inside stayed on the conveyer belt, and the empty boxes he put on the belt for the demonstration immediately were blown off the line.

Entrepreneurs are always thinking about What if? and they're always looking for better ways to accomplish tasks. They're not afraid to get their hands dirty in creating something novel and effective.

Put another way, they're like tigers on the hunt. They instinctively know what they want—a healthy chunk of meat—and their hunger drives them to go to all lengths to find and capture it.

Trait #2: Entrepreneurs Are Optimistic

Entrepreneurs are optimistic that their goals can be accomplished.

ENTREPRENEURS SEE RISKS DIFFERENTLY

Jeff Bezos, founder of Amazon, had a successful job in New York when he quit to sell books online. He had no idea how he was going to accomplish his goal, but as he told The Academy of Achievement in an interview, "I knew that if I failed I wouldn't regret that, but I knew the one thing I might regret is not trying" (see www.achievement.org/autodoc/page/bez0int-3). Bezos had a creative idea to fill a niche on the relatively new platform of the Internet, was optimistic he could make it work, and went about acting on it. The result is history. Entrepreneurs face failure all the time, but it doesn't stop them from trying—and this is what also leads to their success.

Remember from Chapter 4 that positive thoughts not only change how we see things, they also change reality. It's called *self-fulfilling prophesy*. Entrepreneurs bring a hope-filled, can-do, optimistic attitude into each venture. "If anyone can do this, I can" is the mantra they follow. They're excited to get started. Understanding the value of positive, self-fulfilling prophesies, they envision success.

Many jobs require optimism in order to operate. Sales is one of them.

TWO SALESPEOPLE

The story of two shoe salesmen venturing into Africa at the turn of the 20th century bears repeating. On arrival, one shoe salesman noted the barefoot natives and wired a message to his office that read: "Situation hopeless. The locals don't wear shoes." The other salesman took a quick look around and excitedly wired a different message back to the office: "Glorious opportunity! They don't have any shoes yet!"

Without optimism, salespeople would quit after making 10 calls that produced nothing—and they would therefore miss out on the 11th call that leads to the big sale. This is why many sales training courses require starting each sales call with the attitude of "I get to help 100 people find the information they need today" instead of "I've got to make 100 calls today." When we change an obligation into an opportunity—even changing the words we choose to describe our tasks at hand—our entire outlook changes, and the results can be heard in our voices. Our customers hear this tone, and act on it. In fact, as we discuss in Chapter 8, 93 percent of communication is nonverbal!

This is yet another way that success follows our happiness ... or our attitude. Foster entrepreneurial optimism by:

- Encouraging your employees to present you with solutions to problems rather than just complaining
- Focusing on progress over perfection
- Celebrating successes, even when small

Option The dictionary defines *option* as "the right to choose; freedom of choice." It also enhances employee engagement. When your people realize they have options—as in the ability to select a solution from a variety of alternatives—they're more apt to engage creatively and to feel they own their decisions and actions.

 KEY TERM

Psychologist, neurologist, and Nazi concentration camp survivor Viktor Frankl lost his wife and parents to the Nazi reign of terror. In spite of losing his family and freedom, Frankl survived to write this in *Man's Search for Meaning* (New York: Simon and Schuster, 1997): "Everything can be taken from a man but one thing: the last of the human freedoms—to choose one's attitude in any given set of circumstances, to choose one's own way."

If Frankl could see the options to choose his own attitude in the worst of circumstances, imagine how much easier it can be for us to choose optimism when we acknowledge that we run our lives and destinies with the attitudes we choose!

Trait #3: Entrepreneurs Are Unwavering

Entrepreneurs live by the Japanese proverb that says, Fall down seven times, get up eight. They don't let failure one day lead to defeatism the next day. They're resilient enough to make 100 sales calls to get to the one sale. Entrepreneurs are the type of people who are willing to save money for 10 years before breaking out on their own to launch their businesses. They continue to align themselves with their overall goals and dreams, and they keep trudging. In his bestselling book, *Quitter* (Brentwood, TN: Lampo Press, 2011), author Jon Acuff shares the lessons he learned in 12 years of "cubicle living" on his route to "cultivating a dream job that changed my life." Twelve years? Acuff practiced resilience.

Part of unwavering resilience is keeping the adage in mind: What doesn't kill me will make me stronger. Entrepreneurs may have to readjust based on setbacks, but they don't cry defeat prematurely. They learn from their mis-

SOWING AND REAPING

FOR EXAMPLE

When my business partner worked in advertising sales, she told me that more than once she spent five years cultivating a contact before it paid off. Five years! Talk about resilience, optimism, sales-orientation, and an internal locus of control! Why did she do it? She *owned* her work. She knew that the work she invested today would pay off tomorrow. And many times it did.

TRICKS OF THE TRADE

FOSTERING RESILIENCE

To breed resilience, give your employees challenges that require a stretch. Allow them the opportunity to fail and to see that life—and their jobs—go on. Help them learn from their mistakes and failures—applying the lessons to the next tasks.

When I was five, my parents let me wash the dishes for the first time. I felt so proud of myself. I later learned that they had to rewash everything that I "cleaned." But what mattered most is that they let me try until I eventually demonstrated competence commensurate with my confidence!

takes, pay attention to their successes, and trudge on to victory. Remember the hungry tiger? A hungry tiger doesn't complain that his prey runs too fast. A tiger that plans to survive doesn't become a vegetarian when prey is hard to find. Instead, he practices resilience.

Trait #4: Entrepreneurs Are Realistic

Many mistakenly believe that entrepreneurs jump out of the gate with no clue what they're doing or that their whole lives consist of bungee jumping off cliffs. The reality is, while they may take some initial risks in getting started, they quickly learn the required skills to get to their destination and they're willing to fulfill the sometimes-tedious requirements to get there. They make plans, create budgets, and act with urgency at times in order to do what's necessary to maintain survival. In short, entrepreneurs must be realistic. Like any leader, they must drill down their goals into strategies and tasks. They must manage their assets—whether money, people, or time. They often must see the larger picture of a project or goal—and realistically determine how to navigate.

Entrepreneurs aren't interested in any sort of get-rich-quick schemes. And they're not pie-in-the-sky dreamers who quit their jobs one day and expect to make a living overnight writing poetry or baking herbed bread. In fact, entrepreneurs understand that the seeds sown today may not be harvested until much later. They make plans accordingly, work hard, and assess as they go.

Amazon's Bezos, whom I mentioned earlier, explained when interviewed by Daniel Lyons for *Newsweek* about the success of Kindle even amid a down economy, "I always tell people, if we have a good quarter it's because of the work we did three, four, and five years ago. It's not because we did a good job this quarter" ("We Start with the Customer and We Work Backward," December 24, 2009). Entrepreneurs understand that an investment made now may not pay off instantly, but they're still willing to invest now. They see realistically how the work they produce today fits into their overall goals. Promote realism by:

- Providing honest assessments of where your company is and what needs to get done
- Showing employees how they can contribute to the bottom line
- Delivering necessary bad news on time and in a proactive manner

Trait #5: Entrepreneurs Are Sales-Minded

Unless your job has the word *sales* in the title, your picture of salespeople might include an old, outdated experience you had with a dishonest, thieving, used car lot huckster. It's time to challenge that stereotype. We're all in the business of sales:

- When a minister delivers a sermon, he's selling something.
- When you share an opinion about a sports team, a restaurant, or a cell phone carrier, you're selling something.
- When a politician lays out her agenda for the upcoming term, she's selling something.
- When you talk about business at a dinner party, you're selling something.

No one pays you to engage in the activities like hobbies that most excite you. When you talk energetically and passionately, is it your desire to sell something or is your enthusiasm simply spilling out? The only difference between you and a salesperson is that the salesperson has an opportunity to make money directly by promoting a particular product. Entrepreneurs are natural salespeople because they have a deep, abiding passion about what they're doing. That enthusiasm comes out. It's hard for them to *not* talk about their business because their passion is what makes their hearts beat! As Norman Vincent Peale wrote, "Enthusiasm spells the difference between mediocrity and accomplishment."

NORMALIZING "SALES"

TOOLS

Those who aren't in sales often see it less than favorably—as if it's manipulative. But selling is really about communicating information to a prospect positively—and that's something you want all your employees to do, even if only to one another! Encourage your employees to talk about how great your company or its people are. Ask them to write a small "pitch" including their three favorite aspects of your organization, and post these in a break room for all to see. Then, tell them all they're in sales—sort of—in that they're all able to promote the company in a positive way!

Trait #6: Entrepreneurs Are Empowered by an Internal Locus of Control

Entrepreneurs don't wait for good fortune; they create good fortune. Compare these two proverbs. Then ask yourself which demonstrates an internal locus of control:

- Proverb #1: If God does not bring it, the earth will not give it.
- Proverb #2: If a man works hard, the land will not be lazy.

IS YOURS INTERNAL OR EXTERNAL?

Check the answer that best describes your belief:

In school, you received high marks on a test. You tell yourself:

❏ I studied hard, and it paid off.
  or
❏ The teacher was lenient and made the test easy.

TOOLS

At work, you were overlooked for a promotion. You tell yourself:

❏ I don't have the experience required for the job at this time.
  or
❏ The boss played favorites by choosing his friend.

If you checked the first choice in each one, you have an internal locus of control. When good—or bad—things happen to you, it's because of things within your control. If you checked the second choice, you have an external locus of control, meaning you credit—or blame—fate, chance, or "powerful others" for the result.

Proverb #1 seems fatalistic and pessimistic. God gets the credit or blame for the harvest. Proverb #2, on the other hand, demonstrates a strong correlation between personal effort and reward, and it accepts responsibility for outcomes.

Entrepreneurs appreciate the connection between hard work and rewards, because they make their own fate and create their own successes. They're empowered to act outwardly on their internal drives. They're so strongly driven by their internal locus of control that they trust their "gut instincts" as being the best source of wisdom they have in deciding how to act on an opportunity or challenge.

Entrepreneurs don't expect to have a fully stocked supply room, an information technology department to troubleshoot hardware and software problems, or pockets deep enough to hire consultant specialists or market researchers to answer every question that arises. Rather, entrepreneurs use their inner strength and drive, and tap into whatever external resources they can find to help them.

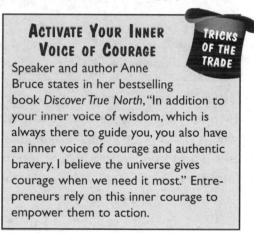

ACTIVATE YOUR INNER VOICE OF COURAGE

Speaker and author Anne Bruce states in her bestselling book *Discover True North*, "In addition to your inner voice of wisdom, which is always there to guide you, you also have an inner voice of courage and authentic bravery. I believe the universe gives courage when we need it most." Entrepreneurs rely on this inner courage to empower them to action.

Grant Appropriate Control and Autonomy

To foster an internal locus of control and sense of empowerment, provide your employees with a sense of control over their environment and choices. In *The Happiness Advantage*, Shawn Achor points out that employees who believe they have a higher level of control at work report greater personal happiness and job satisfaction. But the positive benefits don't stop at work. Research also indicates that those who feel they have control at work report greater satisfaction with family and other personal relationships (p. 130).

The biggest surprise for researchers is that the actual level of control people have at work matters less than how much they believe they have.

ENTREPRENEUR-INTRAPRENEUR CONNECTION
One night I had dinner with a friend named Austin who's the senior vice president of a large insurance company. I was curious how he got his start in the industry.

Austin told me a familiar story about how he took a job with the company right out of college, and he planned to stay for a brief time before moving on. However, his boss gave him an opportunity. "How would you like to manage your own office?" Austin's boss asked.

Austin found himself temporarily relocating from Chicago to Danville, Illinois—a small town on the Indiana border. Austin related with fondness that one moment he might be making decisions involving hundreds of thousands of dollars, and the next he would be heading to the corner store to buy toilet paper or coffee filters for the office!

That self-reliance and sense of empowerment Austin practiced in his early career developed him as an intrapreneur—one who practices entrepreneurial leadership inside a corporation. He brought that same determination and self-reliance with him as he climbed the corporate ladder.

No, I'm not suggesting that you go out and lie to your employees by telling them they have complete autonomy when they, in fact, have little. But when a leader is less autocratic and more democratic and when a leader uses positive reinforcement as a teaching tool instead of punishment, employees feel more control over their work environment.

Promote empowerment by:

- Allowing your employees to make appropriate decisions without approval
- Providing opportunities for your employees to independently research solutions for problems and present them to you

What Does This Have to Do with Engagement?

Review the list of entrepreneurial traits:

- Creative
- Optimistic
- Unwavering
- Realistic
- Sales-oriented
- Empowered with an internal locus of control

First, engaging leaders possess these qualities. Which of these traits do you have as a leader? Are you on the right C.O.U.R.S.E. to engagement? Chances are good that your leadership involves most if not all of those attributes. When you bring those characteristics to work or play, people seek your leadership and your company.

Possessing those traits gets you halfway there. But to maximize employee engagement, you must enable your employees to act like entrepreneurs, as well as do as Chouinard says and "work like demons to produce something of the highest possible quality." This causes your employees to hunger for your organization's success as badly as your CEO does.

And how is this done? What makes entrepreneurs different from "drones who will simply follow directions"?

Entrepreneurs are owners in a company—driven by the link they see between effort and reward. They know the decisions they make today affect the results they receive tomorrow. They feel personally invested in their efforts because they know their hard work today will bring the outcomes they'll enjoy later. They're like the farmers who not only order the seeds, but sow them, and later sell the crop for profit. They realize the key choices are theirs, and the effort they put into making the wisest choices and engaging in the right behaviors are the best determinant of the payoff at the end of the year.

Back to the dance metaphor: Entrepreneurs are stage managers who transform the dance floor into a magical place. And they themselves are dancers, knowing how to "bust a move" with the best of dancers. But additionally, entrepreneurial leaders are the party planners, emcees, and caterers. They might outsource or insource parts of the work, but they retain a mindset that the end result is something they alone control. Their minds are constantly bookmarking ways to optimize processes and performance because they're curious about how all parts of the organization work together.

To engage employees to act as entrepreneurs, engage them to become owners in the company.

Empower Employees to Be Owners, Not Renters

Think of a time you rented a car. How did you drive it? Did you wipe every smudge from the exterior between each drive, and if ever a liquid spilled around the cup holder, did you mop it up immediately with a soft, lint-free cloth? Did you exhibit a light touch at bringing the car to a complete rest at stop lights? Did you accelerate and turn corners so smoothly that you could drive around with a full cup of coffee on the roof without spilling a single drop?

One time the rental car company I used didn't have the class of car I had reserved, so I got a free upgrade to a two-seat convertible sports car. Normally, I'm fairly responsible and I drive rental cars like I would drive my own car. But a two-seater convertible with a turbo-charged engine under the hood?! I'm only human. I couldn't resist opening her up to "see how she rides." I drove like a bootlegger, picturing myself outrunning and outmaneuvering my invisible pursuers, rubber smoking off the tires when a red light turned green, and the tachometer approaching the red line in between my rough shifting of the gears and clutch.

Have you heard the saying Drive like you own the car, not like you own the road? Well, I have to admit, I drove like I owned the road in a car I merely rented!

Okay, how about you? Do you drive a car differently when you own it as opposed to renting it? If you own a car, you likely carefully tuck it away in the garage—well out of reach of Billy's junior mountain bike and Sally's rollerblades. It gets washed on weekends. It gets tuned up regularly. And if your teenage son drives it too hard, you're on his case like a fly on a sweaty horse's behind.

Most people don't treat a car they rent with the same care they do as a car they own. When you're a renter, you're a passer-through—temporarily in need of taking whatever it is for your own use. When you're an owner, you're an occupier—in a long-term relationship (LTR).

A Lesson in Fostering Ownership: The Best Meeting Ever

Years ago, I had minor yet unavoidable surgery scheduled during a critical time at work: the planning phase of the year-end leadership meeting. My team and I were responsible for nearly every aspect of the meeting, from content development to theme, from speaker to menu selection. And sad for me, the retreat I had planned with my team to brainstorm about this event fell at a time when I would be out.

I charged my team with this: "Let me know what you come up with. I can't wait to hear what you decide!" I said this with more confidence than I actually felt. And my first response when I saw their ideas was a little concern because those ideas looked nothing like ones that I would have come up with. But after a few minutes, I realized they were perhaps even better! I went with their ideas, getting behind them 100 percent. My role shifted from project owner and manager to that of cheerleader and "Let me get out of your way!"

By all accounts, this was the best meeting my team ever produced. But for that to happen, I had to believe in my people and let go; my people had to believe that I believed and run with it.

Believe in your people and see how their engagement improves as they become owners in their task!

Ownership Is Like an "LTR"

Consider a dating relationship you might have had in junior high school. Were you sure it would last until death did you part? Did you give it everything you had to make it work? Maybe, but more than likely you were in it to experience what it was like to get to know a romantic partner on a basic level—maybe passing notes at lunch—while you went about developing other aspects of your life.

By the time you got to high school, if you were in a relationship, you were also still worrying about bigger issues like the junior prom, getting into college, and passing your driving test. Your beau or "sweet baboo" probably didn't yet serve as an anchor for most of your major decisions. In fact, you may have dated several people, or none at all!

Once you got into college or possibly graduate school, did anything change? How about when you got your first job, or a little later? This is the time when many begin thinking about settling down with one person. What changes? The commitment level. And why? Because we want it to change; we want it to grow. We begin to think about what we'll get out of the relationship long term: outcomes like security, companionship, children, and someone who travels alongside us on our journey.

Finally, if and when we commit to someone, we pledge our full engagement to that person. We intend to do everything we can to make the relationship as strong, lasting, and productive as possible. Through that commitment, we decide to make big life sacrifices to preserve the relationship. We are owners—invested in a lifetime with this person.

Similarly in the workplace, when employees see their role as having LTR potential, they begin to picture themselves as co-owners—giving themselves over to "for better and for worse" as in traditional wedding vows. As a manager, be aware that some of your employees are merely passing through, playing the field, and courting better options—but treat each of them as if you want them to stay forever and make this company their own company, their most meaningful LTR. Even those on their way through may still commit fully to their tasks at hand—so they can still act as owners today.

Entrepreneurs own the company. The most effective and engaging leaders act as if they own the company and inspire their employees to become owners, too. Entrepreneurial employees embody a sense of ownership—not only of their stapler, their roles at work, and their hours—but also of the decisions they make. If you engage your employees to feel they own the outcome of the company—and that the things they do and

---

THE VALUE OF OWNERSHIP

FOR EXAMPLE

A former colleague of mine named Scott Alexander told me over dinner one night the story of how he came to own a Dodge Viper. He explained that while having a beer with his friends in college, he saw a commercial for a soon-to-be-available car called the Dodge Viper. Scott announced to his friends that he would own that car one day. His friends laughed at what they assumed to be more a fantasy than a serious goal.

But from that moment on, Scott chose to forgo vacations, dining out, and all the luxuries his friends enjoyed because he was saving for that dream car. And what served as Scott's dream car didn't remain in the dream world. Shortly after graduating from college, he purchased his first Dodge Viper. *First?!* Yes, first. Years later when I told Scott how often I shared his story with others, he updated me that he now owns two Dodge Vipers—one for "everyday driving" and another that he takes out on the race track on weekends! Scott took ownership of his dream and made it reality.

sometimes even the things they don't do make all the difference, then you're fostering engagement.

Fostering a Culture of Entrepreneurial Engagement

To house entrepreneurs within your corporate walls, you must be willing to foster a culture of entrepreneurial engagement. Entrepreneurs do it as second nature. Successful companies like Google, Southwest Airlines, RedHat, SAS, and Zappos do it in the policies and procedures they create. In this section, I outline Four Steps to Entrepreneurial Engagement.

Four Steps to Entrepreneurial Engagement

Step #1: Promote the positive. Remember what happened with the entrepreneur who got stranded on a deserted island? Entrepreneurs must remain positive so they can see the possibilities, be resilient even when they face sharks, and act to bring home the bacon, er ... mahi.

How do we do this as leaders? It's a simple concept I repeat in this book, because it's so crucial to engagement: Happy people are engaged; engaged people are happy! Revert to the positivity to refresh yourself on how positivity and happiness create success, not the other way around.

Practice and reward the actions that bring about positive emotions. We discuss humor and fun in the workplace in Chapter 9, but basically, practice, practice, practice.

Step #2: Foster creativity. How do you inspire great art? Encourage little Van Goghs to dabble with their paints. How do you inspire entrepreneurship and great leadership ideas? Allow employees time to think outside the box and experiment. Be like Google and give your employees ample time within their workday to pursue creative endeavors and interests outside their tasks or roles. (If you want more on how they handle creativity at work, Google it!) Obviously your employees can't abandon their basic tasks, but provide them with time and tools to explore when possible.

Step #3: Activate authentic communication. To activate employees' creative ideas and communicate effectively about your adapting goals, strategies, and tactics, it's crucial to implement policies that allow for authentic dialogue.

Step #4: Orient toward entrepreneurial action. Find ways to engage your

KEY TERM

Authentic dialogue This is honest communication allowing for the airing of emotions for the purpose of resolving key issues. Lawrence Polsky of People NRG, a change consulting firm, told me in an interview that when he goes into a company to solve issues regarding stagnated change, the biggest key to breakthrough occurs when leaders not only allow but initiate authentic dialogue that unleashes emotions, even the negative ones.

employees by activating the C.O.U.R.S.E. Traits of an Entrepreneur. Even the most creative and talented individuals practiced extensively to experience their success. Rarely does a prodigy fall out of the sky. Even the Beatles weren't just lucky. They practiced for thousands upon thousands of hours and had to perform in nonnative speaking lands (to overcome rejection and work on their charisma) before they became a sensation. Encourage your employees to take action on their creative ideas and take ownership, rather than waiting for luck to drop solutions out of the sky.

Autonomy, Complexity, and an Effort-Reward Connection

Malcolm Gladwell, author of *Outliers*, states that in addition to showing employees a link between efforts and results, the other key element essential to giving a job meaning is that it includes a level of autonomy as well as some complexity.

You can't necessarily change the nature of a job to suit an employee's sense of purpose, so what can you do?

Promote Autonomy

I would tell most of my new employees that I practiced earned autonomy: "Once you show me that you can handle something with little help from me, it's all yours!" Isn't it more of a Theory X leader's belief that employees work harder when they're watched and micromanaged? But they don't. In fact, they work slower, more afraid of making a mistake and more interested in watching you watch them.

By turning over as much decision-making power to them as you can, you give them an incentive to act like owners—to behave as if they had skin in the game. Stretch your comfort level by turning over control to those who demonstrate they've earned it. They might not structure, prioritize, and complete work the same way you would, but since they're closer to the work than you are, they often find a better way.

GET OUT OF MY STUFF

SMART

MANAGING

While still a relatively new manager, one of my employees named Jamie pulled me aside and gave me a little advice: "Scott, I love you, but can you get out of my stuff?" She said it without a trace of disrespect. Jamie went on to explain that she knew her job well, and that one reason that she wanted to work with me is because she liked what she saw our team do, she believed in her ability to positively contribute to team success, and she hoped to have some freedom over the direction of her work.

So, of course, I had no choice but to fire her. No! Thanks to Jamie, I started to let go. And I kept letting go until the times when she'd say, "Um, this is probably something you should be involved in." Know when to be involved and when to let your employees shine and do their thing.

Provide Complexity

Imagine calling an employee into your office and saying, "I have an assignment so simple, a monkey could do it. So, how would you like to ...?" Pretty demeaning, right? But this happens all the time at work. While it's true that people most enjoy things they're good at doing, there has to be a level of challenge.

When the job is too simple, employees shut down or disengage. Unless your job involves asking employees to prop open a door, you want them thinking and engaging!

Back in the day when video games were housed in arcades at the mall, I would shovel handful after handful of quarters into my favorite game. Obviously, I didn't find conquering the game easy; otherwise, I would have finished it with just one quarter. Not in spite of it being a challenge but because of it, I was fueled to win!

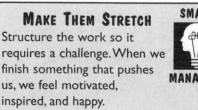

MAKE THEM STRETCH

SMART

MANAGING

Structure the work so it requires a challenge. When we finish something that pushes us, we feel motivated, inspired, and happy.

Recognize Progress

In addition to Gladwell's list, employees need to have some sense of accomplishment at work, a concept that Teresa Amabile and Steven Kramer call *progress* in *The Progress Principle: Using Small Wins to Ignite Joy, Engagement, and Creativity at Work* (Boston: Harvard Business Press Books, 2011). The authors make a strong case for progress as a transformative source of happiness and engagement at work. Here's one of the most important conclusions they make from their research based on 238 individuals inside seven companies: What motivates people most on a daily basis is *making progress on meaningful work.*

I've never seen a job posting that tried to lure new employees for the opportunity to work "in the fascinating world of finding needles in a haystack." Yet, many jobs are structured using some of the same elements of the needle-in-a-haystack position that I refer to as R.O.T.E.: Repetitive, Overwhelming, Thankless, and Endless. These are positions that may not be automatically fulfilling or engaging in themselves; therefore, R.O.T.E. jobs require even more engagement efforts on the part of the leader.

SMART MANAGING

SHOVELING THE SNOW

In February 2011, I woke up at home in Naperville, Illinois, with 22 inches of fresh, heavy snow on the ground— and a 150-foot driveway from the street to the garage! Snow drifts reached more than six feet in places. How did I dig out? One scoop at a time! Instead of looking at what I had left to do, I used the clean driveway behind me as a measure of how far I'd come!

Even employees in R.O.T.E. jobs can become engaged when they have a well-defined outcome, meaningful rewards, and a way to monitor and measure their progress.

Years ago, my manager asked me to be part of a merger integration team responsible for designing and conducting leadership workshops across the enterprise to pave the way for an impending merger. I hadn't been with the company for six months, but I drooled at the opportunity to work with this team.

This project allowed me to receive ...

- Exposure to senior leaders and the top strategic minds of the organization

- Insights about the whys and wherefors behind the merger
- Recognition for developing and delivering communication and training

  More than that, the project allowed me to give ...

- My opinions on effective change management methods I learned in my previous career
- Mentoring to new coworkers and team members
- 100 percent to an assignment that paid me back

Do you think I came in to work early and stayed late for a month for the paycheck? Or because I had to? Of course not! The work itself created excitement, rewards, and opportunities that made me want to be part of every moment! If you want to engage your employees to be entrepreneurial, encourage them to grow outside their comfort zone in areas that offer rewards.

COOKS COOK; CHEFS CREATE

A cook knows how to cook an over-easy egg; a chef knows hundreds of more interesting things to do with an egg. Chefs get good because, as artists, they master their craft in a world that allows creativity and experimentation. Similarly, an entrepreneurial employee must be empowered to create something from his cabinet of ingredients instead of merely following orders.

Flexibility Sells

Back in the late 90s, the picture of an entrepreneur was a 20-something Gen Xer who could be at a board meeting at 10 a.m., and then back on his surfboard by noon—making him the envy of all his cubicle buddies back at the old corporation.

With recent layoffs, the picture may have changed. People from all walks are starting their own consulting firms, small businesses, and creative pursuits to bring in cash. But we can learn something from the stereotypical entrepreneur depicted during the boom. That is, entrepreneurs have flexibility. Even if they pull all-nighters, they're doing so because they know a job needs to get done and they feel motivated to finish it. But when it's done, they can take that ski trip or visit their daughter's preschool without guilt, and without having to ask for permission.

SMART MANAGING

NOTHING FOR FREE

Entrepreneurs don't expect a payoff unless they give of their effort, time, and creativity. They know that they get out what they put in. And they know that the best odds of getting the best results come through giving their best.

As I've mentioned, many companies have initiated policies like flex time to provide this entrepreneurial perk in the workplace. Provide employees with as much control and flexibility as appropriate, while still protecting your major deadlines and goals. Gone are the days of requiring arbitrary hours for each employee, unless it's a necessary part of your business operations.

But What If They Leave—With All Their Creative Ideas? Handling the Fear of Talent Abandonment

I've worked with and consulted leaders who were afraid that if they encouraged too much creativity in the workplace and empowered people too much with knowledge about the goals and tactics of an organization, that employees would leave—along with all the best ideas and company secrets. While this is a risk, the risk is greater if you allow that same talent to languish by not encouraging it to flourish. If you remain authentic with your people, they're more apt to become future partners or collaborators than competitors. Most people, after all, don't bite the hand that feeds them; but I've known plenty of disgruntled employees who wouldn't mind scooping the best ideas from a company that treated them poorly.

Invest in your employees and treat them with the autonomy of entrepreneurs. They're more apt to remain loyal to you and to return your support with their support to you and the business. Even if they leave you, you'll keep those relationships for life.

Manager's Checklist for Chapter 5

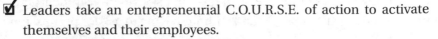

☑ Engaging leaders practice entrepreneurial leadership, acting like they own the company instead of acting like they own the employees.

☑ Leaders take an entrepreneurial C.O.U.R.S.E. of action to activate themselves and their employees.

☑ Entrepreneurs don't have jobs or careers, they have callings.

☑ Engaging leaders create an environment that invites employees to partake in an LTR—a long-term relationship.

☑ Engaging leaders allow employees flexibility and creative risk-taking opportunities.

Aligning Employee and Organizational Values, Missions, and Goals

In Chapter 4, I talked about tapping into the positive as a way to make people happier and more engaged. Wouldn't it be great if the only ingredient required for business success and profitability were positive, happy people? If that were the case, companies would hire Chicago Cubs fans off the street every time their team won, Google wouldn't expect more from new hires than a broad smile, and airline pilots would be selected based on charm and warmth instead of an ability to get passengers safely to their destinations!

Happiness and positivity are essential elements of engagement. As a leader, you can promote a more positive, engaging culture if you feed the positive and starve the negative. However, we hire employees to help us get business results, and all the happiness and positivity in the world won't get you much unless you align that positive energy with accomplishing the vision, mission, and goals of the organization.

In Chapter 5, I discussed engaging employees to act as entrepreneurs or intrapreneurs. While this is ultimately the goal, it's easier to do once you establish the context for how their roles fit into the bigger picture of the organization and how their roles feed their own personal priorities and values.

To maximize performance results and employee engagement, it's time to help employees align their personal values and goals with the values, goals, and mission of the organization. Why? People care more and give more when they see a line-of-sight between their personal values and work. Aligning employees to your organization's mission, values, and goals will help them feel more deeply engaged and satisfied at work. They'll know why they are showing up for work each day—why they're working for your company and why it matters to them as individuals.

Let me use fishing as an example. I've never been interested in fishing, so I know nothing about it. I can hardly differentiate between bobbers and bait. Because fishing isn't important to me, I have no reason or desire to read books or magazines about it, collect the tools of the trade, or create goals that have anything to do with fishing. Why? My life doesn't depend on learning to fish. But if I were stranded like the entrepreneur on a deserted island, I would have a very personal reason to become a skilled fisherman—and to push past the breakers and the barracudas to catch a snapper for supper!

The principles in this chapter will help you maximize the "reason" your employees show up at work, by making the "why" personal to them. This chapter outlines

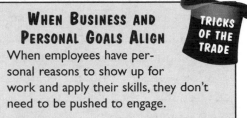

WHEN BUSINESS AND PERSONAL GOALS ALIGN
When employees have personal reasons to show up for work and apply their skills, they don't need to be pushed to engage.

TRICKS OF THE TRADE

practical tips for aligning your employees to the organization's values, mission statements, goals, and finally, their own roles—so their motivation is maximized.

What Values Are and Why They Matter to Engagement

Before we can begin work on aligning to a company's values, let's discuss what they are. Many companies today have values posted on websites or even integrated into communications—which is great. If this is your company, revisit them now so you can apply the tips in this chapter.

If the word *values* reminds you of something only the more conservative half of the country talks about at election time, you're missing the context here. Values, as related to the workplace, are the deepest, most intrinsic motivators toward action. They are what drive us to make big changes—

WORDS AREN'T ENOUGH

Glossy prints of corporate values are nice. But they aren't enough. A list of core values is only an antecedent—just words—unless your corporation actively models and promotes those values. As a leader, you are the first "value statement" your employee will read. So make sure you not only represent the right words, but also the right behaviors.

including the changes that require long hours. They are the intangibles that make us get up in the morning, and act toward something tangible. These drivers are our *personal values.*

One of the most memorable descriptions of values comes from an oft-repeated story of a philosophy professor. As the story goes, the professor stood before his class with an empty glass jar and filled it with large rocks.

"Is the jar full?" he asked. His students agreed the jar was full.

The professor then poured pebbles into the jar and shook it until the pebbles filled in the open pockets between the rocks. He asked his students again if the jar was full. Laughing, the students nodded with a little less certainty than they had the first time.

Finally, the professor picked up a box of sand and poured it into the jar. Of course, the sand filled up all the remaining space.

The professor explained his demonstration by saying this: "The rocks are the important things—your family, partner, health, children—anything that's so important to you that if it were lost, you would be nearly destroyed. The pebbles are the other things in life that matter, but on a smaller scale. The pebbles represent things like your job, your house, your car. The sand is everything else—the small stuff.

"If you put the sand or the pebbles into the jar first, there is no room for the rocks. The same goes for your life. If you spend all your energy and time on the small stuff, you'll never have room for the things that are truly most important."

In other words, the things that matter most to you—the rocks or maybe even the bigger pebbles—are your personal values. They are what get you out of bed each morning. They might be things like your family, health, service to others, advancement, education, achievement, or convictions and beliefs in a cause like environmentalism. While it's possible to lose sight of your values from time to time, happiness comes from staying aligned to your core values, not letting short-term results dictate where you spend your finite time and energy.

Similarly, corporate values provide the motivation for a business to turn on its lights each morning to offer a differentiated product or service to its customers and clients. Companies typically operate to make money; values, however, serve as the deeper, philosophical fuel that drives and directs how every corporate citizen engages with one another—and with their customers who pay the bills.

A mission statement is the action-oriented part of those values—illustrating not only why a company operates, but also how it wishes to engage long term. It's the list of ideals

> **UNCHANGING VALUES** **SMART**
>
> It takes an element of self-awareness to define the values that lie at your core. Opinions change; values rarely do. **MANAGING**

it strives to maintain. It's the clear statement that defines how a company fits into the workforce, community, and globe.

Connect employees to the mission of their company by broadening their knowledge of the business and developing their skills and competence. When an employee knows the strategic goals and vision of the organization, and they have highly refined skills they can bring to their work, the company wins. Oh, and the employee wins, too, because not only do these employees add value to the organization, but when you

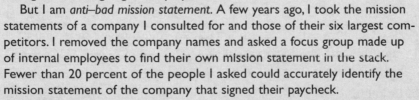

> **WHEN MISSION STATEMENTS DON'T WORK**
>
> **CAUTION**
>
> I'm not anti–mission statements. "Aim at nothing and you'll hit it every time." A company without a carefully crafted mission statement isn't going to have focus in setting priorities, differentiating itself, or aligning its employees.
>
> But I am *anti–bad mission statement*. A few years ago, I took the mission statements of a company I consulted for and those of their six largest competitors. I removed the company names and asked a focus group made up of internal employees to find their own mission statement in the stack. Fewer than 20 percent of the people I asked could accurately identify the mission statement of the company that signed their paycheck.
>
> Make sure your mission statement speaks directly to your organization's values, goals, and operations.

How Is Your Mission Statement?

Test the strength of your mission statement to see if it's meaningful and effective. At your next staff meeting, do this:

TOOLS

1. Ask your employees if they can recite all or any part of your mission statement.
2. Ask your employees to pick your mission statement out of a stack that includes those of your closest competitors.
3. Ask your employees to tell you two or three things they do each day that enable and drive the mission.

If you need more confirmation, give a copy of the statement to your friends or family. Ask them to give you one word to describe how the statement connects with them. If you hear words like "So?" "Snooze," or "Duh," don't rely on your mission statement alone to connect with the hearts and minds of your employees or your customers. Work to improve it.

---

focus on employees' growth and learning, you increase employee engagement. It's a win-win.

How About a ButterBurger?

FOR EXAMPLE   I like the mission statement of the privately owned casual restaurant chain Culver's: "Every guest who chooses Culver's leaves happy." Does that sound too vague? A customer who visits a filthy bathroom won't leave happy. A guest who gets the wrong flavor ice cream in his milk shake won't leave happy. A guest who is ignored at the counter while the person who should be on the register engages in a personal phone call won't leave happy. The Culver mission statement *is vague* ... and yet every employee at every level understands how he or she delivers on helping guests leave happy.

Do your employees know what to do when they read your mission statement? Maybe you should go to Culver's for lunch to think it over.

Revisit Your Values, Goals, and Mission Statements

Today, some companies integrate their values into their marketing campaigns. The powerful thing about values is that they are deep and intrinsic, and they are the fuel that drives each human being. Most of us are engaged by our values—whether of family, leaving a legacy, or having fun. While values differ from one person to the next, and while many people may not have stopped to define theirs, several values are nearly universal to all mankind. For example, most of us want happiness, health, a sense of accomplishment, and positive relationships. As Dr. Maya Angelou said in her interview with my partner, Jocelyn, "Everybody wants a job, a good job, wants to be needed in the job, wants to be paid a little more than she's worth ... Everybody wants someone to love, and maybe to get love in return. Everybody, from Birmingham, Alabama to Birmingham, England. Where we are dissimilar is tangential" ("An Inspirational Conversation with Dr. Maya Angelou on Courage, the Economy, and Fear of Large Dogs," *Attitude Digest*, magazine, Spring 2009).

A MISSION YOUR EMPLOYEES SUPPORT

In explaining why the word *profit* doesn't appear in the Patagonia mission statement, founder Yvon Chouinard says in his book, *Let My People Go Surfing*, "In many companies, the tail (finance) wags the dog (corporate decisions). We strive to balance the funding of environmental activities with the desire to continue in business for the next 100 years."

If the mission of your company is one that your employees embrace on a philosophical level—and not just a monetary one—they will support it with full enthusiasm and engagement because the mission of the company is aligned with their own.

If your corporate values and mission statement can be written in such a way that they communicate universal principles that most humans want in their lives, you'll motivate your employees to feel a deeper tie to your organization.

Brand Your Values

Once your corporate values are set, brand them for your employees. You could do as Zappos does, and become known for hiring only employees who fit into your corporate values system. Zappos' values are readily communicated throughout the company and published each year through a Culture Book highlighting employees' experiences. In the 2010 version, employee Frances M. states, "By being honest, positive, never shutting out change, accepting differences, and finally, ALWAYS thinking of our friends, we spread LOVE. That is what we're all after, right? Finding a little bit of love in the world?" (p. 41). Frances, like thousands of others at Zappos, is engaged in her work, because she clearly sees and

BRANDING VALUES

Consider creating internal branding and communications such as newsletters, videos, events, and social media that promote your story. I'm a partner in a communications firm, Spiritus Communications (www.SpiritusCommunications.com), which does just this. As a side benefit, many of our clients (the company owners) note that they become more engaged in their own leadership when they're able to clearly define their mission and goals through a tagline, mission statement, or values list.

feels how it directly ties into her values and those of her customers. It's no secret why Zappos is consistently rated one of the best places to work by a variety of surveys and is regularly used as an example of engagement in action.

The Power of Story in Branding Values

Successful companies use storytelling to both internally and externally brand values, goals, and mission statements. Employees are engaged when they see how their jobs contribute to more universal principles—such as a desire for community, wellness, or peace. Walmart's mission statement, for example, is "We save people money so they can live better." Who doesn't want to save money or live better?

If your company continually tells its values-based story to both its customers and employees, you ignite an entire community of engagement. In fact, if your engagement culture is one of your values, you have something even more powerful to brand! Read the sidebar about Patagonia for an example.

When I worked as chief of staff, I oversaw the development of a large internal communications campaign designed to tell employees the story of how we were helping our customers. The goal was to show employees how they fit into the bigger picture and to help them better deliver the service we offered.

As a health insurance provider, this involved creating strategically aligned videos to tell our customers' stories—including those who had overcome illness or even bereavement over the loss of a spouse. We simultaneously trained our employees in how to help these people— instilling a culture that reflected our values as well as our goals. At the time, our goals were to improve our corporate culture and customer serv-

> ## LET MY PEOPLE GO ... SURFING
>
> Yvon Chouinard, founder of the environmentally and socially conscious outdoor company Patagonia, is also author of the book *Let My People Go Surfing: The Education of a Reluctant Businessman*. The phrase *Let My People Go Surfing* started as the company's tagline and motto of sorts—allowing for flex time and fun in the workplace. Chouinard valued this and reflected it by giving employees a chance to take a break to surf at any point during the day. In an exclusive book excerpt published in *Outside* magazine in 2005, he stated:
>
> > Since I had never wanted to be a businessman, I needed a few good reasons to be one. One thing I did not want to change, even if we got serious: Work had to be enjoyable on a daily basis. We all had to come to work on the balls of our feet and go up the stairs two steps at a time. We needed to be surrounded by friends who could dress whatever way they wanted, even be barefoot. We all needed flextime to surf the waves when they were good or ski the powder after a big snowstorm or stay home and take care of a sick child. We needed to blur the distinction between work and play and family.

ice. These videos were only one part of the larger story we sought to tell our employees so they would clearly see how they fit into the picture. This internal communication effort was partially responsible for helping us lower our attrition to 6.5 percent—an unheard-of rate in the customer service industry—while at the same time helping our customer service scores skyrocket. Coincidence? Hardly. Remember the case for engagement in Chapter 1? Engaged employees create engaged customers.

In effect, we were defining our corporate values: *We exist to help our customers navigate the complicated healthcare system and processes*. We were communicating those values to our employees by starting with the end result: a satisfied, loyal, engaged customer.

We didn't get there overnight. Progress started when senior leadership got clear on the vision and mission. Next, organizational leaders developed strategic plans that aligned with and enabled the corporate vision and mission. Finally, we involved the employees as a big part of the process.

I listened to the then-president of the company say to a group of employees something like this: "I tell my board members that if they want to know about what's important to our organization, I hope they can turn to any employee here for an answer."

BUT I CAN'T AFFORD THIS

Your efforts don't have to involve million-dollar videos or conferences. Your "campaign" can start with a list of values circulated by e-mail throughout the company and posted in a common area. Create a recognition program and e-mail box for employees to recognize coworkers when they are observed living those values in a remarkable way.

In effect, we created a community of engaged leaders, customers, and employees—all by creating a campaign that told a story tied into our values and mission statement.

Create Learning Maps to Get at the Mission

In my division, we created an interactive learning activity called a learning map. This map visually depicted our current world, while showing our future world. Employees were involved in creating the map as well as testing it. And in the all-employee sessions we ran for the thousands of employees in the operations division, many employees served as group leaders. We partnered with Root Learning, a consulting firm that specialized in helping organizations navigate the waters of change. As their website says, "Strategy without execution is meaningless and execution without engagement is impossible."

The best part of the learning map experience was that it wasn't just another training program, and we didn't *talk at* employees about the mission of our company. Rather, the process helped us *show* the mission, and as a result, *employees saw where they fit into the mission* of the company.

After the session, one employee said: "I learned more in this session about our company and my role in supporting the mission than I've learned in 20 years!"

Brand Your Values for Your Customers

Once your employees are clear on your values, brand them for your customers. Remember those videos I mentioned earlier that we created for internal communications? They are now used in external marketing—to build customer engagement! Do you see how engagement is a community affair? And values are the threads that tie it together.

SOMETIMES A CUP OF COFFEE IS MORE THAN A CUP OF COFFEE

FOR EXAMPLE

I love Starbucks coffee, and I drink it at home each day—several cups (in fact, somewhere around 8–10 cups!). Recently while speaking at a meeting, an audience member asked if I had read a certain book that had Starbucks in the title. Hours later, I couldn't remember the exact title she mentioned (likely, I hadn't had enough coffee!), so I looked online to trigger my memory. I found these:

- *Onward: How Starbucks Fought for Its Life Without Losing Its Soul*
- *The Starbucks Experience: Principles for Turning Ordinary into Extraordinary*
- *It's Not About the Coffee: Lessons on Putting People First from a Life at Starbucks*
- *How Starbucks Saved My Life: A Son of Privilege Learns to Live Like Everyone Else*
- *If It's Raining in Brazil, Buy Starbucks*
- *Starbucks Nation: A Satirical Novel of Hollywood*
- *The Story of Starbucks*

Incidentally, these titles were some of the books with Starbucks in the title from the *first page* of my search only!

Now if you are Starbucks, do you see the advantage of having this many people talking about you, reading about you, and searching for you? Starbucks doesn't rely solely on traditional marketing; it has shelves of books that help tell its story and keep its product and company in the minds of consumers!

Where Do Goals Fit In?

Values feed goals. Keep your company goals aligned with your stated values. Employees commit more deeply when they work for a company that practices what it preaches—and a leader who practices what he or she preaches. How do you do this? During all strategic sessions that involve major change, ask yourself, "Does this new project align with our corporate values?"

And be warned that employees have a built-in BS-ometer, and when they sense that their leaders are being self-serving or Machiavellian, they disengage immediately. A friend told me her company just completed the move of its corporate headquarters to a new building. Since her area of expertise lies in change management, she spent countless hours with senior leadership, human resources, public relations, and internal com-

; to make sure her change and communication plans were
consistent at every level and with all groups, both internal
l. The key message of the move was this: "By replacing offices
with an open floor design plan, members of management and employees
will have the opportunity for increased interaction and involvement, creating the kind of environment that nurtures engagement."

This sounds awesome, right? In fact, it sounds like a best practice for
fostering a sense of team, promoting shared values, and igniting an *us*
culture instead of a *them vs. us* culture.

Sadly, the stated goal around the new headquarters turned out to be
far out of alignment with the reality of the new headquarters. Managers
and employees indeed were placed in proximity with one another.
According to my friend, *quite* close proximity—as in cramped. She told
me that managers grumbled more than employees, because employees
were accustomed to having little space or private offices. However, both
employees and managers were equally outraged when they became
aware of the discrepancy between their new workspaces and those of
their senior leaders. The top executives were housed on their own floor,
each with a large, well-appointed office that connected to private bathrooms with showers. Those bathrooms connected to a complete workout
facility with a swimming pool. None of these amenities were available to
employees or nonsenior leaders. Worse yet, senior leaders attempted to
keep news of these "little perks" away from their employees!

As a manager, you might not be able to influence the alignment of corporate goals with the stated cor-
porate values. However, you
have the power to practice
alignment between what you
say and what you do. That's how
trust is built, remember? Even if
the senior leaders of your company don't model alignment,
you have the ability to build
engagement with your team by
practicing what you preach.

HOW IMPORTANT IS A MISSION TO ENGAGEMENT?

FOR EXAMPLE According to Gallup's research, the mission of a company is *very* important to employee engagement—so important, in fact, that one of the 12 questions of the Gallup Q12 Index I mentioned in Chapter 1 asks about it directly: Does the mission/purpose of your company make you feel your job is important?

Keep your company goals aligned with the values of your customers and employees. A former teacher of mine led a development team within a large, well-known computer company. Corporate leaders wanted the product launched as soon as possible, and even though the project team members had reservations about the product's stability, it was released. It bombed. The company had done nothing illegal or unethical. But by pushing out the product to consumers (many of whom hated it) over the protests of the development team, some customers and employees disengaged from the company. Why? Some felt the product wasn't a good value (in the dollar-and-cents meaning), nor did it show the best company values when instead of fixing the issue, the company shortly afterward released an entirely new product to replace the flawed one.

My boss, Ray, did an outstanding job of aligning goals with values. Around the same time terrorists attacked the World Trade Center, other terrorists fomented fear in the hearts of U.S. citizens by using the mail to deliver anthrax. In most cases, the powdery substance found inside the envelopes turned out to be harmless—things like powdered laundry soap. But the threat of anthrax created psychological terror in the hearts of many employees within our company, especially those individuals in the mailroom who opened and sorted mail.

My boss acted immediately in a way that demonstrated care for his employees by appealing to our customers to help us protect our people. He championed an electronic claim submission process that removed paper claims almost entirely. By reducing millions of pieces of mail from entering our offices, the threat and risk to our employ-

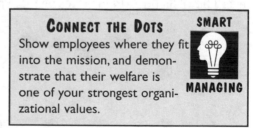

CONNECT THE DOTS   SMART

Show employees where they fit into the mission, and demonstrate that their welfare is one of your strongest organizational values.   MANAGING

ees was greatly reduced. Employees were grateful, and most customers readily abandoned paper claim submission in lieu of electronic claims submission. My boss protected his employees, but this change also proved a less expensive, more accurate, and more efficient solution for all parties. Put another way, Ray did not only do *things right*; he also did the *right things*.

Bringing the Employee into the Mission

How do you make these values, goals, and mission statements personal for each employee?

For an employee to be fully engaged in the mission of your organization, he or she needs to know why it matters on a personal level. They each want to know, What's in it for me? It's your job to make the connection between what they're doing and why they're doing it. The more you can tie this to employees' own personal drivers, the more engaged they'll be in their roles.

Who Do You Want to Be When You Grow Up?
A Values-Assessing Engagement Tool

Do you ever take time to assess if you're aligned with your core values or if perhaps you've strayed from them? Or maybe the question is this: Have you taken the time to identify what your core values even are? No, it's not imperative that you write down your values in order to live by them, just as you don't have to remotely understand the workings of a fuel-combustion engine to drive your car to the grocery store. But many people find it helpful to take an intentional look at their values and behaviors to see if they're out of whack in any way. Why? Have the wheels of your car ever been out of alignment? Mine were recently. At highway speeds, the car pulled to the far right in much the same way my bowling ball pulls to the right gutter whenever I bowl! Figure 6-1 illustrates being in and out of alignment.

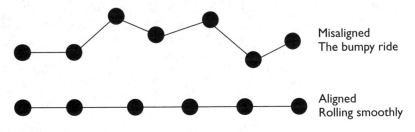

Misaligned
The bumpy ride

Aligned
Rolling smoothly

Figure 6-1. Alignment

When you drive a misaligned car, you use more energy to keep the car pointed in the right direction. But in addition to using extra energy, misaligned wheels wear out your tires. Likewise, when you're out of alignment, you're inefficient, and it can wear you out.

I developed a short tool as a way to help people begin the internal work of evaluating their personal values. First, you can use it to get clarity on your own core values. Second, you can share these same questions with your employees to promote thinking more deeply about their own values. Employees aren't likely to tell you what their core values are, and which of your corporate core values they most align with. In fact, in many cultures, it may be inappropriate to ask for this information. But as an engaging manager, you can share this with them, explaining that you found it a helpful tool, to get them thinking about how to align personal values with roles at work.

Value

1. Name someone you most admire (living or deceased).*
2. Why do you most admire this person? List 3–5 traits this person has that you find most admirable.
3. Think of a company you admire. What 3–5 traits does this company have that you find most admirable?
4. Next to the traits above, list actions you can take at home and/or at work to embody these traits.
5. If you were to do these things for the next year, how would you expect your life to change, if at all?

   *Often the people we most admire embody traits synonymous with our core values—or what matters most to us. If we bring these traits into our lives and the workplace, we're more apt to find meaning and joy in what we do.

Mission

Read your company's mission statement: [Insert here]

1. Based on the questions you answered above, what traits within this mission statement do you most admire?
2. In what area of your job do you most struggle to stay motivated?
3. In what way do your job description or daily tasks relate to these traits you most admire (how do you contribute)?
4. What 3–5 things can you do to further your involvement in these core areas, and minimize or reframe the aspect(s) of your job that demotivate you?

   Note that a similar exercise can be created around goals.

What If the Company's Mission and an Employee's Mission Don't Align?

I've counseled countless individuals on this very topic, and it comes down to clarifying what it means to be *not aligned*.

Incompatible (Not Aligned)

If you or an employee has personal values that directly conflict with company values, it's time to leave. Engagement can't occur when you're in a perpetual state of incongruity. It's like thinking about food when you have the stomach flu. It does strange things to your body. So if you're a member of PETA (People for the Ethical Treatment of Animals), you probably won't feel comfortable working for a company that manufactures fur coats. You might not even feel comfortable working for an organization that *sells* fur coats. Do everyone a favor and find a company whose mission doesn't turn your stomach.

FOR EXAMPLE

INCOMPATIBILITY HURTS EVERYONE

My wife was at a local restaurant with friends. This establishment got high online ratings for its cuisine—especially its vegetarian dishes. One member of my wife's party asked the server for her thoughts about a particular dish that was *not* vegetarian.

"I don't know," the waitress said, seemingly annoyed. "I don't eat anything with a face," she replied before leaving the table.

That's the only time in her life that my wife left a negative rating for a restaurant. And not surprisingly, we have not been back.

If you can't support the mission of your company, find a new company.

Innocuous

More common than a mission being painful is one that inspires indifference or even boredom. Let me use a fictitious janitorial company as an example, one whose mission states: "We are dedicated to delivering excellence in cleaning care to our customers in a manner that shows dedication, quality, reliability, and environmental responsibility at all times." It's a nice mission statement. It includes many descriptions of excellence that employees would want to be associated with regarding their work output. And it's green—conscious of its environmental footprint. But some employees might see it this way instead: "I'm just a janitor. I scrub toilets."

Linking the Mission to the Employee

So what if the mission of your company doesn't make people feel important, valued, or as if they contribute to a worthy cause? If an employee says or indicates that the company's mission isn't important or isn't aligned in a dynamic way to his or her values, help connect the dots. Not everyone is burned up about your corporate core values and mission statements. And that's fine. You don't need to push the words *values* or *mission* around to promote the concept. But, *do* find out what internal drivers matter to employees. Find whatever *does* motivate them to show up each day. And help them remember it. Maybe it's:

- Feeding the family
- Advancing a career
- Funding a passion or hobby
- Learning new skills

Again, helping your employees discover how their jobs fit into their own personal needs (which are, actually, indicators of their values) will help them answer the questions, Why am I here? and Why should I care?

WHY AM I HERE? ALIGNING TO A ROLE

Provide employees with the following worksheet, and let them keep the answers confidential.

- What tasks do you engage in each day in your role at work?
- What matters to you most beyond your daily job? (Name at **TOOLS** least three things. They could be work-related or not, for example, advancing my career, being with my family, learning new skills.)
- In what way is my job contributing to these life goals or priorities?
- What adjustments do I need to make so my job or view of it fits into the bigger picture of my life?

Aligning to Goals by Getting Employees in on the Action

After speaking to a group of business leaders in Memphis, a woman came up to talk to me about her new job in a local company known as

FedEx. She told me she knew more about FedEx from the eight weeks she worked for them than she knew about the former employer she'd been with for years.

Did you know that FedEx started delivering overnight packages with only 14 airplanes and service to only 25 cities in 1973? Did you know that today, FedEx employs more than 280,000 employees worldwide and they do business in more than 220 countries?

This woman knew that and more. She also knew that one of FedEx's core values involves loyalty: "We earn the respect and confidence of our FedEx people, customers and investors every day, in everything we do." How does that value drive how FedEx leaders engage their employees? They treat employees as an asset to the FedEx strategy, not a liability on their financial statement.

FedEx wants its associates to understand the business. But they want more than that. According to this employee, they want people to engage with it. Perhaps that's why she said that as a new employee in the Memphis area, she toured the FedEx "Superhub"—a place that processes more than 2 million packages each day. After seeing the guts of how the company operates, this woman had a higher level of passion and excitement about being part of the FedEx family as well as an increased appreciation for the work her colleagues perform. In a sense, she was able to see the company's goals in action, firsthand, and align her work to the bigger picture.

Managers, do you want to enhance the engagement level of your employees? Invest in them by educating them about your business and trusting them with your goals.

Engaging Through Social Service

So far, this chapter has focused on how managers can align employees around their own values and those of the company. Wouldn't it be cool if the passion and values of an employee could actually expand the values and goals of the company and its leaders? One of my employees did just that.

Tracy heard some of the worst news a parent can hear: Your daughter has leukemia. In the middle of caring for her precious 5-year-old daughter, Carly, Tracy told me how impressed she was with the level of care she received at the hospital. "When we checked in, they gave her this packet from a local charity that had a coloring book, stickers, crayons, and other things like that. It made her feel like she was at Grandma's instead of the cancer ward of a hospital. When this is all over, I want to do something to give back."

This spawned an idea. We worked for a healthcare company, and we dealt with millions of people through the claims they submitted each year. Wasn't our mission to help care for others—to demonstrate compassion for their emotional well-being as well as their physical well-being?

I asked my boss if we could help. He readily agreed. I asked all the employees in our division if they would purchase and then donate items for local children's hospitals to give to incoming patients. Then, I asked if we could use time at an upcoming leadership meeting to assemble those materials into packets.

The corporation's employees acted en masse. We collected so many materials that the 500 leaders who showed up to assemble packets spent more than two hours before they finally ran out! More than 13,000 employees across four states in more than 20 offices spent their money buying materials, and more than 500 leaders took their time joyfully putting together packets. Why? Because an employee was touched by the kindness of strangers, and her experience served as a catalyst to ignite the values and behaviors of an entire organization.

VALUES START SOMEWHERE ... AND SPREAD!

The St. Baldrick's Foundation started in 2000 when three Irish-American executives in New York decided to turn their St. Patrick's Day party into a fundraiser for pediatric oncology research by shaving their heads, thereby showing solidarity with children undergoing chemotherapy treatment. Nearly 190,000 volunteers have since held events in 28 countries, raising more than $117 million for the cause.

My son and I have twice shaved our heads to raise money for St. Baldrick's, and I recently donated my speaking fee to them at a charity event. It started with Tracy and Carly's story, which touched me on a personal level.

Tap Into Your Employees' Need to Give Back

Maybe your own passion and values can't drive the goals of your entire company. But you can start in your own department by helping your employees see some of the things they value come to life. If your employees are motivated by a particular cause, try to find opportunities to support giving to it. Note the following examples.

- David heard many complaints from his employees about holiday gift-giving. Even though company policy made it clear that it in no way endorsed exchanging gifts, employees felt compelled by peer pressure to do things for each other. One employee suggested to David that they try something different. "Why don't we promote Toys for Tots instead? I love that charity, and I'll do all of the work with communication and coordinating. What do you say?" David said yes. The employee took care of everything.

  Win-win-win. David heard fewer complaints about gift exchanges, but he heard several thank-yous from his employees who were grateful for having a constructive, charitable alternative. The employee who brought the idea to David was gratified to see a charity she loved get such participation from her coworkers. And of course, the children who received gifts from anonymous donors that holiday benefited, too.

- Or maybe you can do what Mickey did to help a cause she supported—a local domestic violence shelter in her hometown. Many abused women flee during the middle of the night with their children to escape abuse, and they don't bring anything but the clothes on their backs. Mickey's job put her on the road and in hotels nearly five days a week for two years. So she decided to put those little bars of soap and bottles of shampoo to good use: She collects them and drops them off at the shelter once she acquires a bunch.

  One day her boss saw the bag in her car and asked about it. Once Mickey explained what she did with them, her boss wanted to help. Since her job, too, put her on the road, she coordinated with all the other roadwarriors to collect supplies. Over time, collecting these items became a routine practice, and countless women and children reaped the rewards because the values of one person ignited a movement.

Some companies fall short on living up to their values. But that doesn't mean your company should abandon the practice of creating and distributing a values list. As parents, we set up rules for our children based on basic social mores—such as being kind to others, eating healthy food, saying *please* and *thank you.* Do our kids fall short? Absolutely. But we still hold them to those basic standards—hoping for growth, improvement, and internalization of those values. Ultimately, we hope those rules or guidelines inspire lifetime success and even the opportunity to leave a legacy.

Similarly, your corporate values and mission statements aren't a stick to whack

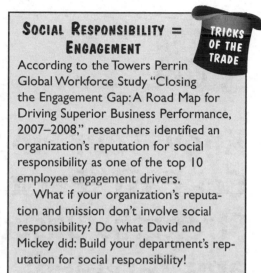

SOCIAL RESPONSIBILITY = ENGAGEMENT

According to the Towers Perrin Global Workforce Study "Closing the Engagement Gap: A Road Map for Driving Superior Business Performance, 2007–2008," researchers identified an organization's reputation for social responsibility as one of the top 10 employee engagement drivers.

What if your organization's reputation and mission don't involve social responsibility? Do what David and Mickey did: Build your department's reputation for social responsibility!

employees over the head with if they fail. Instead, use those values and mission to inspire greater levels of fulfillment and joy. Those values and mission statements provide inspiration, structure, and direction to you as a leader, as well as to your employees and even customers.

Now that we've helped employees align to your organization's values, mission statement, goals, and their roles, it's time to move on to lighter, fine-tuning subjects in future chapters—like having fun in the workplace!

Manager's Checklist for Chapter 6

☑ As a leader, you have the ability to align employees' values and goals with the organization's values and goals to foster deeper engagement.

☑ A meaningful corporate mission statement can motivate your employees to feel a deeper tie to your organization.

☑ Employees commit more deeply when they work for a company that practices what it preaches—and they work for a leader who practices what he or she preaches!

☑ Show employees where they fit into the mission and demonstrate that their welfare is one of your strongest organizational values.

☑ You can start a social revolution in your own department by finding out what causes your employees believe in and getting behind those causes.

Chapter
7

Know Your Employees: Get PSST (Personal, Strengths-Based, Social, and Targeted)

Do you remember when I said that engagement is like a dance? Everything you've read and applied up to this point served one purpose: to prepare you for the dance. You're dressed and you look great. You've practiced your moves and you can dance with the best of them. Most of the people you invited have shown up to join you, and the discotheque captures the perfect balance of light and darkness, slow and fast music, salty foods and sweet beverages. And do you know what? People are having fun! They're relaxed, laughing, and swaying with the music.

But your work is not done. People are at the dance, but they're not yet dancing. It's time to court them. And remember, you can't invite them collectively by screaming, "Okay, people, listen up! I need all of you to dance with me right now!"

All our efforts to build an engagement environment won't create benefits if you fail to capture each employee's desire to join you one-on-one. Engagement happens *one-on-one*.

Get PSST!

Before you can engage your employees as individuals, you first must really know them. In the last Chapter, I covered how to help employees

156

know themselves—how their values and goals fit into the organization. In this chapter, we talk about how you can know your employees. Make it your priority to get PSST:

- Get Personal—Know and tap into their preferences and passions.
- Get Strengths-Based—Focus on their areas of greatest strengths.
- Get Social—Encourage friendships at work.
- Get Targeted—Concentrate coaching on where the employee wants to head.

Relationships Are Built on Getting PSST!

Imagine that your spouse of nearly 20 years leaves you a voicemail saying something like this: "I know we've been too busy this week to discuss plans, but would you be willing to make the arrangements so we can celebrate our 20th anniversary with a nice dinner? Thanks, Honey!"

Would that be a hard task? Hopefully not. Why? You have a relationship lasting 20-plus years! You should have no problem making plans your partner will like. When you're in a close relationship with someone, you observe and remember the things that are important to that other person. You know that person's passions and preferences.

But now imagine this was your first date, and you were told: "I'm open to having dinner anywhere you think I'd enjoy." That changes matters, doesn't it? Wouldn't it be nice to have a little insight like:

- What kind of foods do you like? Or dislike?
- Do you have any food allergies?
- What time do you normally eat?
- What kind of message does it send if I make a reservation at a place that's too expensive? Or too cheap?
- Would it be weird if I made a home-cooked meal instead of going out to dinner?

Isn't it easier to please someone whom you really know, as opposed to someone you're meeting for the first time?

As a manager, that's the relationship advantage. And how do you build a relationship? You get PSST!

PSST!

I love acronyms and other mnemonic devices because they make things easier to remember. I use the PSST! acronym for more than a memory aid. The definition contains an additional key principle: PSST! is the sound used to get a person's attention without other people noticing.

Without other people noticing. When you think of PSST! remember that it's one-on-one, not one-on-masses.

Passion and On-the-Job Performance

Once you hire an employee, you have a front row seat to witness his or her work performance. But in addition to observing what that employee accomplishes, you have an opportunity to see *how* he or she gets things done.

As a leader, I want to know the *what*, the *how*, and the *why*, so I can tap into an employee's passions at work.

Former head of the psychology department at the University of Chicago Mihaly Csikszentmihalyi is considered one of the most influential positive psychologists in the world. He's best known for his research on the concept he dubs *flow*, which directly ties into passion as I describe it in this chapter.

What gets you into the flow? Spend a moment thinking about some activity in your life to which you willingly and nearly obsessively dedicate

SMART MANAGING

A Job, a Career, or a Calling?

Researcher Amy Wrzesniewski published her findings in a 1997 article "Jobs, Careers, and Callings: People's Relations to Their Work" in the *Journal of Research in Personality* after studying employees who identified with those three distinct work orientations. She found that employees who classify their work as a *job* view their tasks as chores that they *have to do* (does that sound like they operate under negative reinforcement?), and the reward is the paycheck. Those who classify themselves as having a *career* work because they *want* to get ahead and succeed (as in positive reinforcement). However, employees who view their work as a *calling* don't work for any external reward. These individuals love the work itself because they see how it contributes to the greater good, and they're excited to do what they love doing every day at work! Their motivation is entirely intrinsic. Not surprisingly, these employees are the most highly engaged, and they work harder and longer because they no longer see work as work but *work as play*.

Employees who are invited to apply their passions at work are more likely to believe they have a calling rather than a job.

your time. Would you call that activity work, a to-do, or a chore? Probably not. Would you engage in it even if it not only didn't make you money but actually cost you money? Most certainly! One might call these types of activities hobbies or obsessions, and many people take great pains to safeguard time around those activities because it's where they go to escape and find a release from the cares of the world. Why? Because people have a passion for those activities!

As an example, let's say you're passionate about skiing. If skiing is your passion,

> **Flow** Csikszentmihalyi told *Wired* magazine that *flow* is "being completely involved in an activity for its own **KEY TERM** sake. The ego falls away. Time flies. Every action, movement, and thought follows inevitably from the previous one, like playing jazz. Your whole being is involved, and you're using your skills to the utmost" (found at www.wired.com/wired/archive/4.09/czik_pr.html).

> **Passion**
> 1. A powerful emotion, such as love, joy, hatred, or anger.   **KEY TERM**
> 2a. Ardent love; b. Strong sexual desire; lust.
> For purposes of this book, assume that any time you see the word *passion*, I'm referring to the first definition and not the second one!

you're in the flow when you're skiing. Harnessing a little of my psychic abilities, I offer six predictions about your thoughts and behaviors as related to skiing:

1. You think about skiing when you're not skiing, which is why you've already scheduled your next ski outing.
2. You regularly check mountain conditions and temperature and read up on the latest ski technology.
3. You keep a journal about where you've been and where you plan to go.
4. You have a ski rack on your vehicle, and you own boots, skis, poles, goggles, and attire—all kept in optimal condition, replacing things as they wear out.
5. You still have the lift-ticket on the zipper of your ski jacket from your last outing.
6. You seek the company of other skiers. Many of your closest friends are skiers.

Wouldn't it be awesome if you could command the same flow in yourself and your employees around work activities? Well, on some level that happens. Some of the following items can be done without flow—without being in the zone. But if you do all of them, there's a good chance you find those work activities your areas of strength (which we discuss later in this chapter), and those that are most engaging to you personally.

You Might Be in the Flow with a Task or Role if ...

1. You make room for these activities. If you like ice cream, no one has to remind you to save room to eat some for dessert!

2. You study new trends or developments. Sports fans are more likely to need to limit the amount of time they spend watching ESPN and reading *Sports Illustrated* than they are to require a sticky note reminding them of an important, upcoming sporting event.

3. You set goals for what you want to accomplish. Runners run because they love it, not because they're being chased by wild animals. That's why they set goals and measure their running. It tells them how they're doing and where they're making progress.

4. You keep the right tools handy. A friend of mine loves Sudoku puzzles. Not surprisingly, she keeps a small puzzle book and a pencil in her purse. In the event that she has the opportunity to work a puzzle, she's ready!

5. You save mementos as positive reminders. Have you ever won a trophy or been given a small memento of an accomplishment? Most of us keep those in a cherished place. For years, I've kept a refrigerator magnet that says, "I love you for being my friend" given to me by a teenage girl I counseled nearly 20 years ago. Every time I see it, it reminds me that while I didn't save every child in my care, I did make a difference to that one.

6. You enjoy the social camaraderie of fellow enthusiasts. It's not surprising that hot-air balloon enthusiasts descend on Albuquerque each year for the fall Balloon Fiesta. And it's not surprising that no one has to twist people's arms to get them talking about their shared passion for ballooning.

Before you can engage your employees as individuals, you first must know them as individuals—what makes them passionate. You do that by engaging in the P of PSST: Get Personal.

Get Personal

What does it mean for a manager to build a personal relationship with each employee? It means you know enough about each person that you can tap into their personal preferences and passions.

The items listed in the sidebar hint at the employee's professional preferences and passions. Competent employees with solid performance tend to demonstrate more engagement than those who find themselves struggling to perform. Wise leaders take notice of individual employee preferences and traits to maximize the employee's effectiveness and job performance.

PROFESSIONAL PREFERENCE AND PASSION INVENTORY

There are certain things I want to know about the professional preferences and passions of those I manage so that I can most effectively engage them. Think of one of your employees and ask yourself these questions:

TOOLS

1. Does the employee work best alone or in a team setting?
2. How does the employee respond to feedback?
3. Does the employee perform best in the morning or in the afternoon?
4. Does the employee prefer a highly planned work schedule or does the employee thrive on spontaneous work assignments?
5. Does the employee like doing one thing at a time or a variety of tasks simultaneously?
6. Does the employee prefer to get big tasks out of the way first or accomplish several smaller things to get momentum?
7. What kind of assignments does the employee seem to avoid or delay starting?
8. What kind of tasks does the employee throw himself or herself into with excitement?
9. Does the employee prefer learning-by-doing, asking for help, or reading a manual?
10. Does the employee like to be assigned work or actively begin working on things that need to be done?
11. Does the employee seem to appreciate public recognition? Private?
12. Is the employee liked by his or her peers?
13. Does the employee prefer leading or following others?
14. Does the employee thrive on structure or autonomy?
15. Does the employee demonstrate an internal compass related to priorities, time management, and execution of essential tasks, or would he or she rather have these things spelled out?

If you know what your employees prefer, how they approach their work, how they interact with others, how they learn, and what motivates them, you can give them more of what they want. In other words, you become a part of what engages employees at work.

You engage your employees when you *set them up for success*. You set them up for success when you know and tap into their preferences and passions.

A Tale of Two Employees

A few years ago, the company in which I worked began to undergo a cultural transformation from health insurance claims processor to health and wellness partner. That shift necessitated several strategic messages to broaden our leaders' view of our business. I sponsored a leadership conference for all frontline supervisors so we could begin to institutionalize the key direction the company was now headed.

At the meeting, I relied heavily on two employees: Stephanie and Randy. Stephanie had a strong project management background and mindset. She followed me around with a notebook to make sure I knew the course of events at every turn. Stephanie planned down to the smallest detail. Randy, on the other hand, thrived on spontaneity and he came with extensive training and team-building experience.

Which employee made the event successful? Both. I needed both for different reasons. Stephanie would whisper in my ear to update me on the remaining time during each activity; Randy would grab the microphone, rally the troops, debrief the activity that just occurred, and send people on to the next assignment. Stephanie preferred behind-the-scenes logistics and planning; Randy enjoyed public roles. The success of the supervisor conference would have missed the mark had I not known and tapped into the professional preferences and passions of each employee.

Here are some specific examples of how you can tap into employee personal preferences:

- Do you have an employee who thrives when working "on the fly," who really enjoys working spontaneously? Give that employee your urgent, impromptu assignments.

- Do you have one who works best in the morning? Ask that employee to meet you first thing in the morning for an important discussion around a mission-critical assignment.

- Do you have a born planner on your team? Give that employee assignments that require multiple steps and more sophisticated organization skills.

- Do you have a "social butterfly"—an employee who knows and gets along well with seemingly every member of the team? Tap into that person to gather feedback and opinions from others. The employee will love the opportunity, and you'll get better insights because of that employee's relationship-building skills.

In each case, knowing and tapping into the professional preferences and passions of your employees will increase the likelihood of an outstanding outcome. Oh, and incidentally, doing so also increases that employee's engagement!

Three Ways to Learn About Your Employees: Observe, Test, and Ask

In addition to knowing employees' professional preferences and passions, I want to know personal things about them. What kinds of things? The kinds of things that will allow me to provide customized, positive reinforcement to them.

Here are three easy ways to find out where your employees' passions lie:

1. Observe. What Yogi Berra said is true: "You can observe a lot just by watching." Watch your employees and make note of what you see. Do you see a magazine with a mountain biker on the cover sitting on your employee's desk? How about a picture of a popular musician? Does your employee enjoy working with others? Do you see that others treat that employee as an opinion leader? Use that information to make educated guesses about what excites your employee.

2. Test. Sometimes you aren't able to observe firsthand, such as when an employee works remotely. But you can test to see what kinds of items register a positive response. Does an employee respond well to your praise, acknowledgment, or even a silly joke e-mail? Just as you can test an employee's communication preferences, you can test to see what unique interests and passions an employee might have.

3. Ask. Keeping in mind the example of the dance, what's the worst thing that can happen if you ask someone to dance with you? You'll get a no. But you can always ask, right? And when you do, you'll most likely get a yes. Similarly, ask employees what they prefer.

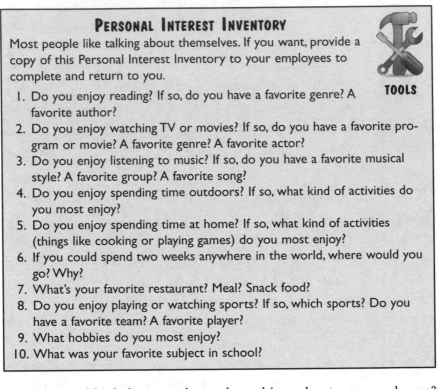

PERSONAL INTEREST INVENTORY

Most people like talking about themselves. If you want, provide a copy of this Personal Interest Inventory to your employees to complete and return to you.

TOOLS

1. Do you enjoy reading? If so, do you have a favorite genre? A favorite author?
2. Do you enjoy watching TV or movies? If so, do you have a favorite program or movie? A favorite genre? A favorite actor?
3. Do you enjoy listening to music? If so, do you have a favorite musical style? A favorite group? A favorite song?
4. Do you enjoy spending time outdoors? If so, what kind of activities do you most enjoy?
5. Do you enjoy spending time at home? If so, what kind of activities (things like cooking or playing games) do you most enjoy?
6. If you could spend two weeks anywhere in the world, where would you go? Why?
7. What's your favorite restaurant? Meal? Snack food?
8. Do you enjoy playing or watching sports? If so, which sports? Do you have a favorite team? A favorite player?
9. What hobbies do you most enjoy?
10. What was your favorite subject in school?

How would it help you to know these things about your employees? I'll answer that with another question: Have you ever struggled to find common ground with another person? The more you know about a person, the easier it is to meet or exceed that person's expectations. It's the relationship advantage. Knowing some of these things about each employee allows you to have a conversation about things in which he or she is interested. It bridges the gap between two people.

Beyond increasing the potential common ground, these discussions enable you to look for ways to deepen your relationship with your employees. For years, I suggested that supervisors use a similar survey for

GUIDELINES FOR ASKING PERSONAL QUESTIONS

CAUTION

If you ask your employees to complete the interest inventory, follow these guidelines:

- Make completing the inventory voluntary. Making something mandatory will create resentment.
- Offer some small thank-you for completing the survey, like a piece of candy.
- Provide a rationale for the inventory, something like: "I want to get to know you a little better so I can tap into your interests. Would you do me a favor and complete this short survey and return it to me? You can skip any questions you don't feel comfortable answering. Thanks in advance for your help!"
- Read, keep, and *use* the results. Don't provide extinction to your employees for their efforts by doing nothing with the results you collect. At least acknowledge and thank them for completing it. Then use that information whenever you can to get to know—and reinforce—them better.

their employees. Later, I asked them to share examples of how they used that information to build relationships. Here are some examples I heard:

- One employee collected salt and pepper shakers. The supervisor found an unusual set at a garage sale for a small amount of money. She gave it to her employee after conducting her performance appraisal and added, "I know it's nothing, but I thought of your col-

FINDING COMMON GROUND

SMART

MANAGING

Earlier, I mentioned my good friend Craig Wortmann, author of *What's Your Story: Using Stories to Ignite Performance and Be More Successful* and a professor at Chicago Booth (in fact, his sales course was awarded a top-10 national designation by *Inc.* magazine in April 2011!). Craig is a zealot on the power of stories to bring people together, and he teaches storytelling as an essential relationship-building tool. He says this: "When two people meet, they begin to tell their stories. Over time, these stories begin to 'pile up behind them,' pushing them closer together. ... [A]nd if you look closely, some of the stories are the same—they have shared experiences that have now created a bond between them."

Do you want to find more common ground with your employees? Exchange some personal facts and share some stories. And over time, build common stories based on your shared experiences.

lection when I saw it, and I wanted you to have it."

- One employee loved NASCAR. The supervisor left a couple of small NASCAR toys on the desk of her employee with a note that said, "I thought you'd like these!"

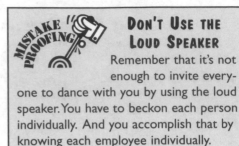

DON'T USE THE LOUD SPEAKER
Remember that it's not enough to invite everyone to dance with you by using the loud speaker. You have to beckon each person individually. And you accomplish that by knowing each employee individually.

- One employee enjoyed gardening. She was given the opportunity to show off her knowledge when the supervisor stopped by her desk with the cutting from a plant. "Do you have any idea what this is? This is growing in my yard, and I want to get some more. I figured that since you're a green-thumb . . ."

- One supervisor asked an employee known for blogging about food for her recommendation on the best Mexican restaurant in the area.

In each case, the supervisor took the information from the survey and used it to deepen the relationship with his or her employees.

Manager, when you know the personal preferences and passions of your employees, you deepen your relationship with them—which is critical to igniting employee engagement.

CAUTION

THE BOSS AS BFF?

In the American television comedy *The Office*, manager Michael Scott (brilliantly played by Steve Carell when he was on the show) often has no boundaries when it comes to the relationships with his employees. Character Michael Scott so wishes to be liked and to have friends that he becomes ineffective as a leader.

As a manager, your goal is not to be *best friends forever* with each of your employees. You'll be accused of playing favorites, and your objectivity will be questioned by others.

Rather, your relationship with your employees should be friendly, which means the same level of warmth is available to each team member. Friendliness creates a sense of security and safety within the team, whereas being extremely friendly with a select few can cause resentment and an inappropriate competition for your leadership attention.

Get Strengths-Based

Let me make a less-than-psychic prediction about you as a person: Given a choice, you prefer the company of those who enjoy you rather than those who criticize you. Put another way, it's likely that you are more engaged when you're around those who celebrate the things you do well instead of those who nit-pick all your faults.

I don't have to be much of a psychic to guess that. Why? All emotionally healthy people gravitate toward positive relationships—those based on strengths and that create happiness.

The second component of PSST requires that you tap into employee strengths. Let me acknowledge that it's not always easy or automatic for us to focus on strengths any more than it is to focus on the positive. Both require a measure of discipline and intentionality.

Martin Seligman, whom I reference throughout this book, is widely considered the father of the modern positive psychology movement—a branch of psychology that, according to Wikipedia, seeks "to find and nurture genius and talent." Whereas traditional psychology can best be described as *problem psychology*—whose main bodies of research and interventions focus on treating mental illness—*positive psychology* strives to elevate those things that are working in our lives and the things that bring us the greatest happiness. Positive psychologists are interested in understanding of concepts like flow, strengths, virtues, talents, and pleasure.

Maximizing Performance

Let me ask you a question about the performance appraisal you use at work: Does it focus on identifying areas for your employees to improve? Most performance appraisal systems do because they're built on these assumptions:

- We all have weaknesses (oftentimes euphemistically known as challenges, development areas, or learning opportunities).
- By focusing our energies on our weak areas, we can improve them, perhaps even turn them into strengths.
- Assuming an employee is pretty good today, he or she will be even better once those weak areas are fixed.

USING YOUR STRENGTHS

Additional research from the Gallup Q12 Index found that highly engaged and high-performing employees can readily answer with a resounding yes is this: At work, do you have the opportunity every day to do what you do best?

Note the wording: every day. Not *at times*, but *every day*.

Do you remember my example about skiing, and how people will spend money doing things they're passionate about? As a leader, your job is to unleash employee passion at work by tapping into their strengths so their work is as exciting as play!

Yes, we all have room for improvement. But imagine your power as a leader if, instead of embracing the assumptions above, you acted on the strengths-based position held by positive psychology: If you do more of the things you do well, the things you don't do well won't be an issue.

Do you remember the performance discussion example I shared in Chapter 2 between Laurence and her boss, Scott? The strength of that performance discussion rested on two pillars: Laurence's strong performance and Scott's focus on all the things Laurence did well—not the things that she's not currently achieving 100 percent on at work. By making Laurence's strengths the focus of the discussion, her performance was maximized.

The Center-Stage Employee

Earlier I mentioned an employee of mine named Tara who could do spot-on impressions of anyone, including me. But I failed to mention this detail: Tara had a degree in performance arts. At the time, I oversaw a communications and change management department. Rarely did my boss call me to say, "Hey, Scott. Do you know what the company could really use right now? A musical!" In fact, my boss never said that. And I don't think he ever thought it, either!

So how could I maximize Tara's preferences and passions for performance art on my strategic communications team?

When a much-loved senior vice president of the company retired, I charged Tara to star in a skit showcasing the contributions of the exiting leader. Tara *loved* it! And the retiring leader loved it too, because Tara's passion was evident.

Strengths Questionnaire

As a leader, I would want to know about the strengths of each of my employees. And I would want to use that information to direct how I maximize their engagement.

TOOLS

I would want to know ...	I would want to do ...
What part of your current role do you *most* enjoy?	Find a way to help the employee do more of these roles.
What part of your current role do you *least* enjoy?	Wherever possible, find a way to minimize these roles.
What top skills do you have that you're able to apply at work most of the time?	This validates the parts of the job that create enjoyment and flow. The more of these, the more engaged your employees will be in the work.
What top skills do you have that aren't currently used at work?	You might find that you have skills among your team that you greatly need but didn't know existed.
What would you do more of at work if you could?	These tasks or activities can be used as motivators for your employees.

No, skits and productions did not make up the bulk of work my team accomplished. But by knowing and tapping into the unique skills Tara brought to the table in addition to the skills that got her the job, I unleashed Tara's passion. Not only did she receive well-earned recognition for the skit she performed, but she also brought more creativity and passion to the other parts of her job. Why? By doing some of what she loved doing, Tara's engagement soared.

I can almost hear some of you saying as you read this: "Back the boat up! We all have preferences. But I don't have the luxury of letting people do 'what they prefer to do.' They have to do what's required—the jobs they were hired to accomplish!"

Keep in mind the words of Confucius, who said: "Choose a job you love, and you will never have to work a day in your life." No, you don't have the power to make every part of what your employees perform each day exciting, dynamic, and customized to their preferences and passions.

TRICKS OF THE TRADE

THE TRUTH ABOUT STRENGTHS

I like playing chess. I like playing racquetball, too. But I don't care much for bowling. Or swimming.

It's not a coincidence that we tend to enjoy the things in which we have strengths, and we're more likely to dislike things in which we don't have a high level of aptitude or skill. Given that, you shouldn't be surprised that I'm pretty good at chess and racquetball, but I'm a lousy bowler and swimmer.

Make a note of what you do well, and make a note of what your employees do well. Those are likely strengths. When people apply their strengths, they perform better, they operate in the flow, and they view what they do as a passion instead of a project.

But you do have the power to align some of their work with the things your employees enjoy and do well. When employees spend time doing what they love to do, they're no longer working, but are rather at play.

The most powerful outcome I've experienced using the simple Strengths Questionnaire was in uncovering strengths that I wasn't aware my employees had. And many of those strengths came in handy:

- Wayne loved charitable work and was extremely involved with his community. How did I use his strength and his passion? I asked him to represent the United Way efforts at work. Not only was he thrilled to be part of it, but his efforts earned him recognition from United Way and our company president.
- Meredith had a creative writing minor and confided in me that she wanted to be a novelist one day. Whenever we needed creative copy, such as a skit or short video to reinforce some learning points, I tapped into her strengths and passion. Not surprisingly, when I had the need for some creative copy, this employee would take the assignment home, working on her own time to deliver something strong and brilliant. She didn't do that for the paycheck or because it was "all in a day's work." She did it because she loved it.
- Randy from human resources had previously worked as a personal trainer—a role that he loved. When our organization entered the health and wellness arena, his expertise came in handy when we set up site visits with new customers to explain our new initiatives. Not only did he know his stuff, he brought a level of passion and excite-

ment that exceeded anything a glossy brochure or sales presentation could have accomplished. He had a chance to do what he loved, and it showed.

- Heather spent years in operations, and she brought that experience with her into my communications department. Once I understood the depth of her operational expertise, I quickly broadened the reach of my own department by offering her to serve as liaison from our strategic area to the business arenas. She had an opportunity to learn new skills in my department, certainly; but more than that, she had a chance to be better than anyone else in the area of her expertise.

- A guy named Chris worked in the department adjacent to my own. By getting to know him, I realized that he had enormous creative talent and I frequently tapped into his skill. I learned that he excelled in photography, a talent that served him well in his graduate studies in graphic design. And it happened to be a talent I needed in-house. I hired him so he could do more of what he loved to do—and what I needed done—full time. How'd that work out? Chris enjoys the creative work so much that in addition to keeping his day job, he's branched out to create his own design shop (www.cpgrafix.com).

No one comes to work wanting to feel incompetent and unskilled. When you identify and tap into the ways each of your employees demonstrates their unique gifts and strengths, it's like giving them a raise. Immediately, their engagement increases because they're getting more of what they want: positive reinforcement and the ability to speak in the native tongue of their own strengths. And, to refer to Chapter 5, this also makes them entrepreneurial!

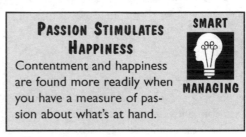

PASSION STIMULATES HAPPINESS
Contentment and happiness are found more readily when you have a measure of passion about what's at hand.

SMART
MANAGING

What a Focus on Strengths Gets You

Earlier I mentioned research by Losada, the psychologist who developed the Losada Line, which says that a 2.9013 positive-to-negative ratio must exist for a work team to flourish. Here's another example of that principle:

Years ago I worked with a group of supervisors in a new office, who struggled to absorb all the technical requirements of their job. The solution from the director was to increase her feedback. To that end, she had her supervisors line up outside her office to receive their performance feedback at the end of each day. And each day, their performance fell a little more.

By the time I got involved, crying was common in the office. The signs of stress were palpable. I met with the director to find out what she was doing.

In a departure from my usual advice that "feedback is our friend," I asked the director to try a new approach: "Call them in at the end of each day for 30 seconds each. Use those 30 seconds to tell each person one thing they did well that day. Just one thing."

Within a month, the performance of every supervisor had improved. By the end of the first year—the standard time by which we expected employees and supervisors to be well into the learning curve—the office was performing better than other offices that had been around for several years.

MISTAKE PROOFING   ### TELL ME WHAT I DID RIGHT

From Gallup's Q12 Index comes another question that highly engaged, high-performing employees answer with a strong affirmative. The question is this: In the last seven days, have you received recognition or praise for doing good work?

Notice that it doesn't say, "In the last seven days, someone coached me, or someone told me all the ways in which I fell short of meeting the standard, or someone made me cry!" No, it's about receiving praise and recognition for something an employee has done well. Put another way, an area where an employee has shown some strength.

What changed? The punitive feedback that dwelt in the world of failures and shortcomings was replaced with a focus on strengths. Once the tears dried up, learning came more quickly, and strengths increased. Once strengths improved at a high enough level, supervisors re-engaged with their roles and their employees.

On a final note, there are several resources available to help you identify your own strengths. (Look these up. One is the book *Now Discover Your Strengths* by Marcus Buckingham and Donald Clifden, Ph.D.

[New York: The Free Press, 2001]. Others include www.viame.org and www.authentichappiness.sas.upenn.edu/Default.aspx.) Leader, if you know and apply your top strengths each day, you can maximize your personal engagement level. And isn't leadership about modeling the right example for others?

If your workplace allows it, make the online resources mentioned above available to your employees to take at work. Offer your employees the opportunity to take the assessment at work if they'll share their results with you. This simple act promotes engagement in many ways. It tells your employees you want to maximize their strengths. It's hard not to respect and appreciate a leader who looks for what you do best! Second, it promotes employee growth and development—another key component of employee engagement. Finally, it gives you the insight to tap into the tasks your employee already does well. Then you can focus more of your time on letting your employees shine, rather than on believing they're all broken and needing to be fixed.

Get Social

Earlier, I shared that one way to know that you're in the flow is if you enjoy the social camaraderie of fellow enthusiasts.

In the groundbreaking book *First, Break All the Rules,* authors Marcus Buckingham and Curt Coffman shared the Q12. According to Gallup's Q12 Index, another question that the most engaged as well as the highest-performing employees respond to with a resounding yes is one that raises some eyebrows when people see it for the first time: Do I have a best friend at work?

Think about that question. First of all, it sounds like grade school a little, doesn't it? What do performance and engagement have to do with friendship? Second, it doesn't just say *friend.* The question doesn't ask about acquaintances, team members, or associates. It specifically states *best friend.*

Friendship has the potential to develop when you have proximity with other people. A friend of mine named Bryan took his first management role more than 20 years ago when he managed an office in Rockford, Illinois. At his first all-employee meeting, he made a plea for people

STRENGTHS: FINDING ... AND SHARING

FOR EXAMPLE Make sharing your individual and team strengths part of your culture.

Every member of my team would take a strengths assessment when they joined my department. At least once a year, I held a team meeting to allow members to share with each other their personal areas of strength. This allowed new members to gain insight about whom to go to for mentoring or advice, and it kept our team focused on what we did well.

to become friends. He said something like this:

The reason we're here is because we aren't independently wealthy. We work because we have to work. And since we all have to work, can we try to make this the best place to work? I want to have fun and build the closest relationships possible. What pulls us together today may be that need for a paycheck; but I want you to want to be here because you care about the people around you, they care about you, and you consider each other friends.

What's interesting about the Gallup research is that employees who are both engaged and high performing report having a best friend at work. What happens when your employees have a best friend at work? Engagement and performance levels increase. Why? While you might not give your discretionary effort just because it's your job or because the boss said to, you're more willing to give your best for a best friend—someone you care about and don't want to disappoint or leave in a bad place.

When I hear the phrase *best friend*, I think of my wife. We share commitment, support, fun, respect, and trust. A best friend will be there in bad times to pick you up and in good times to make them even better. At work, a best friend becomes your sounding board, your confidante, your brainstorming partner, or someone who makes you *a whole person.*

I once managed two employees who were inseparable. Whenever I'd see one, I'd see the other. And it took no time to discover that when I gave an assignment to one of those employees, the other somehow got involved.

These two didn't compete with each other; rather, they complemented one another. One of them jokingly said to me, "Together we make a whole person!"

As a result of their relationship, I got significantly better results than I would have if they'd worked alone. Why? They challenged each other, held each other accountable, wouldn't let the other person down, and together possessed a skillset that was exponentially sharper than either one individually.

People with close work relationships produce better results and exhibit higher levels of engagement because they can tap into the strengths of their best friend.

Remember the story I shared in Chapter 2 about the supervisor named Pat whose employees came in during a blizzard? One reason they came into work was due to their friendship with Pat and with each other. Best friends give employees a reason to get out of bed in the morning and someone they look forward to talking to during the day.

Activities to Foster Social Relationships

While you're not a matchmaker brokering friendships, as a manager you can encourage an environment where social relationships develop. Here are some ideas for fostering more social interactions at work:

> **FOSTER FRIENDSHIPS** **SMART**
>
> Manager, foster social relationships and friendships at work. Those connections increase both engagement and performance. **MANAGING**

Activity #1: Baby picture guessing game. Ask employees for a baby picture. Post them online and ask employees to guess each person from their baby picture. Offer some small reward to whoever guesses the most correctly.

Activity #2: Potluck. Have a quarterly potluck where employees are encouraged to bring in a dish and eat together. In most cultures, "breaking bread" or sharing a meal with others triggers closeness.

Activity #3: Brown-bag lunch. Ask employees to meet in a common place to eat together while sharing a common purpose like listening to a speaker or holding an informal team meeting.

Activity #4: Whiteboard. Display a common whiteboard and encourage employees to post important dates or events (like birthdays or anniversaries), accomplishments, or even inspirational quotes.

Activity #5: White elephant gift exchanges. Many offices build their own holiday traditions like a white elephant gift exchange where each employee is encouraged to bring in a worthless gift to trade and exchange with others.

Activity #6: Brainstorming sessions. An excellent way to speed up the getting-to-know-you process is to give your team a brainstorming project. This allows team members to exchange ideas and thoughts in a nonjudgmental way so they can experience each other's strengths.

Activity #7: Book exchange. In my office, we had a shelf we used to contribute to or check out books that others brought to read. In the process, employees would find others who shared a similar interest or favorite author.

Activity #8: Play a game. At one meeting, we played a quick game called Catch Phrase in which you try to get your team to say a certain word or phrase without using derivatives of any of these words. We discovered a lot about each other, like learning styles, confrontation approaches, sportsmanship, humor, etc. And I learned that I never want to play against my manager, Amy, because she *will not lose*!

Activity #9: Employee Bingo. I was charged with creating a getting-to-know-you game for senior leaders to use at the beginning of a merger, but I wasn't sure if the game would reach its purpose of accelerating a familial environment. It did. People loved it!

See Table 7-1 for an example. Start by creating a 5×5 table and add any information you want people to learn about their team members. Give the group 15 minutes to circulate and gather names for who can truthfully complete the comment inside each box. Offer a small prize for those who get the most names.

The Case of the Clay Alligator

Do you remember in Chapter 3 I said the strongest positive reinforcement includes a tangible as well as a social component? Here's an example of taking something with little cash value and turning it into a way to celebrate and socialize:

A colleague and I traveled to a small town in Texas to do some post-merger training. One of the locals told us of a particular restaurant we should try for dinner that featured locally harvested alligator. Never hav-

Have a twin	Have 4 or more siblings	Love to fly	Don't drive	Read at least a book a week
Have never left the country	Love rock 'n' roll	Exercise 3 or more times each week	Have run a marathon	Ride a bicycle
Lived on a farm	Never ridden a train	Speak more than 2 languages	Love to cook	Hate to fly
Climb mountains	Have visited more than 3 countries	Have lived in more than one country	Own at least 10 movies	Have visited Chicago
Never attended a professional sporting event	Are an only child	Know how to juggle	Have never shopped online	Have a Facebook account

Table 7-1. Employee Bingo

ing tried alligator (or any other reptile as far as I can recall), I had to experience it for myself.

My coworker wasn't keen on the idea of trying the alligator. She said, "I'm good with all the meats in my life," as a way of explaining why she could pass on this golden (brown) opportunity. However, she finally tried a small, crispy piece of fried alligator and she liked it a lot!

As we left the restaurant, we passed a counter of clay alligators, and I purchased one as a memento of our culinary endeavor. Initially, I presented it to my coworker for her bravery in eating the alligator. But I had bigger plans for that alligator. That trophy roved through the office when a team member accomplished something significant.

Until the clay alligator tumbled and broke into many pieces, it represented a powerful, visual social technique for bringing people together around a shared purpose and values.

Get Targeted

After a merger with a company in Oklahoma, it became obvious to me that I needed to have a couple team members who were from that state. Those employees would do more than provide me with eyes and ears; they would be invaluable cultural translators for me while I attempted to initiate major changes.

I charged a couple managers with prescreening applicants for me. Once they had the top candidates narrowed down, they provided me a summary of what they'd learned about each. One candidate named Rod clearly held the right degree, had the right exposure to the business and experience in operations, and had earned the respect of the local senior leadership. Selecting Rod was a no-brainer. Except …

Rod told my managers that his aspirations were to get exposure outside of operations for a couple of years so he could return as a stronger, more capable leader. I could understand why my managers were hesitant to hire someone who had every intention of using the job as a stepping stone. The work of my department included so many broad categories and functions that two years represented the amount of time it normally took a new employee to become fully well-rounded.

I hired Rod not in spite of his desire to leave after a short time, but because of it. How many potential employees will tell a hiring manager whatever he or she thinks the manager wants to hear to get the job offer? Rod didn't do that. I admired his honesty. More than that, I knew that by targeting where Rod wanted to be and what he needed to learn, he would push himself to engage and achieve. And he did.

Within weeks, he assumed highly visible assignments where he co-chaired meetings with the senior vice president of operations in Oklahoma. He became an invaluable sounding board to Oklahoma leadership as well as to my team. Within months, he emceed a large leadership meeting that included supervisors from four states. And within three years, Rod took a promotion back into operations where he assumed his first management position.

By targeting what Rod needed for his next job, who won? Not only did Rod return to operations with a broader, more strategic perspective than any of his new coworkers, but I also solidified my credibility as a leader who could develop employees for bigger and better things. And the company got a "fully loaded" leader with both operations and strategic experience. Win-win-win.

Manager, make it your business to know what roles your employees aspire to obtain. And then help them get there. Engage them in their work by helping them engage their goals. When you become a partner who helps employees get what they want and what they need, you unleash their engagement and ignite their loyalty.

When you help employees get where they want to be, two possibilities exist. One, they might learn and perform well before taking another position. Or two, they might learn and perform well before deciding they want to stay with you.

WHERE DO YOU SEE YOURSELF IN FIVE YEARS?

My partner, Jocelyn, worked for a leading international consumer technology superstore out of college. As part of the goal-setting process, each employee needed to answer this question: Where do you see yourself in five years?

But there was a catch. Wherever an employee might wish to be in five years had to be *within the company*. So what did Jocelyn do? She didn't wait five years to find another job in another company.

Employees are free agents, not under contract to stay with you until you have no use for them. Forcing your employees to make up personal goals that align to the company doesn't engage them; listening to their true goals and aligning their roles to their long-term objectives will.

I've talked with scores of leaders who tell a story similar to this one a vice president named Helene shared with me:

> I studied journalism in college, but the job market didn't look good when I graduated. So I took a job here, intending to stay for a few months, pay the bills, and then move on to my passion. But something changed. My boss supported me and gave me tons of opportunities. The work not only grew on me, but it became one of my passions. And I worked with some of the best people on earth. So of course, I never left.

Getting personal, strengths-based, social, and targeted—in other words, getting PSST—helps engage your employees. Why? Because when you get to know your people personally, when you focus on their strengths, when you make the workplace one of social friendships and relationships, and when you help employees along on the path they target for their own career, they become engaged to you and the work. And if you're not careful, they just might stay until they retire, which is what Helene did after 35 years with the same organization.

Manager's Checklist for Chapter 7

☑ It's not enough for a manager to call people collectively to engagement; people have to be invited and valued as individuals.

☑ Having a personal relationship with your employees means you know enough about each person so you can tap into the preferences and passions of each employee.

☑ Employees who are invited to apply their strengths at work are more likely to believe they have a calling rather than a job, and they are more likely to be engaged.

☑ A focus on strengths encourages you to spend more time acknowledging when your employees shine, rather than trying to fix what you believe is broken.

☑ Employees with more close social relationships and friendships at work are more engaged and perform better than those who lack social connections.

☑ By targeting where your employees want to grow in their careers, you either engage them by helping them get what they want, or you engage them by making them want to stay.

Communication: The Art of Asking Others to Dance

Effective communication is essential to positive relationships in general. Did you know that communication breakdown is one of the top five reasons married couples cite for filing for divorce?

At work, did you know that communication issues similarly make the top-five list for employee dissatisfaction?

Just like a marriage requires communication to survive and thrive, so do relationships in the workplace. Communication is a vehicle that can and should not only inform employees of what's going on, but also foster trust, understanding, and inspiration—all of which translate into engagement. And the best part is that your communication skills—and that means your ability to engage employees—are at your instant disposal wherever you go.

Exemplary communication is more than a tool to enhance employee engagement; it's actually *crucial* to the process. Communication is what you use to invite others to the engagement dance. In this chapter, you'll learn practical tips to turn your communication efforts into dynamic, engagement-building actions.

What Communication Is and Isn't

Aren't We All Better-Than-Average Communicators? What Communication Isn't. You communicate all day long. So you must be very accomplished at it, right?

Maybe. But I think most people rate their communication skills as higher than they actually are.

For years, I've conducted communication workshops. At the start of sessions, I ask group members, "Raise your hand if you think you're a better-than-average communicator." Not surprisingly, most hands go up. Is it really possible for 90 percent to be better than average? No. That would be contrary to the law of averages!

Then why do most people think they are better at communicating than they actually are?

Maybe the reason lies in how they define communication.

Before defining communication, let's be clear about what engaging communication is not. Engaging communication is not:

- **Talking a lot.** Talking all the time doesn't make you a good communicator any more than eating a lot makes you a gourmet chef!

- **Intention-based.** When we open our mouths, we usually have a pretty good idea what we intend to say. But people *hear our words* and *see our actions*; our intentions, however, remain invisible to them. Good intentions about what you *mean to communicate* are irrelevant.

Communication Involves More Than the Words Being Spoken: What Communication Isn't. Communication as it's defined in the sidebar sounds simple enough, right?

KEY TERM **Communication** In its most basic form, communication is *the transfer of information.* For communication to occur, all that's required is a message, a sender, and a receiver.

It's easy only when you send a message that's so crisp and clear that 100 percent of receivers interpret it exactly as you intended.

But 100 percent alignment between sender and receiver rarely occurs without training and practice. Why? Because most of our communication is unintentional. On top of that, process this bit of news: You cannot *not* communicate! As a leader, people are not only listening to you, they're also watching you. When Tara saw my actions and mimicked me, she picked up on stress and even anger, when really what I felt was focused and driven.

Whenever someone is doing something observable that a witness believes to have meaning, communication occurs. Note: This is why it's imperative that you hone your communication skills so they become sharp engagement tools and not just white noise or words that don't align with your actions.

When communication is clear, crisp, and consistent, it looks easy and effortless. Take praising an employee as an example. You might say, "Sierra, you did a fantastic job on this project!" Along with your words, you might smile and gesture with your hands to convey warmth and appreciation. In this case, both your words and emotions convey an obvious, intentional, consistent message of appreciation.

That communication with Sierra—complete with word efficacy and warmth—represents effective, engaging communication.

But communication is confusing when we fail to recognize that we communicate with more than just our words. Have you ever had a conversation with someone whose words said one thing and actions said another—and you were left believing their words to be false? If you have, you realize what research discovered about communication: We tend to believe more of what we *see in actions* and *feel in tone* than what we hear in words.

In fact, researcher Albert Mehrabian discovered (and published findings in his book *Silent Messages*, Belmont, CA: Wadsworth, 1971) that when listeners simultaneously see and hear words, tone, and body language, words have little meaning compared to the other communication channels:

- Words 7%
- Tone 38%
- Body language 55%

Interesting, isn't it? Think back to the speech class you likely had to take during your education. Your class probably emphasized the structure of the speech—such as having a parallel, three-point outline—or the words used in your speech.

But little of the meaning conveyed in our communication comes across in our words. Do you remember the 1996 Bill Clinton versus Bob Dole debate for United States presidency? Forget about what political party you favor. Most political pundits and surveys on both sides of the political spectrum agreed that Clinton won because he leaned casually and confidently on the podium, looked directly into the eyes of the person talking to him, and exuded warmth and compassion with every sympathetic nod of his head. In other words, even those who watched the debate with the sound muted believed that Clinton won the debate.

FOR EXAMPLE

WHO WILL LET THE DOG OUT?

If you want to understand how effective nonverbal communication can be, look no further than Fido. Dogs are highly effective communicators (even if their motives are simply to be engaged in living the best dog life possible). When my dog needs to go out, she lets me know by whining at the door. When she wants to come in, she scratches. When she's hungry, she comes up to me with huge eyes that say, "It's dinner time." Later, she rubs her body against my hand, saying "Pet me," and then says, "Thank you," by wagging her tail. Later still, she lies down to communicate her desire to go to bed. And the tone of her voice—from a bark to a whine to a yip—communicates anything from danger to need to joy. As humans, we learn to filter many of our nonverbal, behavioral reactions—but many sneak by even our own radars! Learn from Fido: Be aware of the power of nonverbal communication.

Good Communication Creates Relationships

Think of a key relationship in your life. Do you remember the first time you met this person? At that time, you were strangers. Maybe you had heard of the other, but you weren't familiar.

And then something happened. That something turned you from strangers into acquaintances. That same something converted you from acquaintances into friends. (In some cases, that same something can pick up enough momentum that—if you're not careful—might cause you to end up going into business together or even getting married!)

So what's that magical something that enables us to bond and build increasingly stronger relationships? And what's the one thing that provides the vehicle for imparting all the other principles in this book? Obviously, it's communication, in all its forms. When you practice open and free communication with others, you get to know them. You discover things you have in common—like shared interests or passions, a similar sense of humor, or a world view.

Sometimes, you discover information that makes you not want to know someone any further! Maybe he or she is of a different political party, or hates your absolute favorite restaurant. But guess what? As a leader, you don't have the luxury of excluding members of your team simply because you don't like something about them! Rather, your responsibility is to enhance your relationship with your team members—and build on their core strengths—as you engage them within the organization. It all happens through effective communication.

TREAT OTHERS AS IF YOU REALLY LIKE THEM

TRICKS OF THE TRADE

Think about a person you cherish. How do you show that person you care? You probably *act like you like this person.*

What does that look like?

The next time you talk with someone you have a close relationship with, make a special note to observe your voice tone, word choice, body language, and even proximity.

In a healthy, caring relationship, you tend to use soothing voice tones, warm words, and safe and inclusive gestures. And you tend to stand at a distance that makes you both feel comfortable—not so close as to be "creepy," nor so far away as to make the other person feel like they have "cooties."

The next time you're talking to an employee, recall the ways you communicate to the person you like. Now, mimic that behavior with your employees.

The Three I's of Communication

Let's start by looking at why *leaders* communicate.

Years ago, I developed a simple model to help leaders evaluate the purpose of their communication efforts. When used in conjunction with self-measurement, leaders can assess for themselves if they're spending their communication time on activities that build engagement or not.

The three I's remind leaders that most of their communication serves one of three purposes: It should *inform, inspire,* and/or *influence* others. See these examples:

Purpose #1: Inform

This involves passing on information. Here's an example of informative communication: "Due to routine, scheduled maintenance, the e-mail system will be unavailable between the hours of 2 a.m. and 4 a.m. next Saturday." Or, "I've looked over your expense report, and there are some errors I'd like you to correct before I sign it."

Purpose #2: Influence

Another important purpose of communication is influence. Influence involves knowing what to say, when to say it, to whom to say it, and how to say it.

As a leader, if you intend to be a game-changer in your office, you have to understand that you have influence. And you have to be willing to use it.

When I served as chief of staff of internal operations, I sat on the budget approval committee when a colleague named Linda presented a business case asking for additional funding for a forward-thinking project.

It was clear to everyone at the table that Linda knew the business, knew where the industry was heading, and knew how to use her influence appropriately. She plainly laid out two options: If you fund this today, our company remains an industry leader. If you don't fund this, our company will be following industry leaders tomorrow. Even though she came to the committee asking for money, her influential power came when she took advantage of the proper timing and audience, laid out her case for change, and backed it up with her final question of: "Who's with me?"

She got the funding.

Purpose #3: Inspire

Of all types of communication, this is your most powerful engagement tool. We all work for a paycheck, but communication that lifts our spirits is like a bonus check on top of our regular pay. As a leader, when you become known for providing inspirational communication, employees will crave your leadership much like houseplants naturally gravitate toward the sunlight. No one has to teach them to get close to you; the process will become automatic because they are wired to seek the company of those who appreciate and value them.

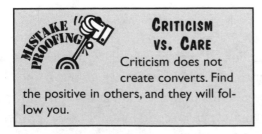

CRITICISM VS. CARE
Criticism does not create converts. Find the positive in others, and they will follow you.

How do you inspire? Try complimenting your employees on a job well done and asking for their insight. Imagine the loyalty you would create if you were to call an employee into your office and say, "Lynn, I've been reviewing your work on this project you just finished. And all I can say is that you're amazing. You thought of everything. Do you think you can spend a few minutes with me later this week telling me a little more of the details behind each step?"

If you spend 15 minutes a day delivering positive feedback and inspiration, your employees will follow you wherever you go!

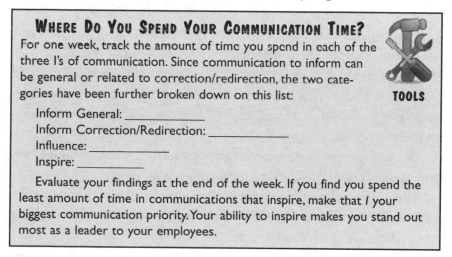

WHERE DO YOU SPEND YOUR COMMUNICATION TIME?

For one week, track the amount of time you spend in each of the three I's of communication. Since communication to inform can be general or related to correction/redirection, the two categories have been further broken down on this list:

TOOLS

Inform General: _____
Inform Correction/Redirection: _____
Influence: _____
Inspire: _____

Evaluate your findings at the end of the week. If you find you spend the least amount of time in communications that inspire, make that *I* your biggest communication priority. Your ability to inspire makes you stand out most as a leader to your employees.

Communication Is Hard: Four Roadblocks to Effective Communication

When I served as the executive director of strategic communications and change management, I got a reputation for shaking my head at various communication mistakes and saying wryly, "Communication is hard."

Did You Mean to Say ...?

Some of the funniest communication blunders happen over e-mail.

One time, an e-mail novice sent out a message to her coworkers asking, "Where do you want to go for lunch?" Sounds pretty simple and straightforward. What could go wrong with that? Turns out, she sent it to the wrong e-mail distribution group. Instead of that innocuous message reaching her peers—the senior examiners—it reached the highest level of the organization—the senior executives—many of whom she had never met and certainly didn't regularly include in her mealtime activities!

Imagine her surprise when several senior vice presidents responded with statements like, "I don't know. What did you have in mind?" And, "I've always liked pizza from Lou Malnati's."

Another time, a senior supervisor sent out an e-mail to all the executives in her division informing us that an upcoming meeting room assignment had changed. To make sure that we as senior leaders could find the right room, she sent us the updated information. At the end of the memo, she added, "I apologize for any inconvenience this change may cause."

Only she misspelled *inconvenience*. Fortunately, spell-check came to her rescue. She accepted the change suggested by her computer. Her actual message said, "I apologize for any *incontinence* this may cause."

Since she was a friend, I ribbed her a little: "Cheryl, some of us may have been put out by the room change, but I doubt it pushed any of us into incontinence!"

One of my employees sent out a statewide employee communication with a subject line that read: Pubic Awareness Campaign.

And I once sent out a quick update for my boss, Ray, to an invite for a staff meeting that read: Rat's Staff Meeting. He sent me an immediate reply: "What are you trying to tell me?"

Now that I'm a little more jaded ... ur ... experienced and I've had time to rethink my previous statement, "Communication is hard," I'll say, "Communication is *easy*. It's *effective communication* that's hard!"

I liken ineffective communication to noise pollution and television commercials. Both are one-sided, hard on the ears, and frequently ignored.

In working with leaders to improve their communication effectiveness, I start by telling them to evaluate their own communication efforts, and tell me where they struggle.

These are the reasons why most communication efforts fail:

TRICKS OF THE TRADE

BE PASSIONATE, NOT ROBOTIC
Communication isn't about going through the motions of checking "I communicated" off a to-do list. Those kinds of efforts are robotic and impersonal. Effective communication accomplishes specific, intended outcomes because it provides needed information, as well as the passion that compels employees to listen, learn, and act.

Roadblock #1. Some Leaders Don't Know How to Communicate

It's not an insult to be ignorant. I'm ignorant about many things. For example, I can't speak Chinese. That doesn't mean I'm a stupid person. It just means that I have had limited exposure to and experience with the Chinese language. But do you know something? If I needed to know Chinese for part of my job or a key relationship in my life, I would push myself to learn at least some basics of Chinese.

Likewise, I tell leaders they don't have to be ashamed if they're not gifted and fluent communicators. Many leaders are promoted for successes they had in previous roles, but they weren't promoted for specific leadership communication skills. According to the storyline on NBC's *The Office*, Michael Scott was the best salesperson in the history of Dunder Mifflin; however, he was utterly clueless about how to communicate effectively with his staff.

Roadblock #2: Some Leaders Don't Know What to Communicate

At times, leaders know the basics of communication, but they don't know what kinds of things need to be communicated to their employees. When Deming said that 80 percent of American managers couldn't

LEARN FROM A COMMUNICATION MENTOR

TRICKS OF THE TRADE

If communication isn't your forte, ask your employees to mentor you. Level with them by letting them know you aren't a natural communicator (this won't be a surprise to them, by the way). Then, you can ask them for help by telling you what kinds of things they want to hear from you, how they want information shared (such as by e-mail or team meetings), or even how often they want to hear from you.

You might also seek out another leader whose communication you admire. Take careful note of how she uses communication to build effective relationships. Make a list of questions you want to ask her, such as "How often do you use communication to inspire your employees?" and "What are some creative ways you've found to engage your employees around business goals?"

I've never been turned down when I've asked someone to mentor me. In fact, you'll likely be engaging this person by letting her know that you admire her skills.

answer the question "What is my job?" that's probably a pretty accurate percentage describing the number of managers who don't know what to communicate. This often happens in large organizations where communication cascades down from the top. Senior leaders spend a day in an off-site retreat crafting high-level employee communiqués. Then the messages get sent through various communication sieves—like human resources, legal, and communications departments. Every department along the path removes anything that can present a legal or PR problem to the point that the resulting communication is devoid of substance.

So, yes, many times leaders may not know the key messages; worse yet, they might miss the context of why it's vital that those messages are shared with their employees. It's no wonder, then, that many employees are left in the dark about matters that directly impact their jobs, their perceptions of their leader and their company, and their engagement levels.

Don't be afraid to ask your boss for clarity. Even leaders have a boss. When you're unclear about either what or how to best communicate a message to your employees, enlist your boss's help.

Years ago one of my employees asked me a question I couldn't answer. "Why do we have to use the corporate travel agency? I always find better prices when I go online myself," the employee told me.

Great question, one that I couldn't begin to answer. And the more I thought about it, the more I realized that I needed an answer. I managed several cost centers, all with travel budgets. Since I had to stay within my budget, I was curious about why I couldn't find cheaper travel alternatives that would save the company money. So I asked my boss.

And then I had my answer. As soon as I left his office, I called the employee who raised the issue and told her what I had learned.

"Turns out," I told her, "that I can save money by you booking flights online. However," I added, "doing that would end up costing the company money." As my boss explained to me, our travel agency gave us a discount at the end of the year based on our total corporate travel expenses. In other words, while I might save $20 on each flight from my cost center, that might end up adding up to a lesser savings than the 1 percent rebate our company would get at the end of the year from the travel agency. That

1 percent of travel for our company amounted to more than a substantial amount of money.

Leaders, if you don't know what to communicate or how to answer your employees' questions, don't ignore them or try to make something up. Make it your job to find answers and get back to people.

WHEN YOU DON'T KNOW SOMETHING, WAIT TO COMMUNICATE

Some leaders fear that if they aren't seen as "having all the answers," their employees will lose respect for them. That's rarely the case. But if you have that fear, try saying something like, "You know, that's a great question, and I want to be sure to answer you fully. Can we schedule time to talk about this in a few days?"

Then spend time making sure that you thoroughly research your answer so you become as much of a subject-matter expert as necessary to answer the question your employees posed.

Roadblock #3: Some Leaders Retreat to "Meville"

Are you familiar with Meville? It's a town whose population grows by one person whenever you focus on your own needs instead of the needs of others. To say "You're in Meville" is like saying, "You're thinking only about yourself."

Leaders are human. Just because you're a leader doesn't mean you're granted immunity from fear and insecurity during times of change and uncertainty at work. Over the last few years, leaders in many companies have had plenty to push them into Meville. When the economy went south and many companies turned to consolidation, downsizing, or staffing and pay freezes, many leaders retreated into their offices, picked up the phones, and called their own bosses to ask, "What's going to happen to *me*?"

The communication topics in Meville are about just one person: me. Guess what, leaders? While you're caring about yourself, your employees are making their own assumptions and drawing their own conclusions. And by the way, whatever it is that they're thinking or saying is likely scarier than the truth.

Yes, leaders are human, and human nature prompts us to think and act in our own interest first instead of being altruistic and asking, "Are my employees going to be okay? I wonder what they need from me?"

The last couple of years have seen many reasons why leaders may wish to retreat to Meville. But leaders: Know that Meville can't become your year-round residence. Think of it like a vacation. You can schedule time off, get out of the office, sit poolside, and sip drinks that come with little umbrellas in them. But that's a vacation, not a lifestyle. You get to do that rarely, and you should view it as a treat—a rare one—not an everyday happening.

Likewise, don't allow your fear of circumstances and uncertainty to make you a permanent resident of Meville. Your employees need you! When you stay in Meville, your employees get information from the wrong sources—like disengaged employees!

SMART MANAGING

CHECK YOUR EXPRESSION BEFORE ENTERING THE ROOM

Do you know the belief that an ostrich will stick its head in the sand when it's scared? I guess it thinks if it can't see the danger, danger can't see it!

Employees are watching your face and reading (and perhaps reading into) your expressions. Just because you can't see your face, don't think that others can't see it. During times of uncertainty and change, times when your employees need your communication more than ever, the look on your face can be the cause for your employees' anxiety or relief.

Check your expression, especially during stressful times. Make sure it's conveying only what you want to convey.

Roadblock #4: Some Leaders Don't See Communication as Their Job

Being a manager means you have responsibilities for administrative functions like payroll, expense reports, budgets, workflows, etc. Most leaders are expected to have a certain level of subject-matter expertise in their field. Most information technology professionals, for example, want a boss with a high level of technical proficiency so that day-to-day needs and issues are clearly understood. Some leadership positions even require you to serve as a thought-leader and strategic visionary for the business.

And what are leaders paid to do? Most of them are compensated for productivity, quality, sales, and other concrete goals that are easily quantificd. Most organizations create compensation structures and goals to improve these key metrics.

Communication effectiveness, however, rarely gets compensated. On one hand, you could argue that communication effectiveness is as much a given for leaders as clothing; companies don't compensate leaders for wearing clothes to work—it's just expected! But if communication effectiveness were truly a given, there wouldn't be so many workshops designed to improve leadership communication.

On the other hand, you could argue that since communication is such a vital performance and engagement competency, it should be a metric on every corporate scorecard. After all, *what gets measured gets done.* Companies spend a fortune gathering data for scorecards so that goals can be met and exceeded; why not create goals for communication and its effectiveness? Communication, while often an afterthought, does affect the bottom line: What's the cost of your employee or customer turnover? How about the increased cost created by low employee engagement levels? Or the exponential cost on your business from dissatisfied, disloyal, disengaged, and vocal employees—or customers sharing their opinions about you?

Leaders, communication is your job. Pretend you get paid to be an excellent communicator. Even if your company or boss doesn't have a communication goal for you, create one for yourself.

Cost of Communication: Even Good Communication Isn't Cheap

As I mentioned earlier, effective communication is a powerful engagement tool. But it's important to know that even the best communication has a cost.

When I was asked to head the strategic communications department within the company I worked for, the first thing I did after hiring staff was conduct a one-day employee orientation for my new communications team. I used this opportunity to make each employee feel special for being selected to join the team, and I wanted them each to comprehend the awesome responsibility we had to the organization. I put together slides to demonstrate the cost of communication so that they could understand how much ROI the organization expected to receive from us.

Employee divisional headcount	7,000 Employees
Time spent reading 1 e-mail/week	5 Minutes
Total time spent reading all these e-mails we send out/year	260 Minutes
Average hourly employee wage	$15/Hour
Divisional cost/e-mail	$8,750
Company cost/e-mail/year	$455,000

Table 8-1. Cost of communication

In other words, the cost of 7,000 employees spending five minutes a week reading an e-mail or newsletter from my department was $455,000 in lost production time. Even if we were the best communicators in the world, that's a lot of money!

Remember, my department's title was strategic communications. How could I create a dynamic, engaged team if I wasn't willing to be transparent with my team? So I showed them the budget.

My team did much more than produce one e-mail/newsletter each week. However, I wanted them to know that our budget plus the time it took our audience to read just one communication we developed each week for a year cost the company some serious dollars ($455,000).

I had two purposes for this meeting, both of them strategic. First, I wanted employees to understand it was imperative that our communications be crisp, precise, relevant, and meaningful to our various audiences. If excellent communication is expensive, poor communication costs even more. Second, beyond challenging them about our need for excellence, I wanted to foster a team identity and sense of pride as a way to engage them.

At the close of the meeting, I asked my team to write down what they got out of our time together. Here are some of their comments submitted anonymously to me:

- I was hand-picked for this job because of what I bring to the table.
- I'm grateful and proud to be on this team.
- No one has ever shown me a budget before. I assumed that was top secret information. I like that you trust us with that.
- [Our division] is spending a lot of money on this team. That means they expect to see great things from us.

Engagement-Building Communication Tips

Every time you communicate with an employee, you have the opportunity to foster engagement and a sense of belonging. And as a leader, you have the "bully pulpit" of rank that makes others want to hear from you.

Use the following tips to make the most of your opportunities:

Tip #1: Be a Storyteller

Stories stick; facts get forgotten. When you want a key point to be remembered, find a story to wrap it around. And when you want to engage others, give them something positive to remember.

First, storytelling works to engage those above you in the organization and to illustrate opportunities for improvement.

As I mentioned in Chapter 1, I began learning about employee engagement in earnest many years earlier when I was challenged to address skyrocketing customer service attrition rates. As you might recall, the cause of the high attrition rate had nothing to do with employees not being paid enough. No, the root cause of attrition came down to poor people-management practices. In other words, some of the managers treated employees terribly, and employees quit as a result.

From my research, I knew attrition percentages of each manager as well as the names of the worst offenders and their offensive behaviors. But I also learned about some great leaders in the process.

My boss asked me to share the information I had uncovered at a manager/officer meeting. At the time, my status level hovered in the grunt category. How would I fare in front of a group of a hundred or so leaders with a message that essentially said, "According to my research, some of you treat your employees like dirt"?

What did I hope to accomplish with my speech? Did it matter that every manager knew the exact attrition percentages? The cost of attrition?

The office locations with the highest turnover?

No. What mattered is that managers understood what led employees to quit. So at the meeting in front of divisional leadership, I told a story.

One former employee I talked to told me about a strong manager I'll call Doug. Doug would say hello in the morning and ask people about their weekends. Doug would pull up a chair and get to know people. Doug was fair, and he seemed to want to see his people succeed.

Then I told the managers about another person I interviewed.

Another former employee told me about her manager, someone I'll call Toni. Toni never established eye contact with her employees. She didn't know any of them by name. One time an employee brought a complaint to Toni, and across the office Toni's voice carried her response: "If you don't like it here, quit. I'll have you replaced in an hour."

Then I asked the group of managers if they thought they were a Doug or a Toni.

I didn't need to name names. I didn't need to single out anyone as a bad egg or a harsh manager. And I certainly didn't need to give these leaders a bunch of numbers and percentages to prove a point. I didn't care if they memorized a number; I wanted them to remember what employees said it felt like to have a good manager and a bad manager.

This approach worked well with leaders who were above me in the organization. Some of them later became my peers. Eventually, promotions took me to a higher level than many of the people in that room. Had I tried to beat up people with facts and figures, the information would have become personal and emotional in a bad way instead of serving as a memorable turning point. Brutal facts would not have engaged them as an audience or as individuals.

The story-based approach worked because it elevated the issue without harping on a specific person. Managers, use stories. Even writing instructors tell prospective fiction authors to "Show, don't tell." In other words, when possible, use examples and tell a story. The same goes for engaging employees—or in this case, superiors.

How do I know that I engaged them? Because many of them sought me out after the meeting to ask for help in becoming more positive, engaging leaders.

Stories bring people together. Storytelling works equally well with employees, and to reinforce a positive experience. When my boss of several years announced his retirement, I wanted to create an event that would honor his work within the company as well as offer my own special thank-you for how he had developed me in my career.

My team and I spent every free moment over a period of three months developing a video homage to our retiring leader. We created a storyboard, wrote a script, conducted interviews with

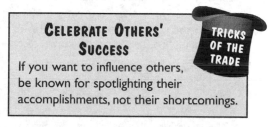

CELEBRATE OTHERS' SUCCESS

If you want to influence others, be known for spotlighting their accomplishments, not their shortcomings.

leaders across the organization, and shot a video called "The Legacy of Service."

The retirement event was a smashing success. There were few dry eyes in the audience of 600 corporate leaders, and my boss's eyes were the least dry! It touched him to be remembered so kindly and in such a fashion.

But it also touched and engaged employees. On my way home from the event, I got an e-mail from one of my newest employees, the project manager on my team named Stephanie who joined the team at the onset of planning. She wrote:

> Scott, thanks for letting me be part of the retirement planning and celebration. While I didn't know [the retiring executive vice president] personally, I feel like I grew to love him and will miss him based on all of the stories you've told us about him. Thanks again for letting me share in such a special event!

That's when it dawned on me how powerful stories can create employee engagement. By telling stories of a great leader—one whom this employee had never met personally—I made him real to her. Then, by including her in the event planning and educating her on the story of who her senior leader was, I not only made her part of the team, but also helped her feel more connected to my boss and the entire company. In other words, in demonstrating my engagement with my boss through storytelling, I increased my employee's engagement with me and the team.

SMART MANAGING

STORIES CREATE INSIDERS

An inside joke is endearing to those on the *inside*. Why? Because if you're in on the joke, it means you have a special relationship with the person telling the joke.

Think of bringing a boyfriend or girlfriend home to meet your family over a holiday. If you're like most families, the dinner table is full of inside stories and jokes. "Do you remember the time you snuck out of the house in the middle of the night and you tried to tell Mom that you were sleepwalking?" your brother teases.

"Let me tell you about my son here ...," your mom might tell your girlfriend like a confidante.

Those stories are being told by insiders. But they are being shared for the benefit of making an outsider a new member of the group.

If you want to bring people together, tell them your stories. And if you want to convert outsiders into insiders, create new memories and stories in which those people are involved.

Tip #2: Be Transparent

In the 1960s television sit-com *Get Smart*, by-the-book government secret agent Maxwell Smart would often insist that his boss follow protocol by lowering "the cone of silence" whenever top-secret matters were discussed. The cone of silence looked like two old-fashioned hairdryers that women in beauty salons used to sit under—except these cones were attached by a small cylinder through which voices were transmitted.

Some leaders act as if they're in the middle of the Cold War. They hold on to information as if every scrap could be used as a weapon. Some still believe that information is power, and that makes them unwilling to give up even the smallest morsel.

The word *transparency* has become a corporate buzzword that means open communication and accountability. In other words, when communication is transparent, you can see right through it. Nothing is hidden or withheld.

Not all information can or should be shared. For example, many corporate workers—those involved in proprietary research or matters involving merger and acquisition deals—must sign nondisclosure agreements with their employers. In those cases, it becomes unlawful to share certain information with anyone who's not designated with a similar security clearance. In addition, you obviously wouldn't want to share personal information confided by an employee going through a hardship.

But as a rule, communicate as if all information can and should be shared with your employees. When someone communicates openly with you, she demonstrates respect for you. Your goal is not to protect your employees from the truth (protection is something that parents do for children); rather, your goal is to demonstrate your respect for your employees by treating them as responsible, mature adults.

What kind of topics require transparent communication with your employees?

Goals and Objectives. Goals often change each fiscal year as old priorities are completed and new priorities are added. If employees don't understand where the company is headed, they aren't likely to be engaged in helping the company get there.

The right hand needs to know what the left hand is doing. When employees within the same department or company lack awareness about the goals they share with others in the area, they have few possibilities to support one another.

Individual Performance. Employees need to know how they're performing. Why? First, if they're struggling, this is an opportunity to offer help. Your job as a leader is to create successful employees—employees who perform well and contribute to the achievements of the organization.

Second, employees need to see progress toward goals. Imagine you've been dieting for two weeks, and when you finally get on the scale, you find out you actually gained weight. Not very encouraging. On the other hand, when you see you've lost weight, your commitment increases. Employees need to know their work makes a difference. As an added bonus, when you take time to discuss their performance with them, you demonstrate that you care about them, which is vital to engaging them.

Negatively Perceived Changes. People have to understand changes before they can support them. I read a case study some years ago about tropical fruit farmers on a Caribbean island. A new law was passed banning a pesticide that local farmers had used for years. Farmers threatened to violate the law by continuing to use their stockpiles of the newly banned pesticides.

Finally, government officials met with a group of farmers and helped them understand the reason for the change. "No North American or European country will buy our fruit if it contains that pesticide," farmers were told. Armed with the whole story, the farmers understood and embraced the change. After all, their economic survival depended on it.

Avoid Playing Favorites

If you've been a leader for any amount of time, you've probably been accused of playing favorites. Whether you have a favorite or not isn't the point. It's all about employee perception.

To avoid the appearance of playing favorites, follow these guidelines:

- Make sure all your employees have equal access to you—both your time and your attention.
- Schedule a set amount of time with your employees one-on-one for open communication, such as answering questions, providing performance feedback, and thanking them for their contributions.
- Make announcements that affect everyone to all employees at the same time. This prevents the perception that the more important employees hear about things before the rest.
- Find individual, unique topics to discuss with each of your employees. If an employee has a picture of his children on his desk, ask him about them. If an employee has a running magazine on her desk, ask her if she's ever participated in a marathon. Be human—not just "the boss," but someone who cares about each employee's interests and activities.

Tip #3: Be an Intense Listener

Earlier I mentioned that talking a lot doesn't make you a good communicator. However, when you listen actively and with intensity, you demonstrate interest in the other person, and that makes you a good and engaging communicator.

Listening is an active sport that requires some technical components, such as the following:

- Good eye contact
- A natural pace that's neither too fast nor too slow
- Clear, audible diction and articulation
- Word choice that fits your audience in education level and style

Effective communication also involves a psychological element. When I practiced as a crisis counselor, there were times when a female client confused the good feeling she got from the help I provided as Scott the therapist and transferred it to Scott the caring male. This is called *transference*.

Why did this happen? It had nothing to do with my being likable or charming or handsome (as much as I wish that to be the case). Rather, it had to do with the feeling of connection we make when we add the psychological component to our listening.

As a leader, your goal is not to have people fall in love with you. But as far as creating engaged employees, you want others to fall in love with how you make them feel when you listen to them.

Some simple ways to increase your ability to connect with others by your listening

- **Stick to the topic at hand.** Don't try to turn the conversation back to you. Remember that the other person is giving you the gift of his or her time, opinions, thoughts, or ideas. Treat it like a gift and not as a burden.
- **Demonstrate interest in what's being said.** Nod, ask follow-up questions, and offer agreement when possible. Don't be thinking about what you're going to say next. Remember how you act when you like someone? Demonstrate those behaviors.
- **Ask open-ended questions to advance the conversation.** Don't ask yes or no questions, since those can be conversation enders. Think like a reporter and ask questions like "How did you ...?" "What happened next?" and "When did you first think ...?" These show intense interest, not just polite conversation.
- **Listen more, talk less.** Don't believe you're more interesting than the person with whom you're talking. Remember what it feels like to have someone you respect ask you for your insights. Hold on to the words of the other person like they were gold.

Tip #4: Be a Two-Way Communicator

Mark Twain once said, "The difference between the right word and the almost right word is the difference between lightning and a lightning bug." That's a pretty big difference, right? Keep in mind that when it comes to effective communication, there's an equally vast difference between a monologue and a dialogue.

Did you ever hold a team meeting and feel as though you're the only one talking? If so, it might be that your staff is used to being *talked to* instead of *talked with*.

THE STUDENT TEACHER

FOR EXAMPLE

In high school, I had a student teacher who taught our science class as part of getting his secondary education degree.

As a joke, I thought it would be funny to see how the teacher would react if the class said nothing. So I asked my classmates to go along with me.

"Don't do anything! Don't raise your hand. Don't answer his questions. Don't raise your eyebrows. Don't express any interest. Just look at him. That's it," I prepared my friends.

The teacher was inexperienced, of course, so for most of the class period he seemed oblivious to anything unusual. In fact, he was probably grateful to be able to teach without the normal disruptions of skittering, chatty kids in each corner of the room.

But near the end of the hour, he was on to us. He asked a simple question. Nothing. He asked for a show of hands on something everyone must know the answer to. Nothing. He asked, "Is anyone awake?" Nothing.

He discontinued his lecture and turned to me. "Okay, Scott. What's going on here?"

This inexperienced student teacher figured out within 45 minutes that *lecturing to students* felt different from *engaging students*.

Similarly, engaged leaders and employees communicate via a two-way channel.

Two quick ways to promote and encourage more two-way interaction in your communications

- **Assign roles.** Employees might be passive because they haven't been asked to get involved. At first you might need to ask employees to take on a role. For example, you can ask one team member to solicit agenda topics, another to create the final agenda, and one to send out the meeting invitation. At the meeting you can ask for a note-taker to jot down important ideas and follow-up steps. You can ask another to keep track of the time so you don't run out before you get through the agenda. Eventually you can ask for volunteers instead of assigning roles. While this is a small, simple suggestion, it engages your team members. Why? It's no longer your meeting, it's their meeting. We tend to think more favorably of things that we shape, own, and control.

- **Ask for feedback.** Did you know that marketing companies use focus groups to test new advertising concepts and taglines? Think about that for a moment. Multimillion dollar advertising firms who attract the best marketing talent from across the globe rely on people like you and me to give them feedback about the ideas they've developed. Why? Whenever we get too close to something, we lose our objectivity. It often takes an objective outsider to tell us if we have a good idea or a terrible one.

    Likewise, when you communicate with your employees, you know what you intend to say, but you might not be the best person to evaluate if your message came across clearly. Ask your employees to help you know if you communicated what you intended to communicate.

A Simple Survey

Early on in my management career, I discovered something about myself that I didn't particularly like: I wasn't a naturally gifted communicator.

So I set out to study and learn. First, I created a survey similar to the one shown here. Second, I explained to my employees what I wanted to accomplish: become a better communicator. Third, I handed this survey out whenever I met with my employees either one-on-one or in a group setting over a period of about six months.

More than anything, this taught me that anyone can become a better communicator if they put forth the effort!

1. What was the purpose of this meeting? *This told me if my purpose for meeting was clearly stated and understood.*
2. What am I supposed to do as a result of this meeting? *If I provided next steps, did the employee hear that?*
3. What is Scott supposed to do as a result of this meeting? *This demonstrated that we were in things together. Rarely would I walk away from meeting with an employee or my team without a follow-up required from me.*
4. Which of the following applies to what I received from this meeting (check all that apply)?

____ Performance feedback on how I'm doing

____ Suggestions on how to improve

____ Praise or encouragement for my work

____ Direction on increasing my knowledge or skills

____ Information on our business or industry

____ Insight into the direction our department is heading

SMART MANAGING

A LESSON FROM BENJAMIN FRANKLIN: ASK FOR HELP

Asking others for help is a powerful engagement tool.

Statesman Benjamin Franklin found himself at odds with a political opponent in the Pennsylvania legislature. Tired of fighting with this colleague, Franklin decided to win him over. In his own words, here's what Franklin did, as described in *The Autobiography of Benjamin Franklin*:

"Having heard that [my political opponent] had in his library a certain very scarce and curious book, I wrote a note to him expressing my desire of perusing that book and requesting he would do me the favour of lending it to me for a few days. He sent it immediately and I returned it in about a week with another note expressing strongly my sense of the favour.

"When we next met in the House he spoke to me (which he had never done before), and with great civility; and he ever after manifested a readiness to serve me on all occasions, so that we became great friends and our friendship continued to his death. This is another instance of the truth of an old maxim I had learned, which says, 'He that has once done you a kindness will be more ready to do you another than he whom you yourself has obliged.'"

How does asking your employees for help increase their engagement? Asking for help demonstrates that:

- You value their opinions.
- You're willing to accept feedback and not only praise.
- You consider them experts on the subject.
- You need them to help you improve.

Revisit this chapter often to brush up on your communication skills and read as much communication material as interest and time will allow.

Manager's Checklist for Chapter 8

☑ Communication is a powerful engagement tool that's available to you 24/7.

☑ Communication can inform and influence others, but its engagement-building strength is unleashed when a leader communicates to inspire his or her employees.

☑ The most effective leaders practice both the technical as well as psychological components of communications to engage others.

☑ Employees become engaged insiders when they are part of a positive, oft-repeated story.

☑ Engaging leaders make certain their employees are informed on the matters that directly affect them.

☑ Communication skills can be learned, and your employees can serve as excellent teachers if you're willing to ask them.

Tickling the Engagement Bone: Stimulating Happiness with Humor, Fun, and Exercise at Work

I once spearheaded a large-scale creative project for a year-end meeting that included more than 600 senior-level leaders from across the country. A linchpin of the event involved a high-end video production with senior leadership interviews. The production met a critical business purpose—serious work, absolutely. It had to be more than good; it had to come as close to perfection as I could deliver. And it had to be fun, exciting, novel, and engaging.

No pressure, right?

I had quite a few liabilities to work around, but the biggest involved timing. The meeting would be held during the first week of December, and we weren't able to finish shooting raw video footage until November 21—the day before the Thanksgiving holiday. That gave us one workweek to successfully complete the postproduction process—a process that the owner of one video editing company told me to expect about two hours of editing work for each minute of finished, edited footage!

I did some simple math using my fingers and toes. I quickly came to understand that what I needed most was more time—more fingers and toes! We planned for a 60-minute final production runtime. If it took two hours to produce each one minute of final video, we would need 120 hours! To pull it off in time, we would need to work 24-hour days during the five days during the last week of November.

But I pulled it off. And do you know what? From all reports, that meeting was outstanding. Do you want to know how I did it?

I didn't. I mean, no one could pull that off. I don't have a magic wand or mystical powers to slow time or create additional hours in the day. If I had the ability, I would bottle some time to master the guitar, speak Mandarin Chinese, and write a few children's books. No, no one person could have turned this into a success. I was no exception. I didn't pull it off.

But my team did. And let me explain how.

Discretionary Effort in Action

Meredith and Angela spent Thanksgiving week living out of a suitcase in Chicago to work on their pieces of the project with the team. This involved the tedious job of last-minute scripting and filming. They drove up from the St. Louis area on the Sunday before the holiday, and they apologized when they left on Wednesday night—explaining that they promised their families they'd be home for Thanksgiving.

Let me say that again, and this time I'll add a couple of details. Meredith and Angela apologized to me for having to leave work on this project to head for home late on the Wednesday night before Thanksgiving. *They apologized to me!* They left after 6 p.m. to begin their six-hour drive home. With ideal, nonholiday traffic, they would get home around midnight. But by the time they left, it was snowing hard. They got home after 2 a.m. Thanksgiving morning.

They weren't the only ones who made sacrifices. Another team member, Chris, set up the video editing equipment in his basement. He invited the team to work out of his house that week. There we sat in the basement eating donut holes and drinking strong coffee for hours on end. While we were downstairs, Chris's lovely and pregnant wife, Agnes, fed us while preparing to have Chris' family over for Thanksgiving dinner.

George was a contract employee who helped us on this project. But we didn't view George as a contract employee; we saw him as a vested business partner and friend. He brought his own video editing equipment so we could work on multiple streams at the same time.

The day after Thanksgiving, Chris, George, and I sat in Chris' basement hard at work once again. This was a paid corporate holiday, yet we worked from 7 a.m. until 10 p.m. More than once, we got Meredith and Angela on the phone to get their feedback before we made important artistic or tactical decisions.

Success often requires sacrifice, no doubt about that. Each one of us on the project worked more hours in the months leading up to that meeting than we had ever worked before. And that's saying a lot because much of our work involved long, nontraditional work hours to get things done.

Do you remember my story about Pat's employees coming into work during a blizzard? They showed up because they enjoyed Pat, and they wished to please her, and they didn't want to let each other down, either. They also came in because doing so felt good, made them happy, and gave them a huge boost of positive reinforcement.

Likewise, the final outcome of what my team achieved required much more than hard work, dedication, and coffee. The outcome required each team member *to do what he or she did because they wanted to*, because it made them feel good to do so. I couldn't ask for the sacrifices they gave. What kind of leader would ask employees to come in on a holiday if there weren't a life-or-death emergency? I certainly wouldn't. But I didn't have to ask. These empowered, dedicated employees asked me if we could work through the holiday and through the night to produce the best possible outcome.

The Engagement Bone

What was the key to unleashing their discretionary effort? Besides the engagement culture that we had already been building in the midst of this deadline, this subset of my team bonded through humor. One morning while the work neared completion, Meredith looked out the window and pointed to something in a faraway tree.

"That's weird. It's an owl," she said.

"No, it's not," I shook my head. "Owls are nocturnal."

"Look at it, Scott," she insisted. "I swear to you that's an owl."

"If it is, it's dead," I said after a glance. "It hasn't moved since we've been looking at it."

"An owl can sit still longer than you can," she persisted.

"I think it's a wasp nest. Or hornet. One of those things that builds a nest in trees. I can't remember," I suggested as an alternative.

"No, it's an owl," Meredith continued.

"It's a plastic bag," I countered.

Chris needed help on a final edit, so he interrupted.

"Scott, can you look this over and tell me …?" he started.

"Chris!" I said sharply. "Can't you see that we're talking about something important here? If you have an opinion about the so-called owl, I'll listen. But come on, Man. Stick to the subject at hand!"

We all burst out laughing. Yes, sleep deprivation can make things seem funnier than they really are. But moments like this kept things light-hearted even when we were crunched, and they gave us many stories that we repeat to each other still when we talk. Without these comic relief episodes, I'm not so sure our team would have been so eager to sacrifice their own personal time and discretionary effort.

Millions of dollars are spent annually on employee motivation, often in the form of humor. The company I worked for hired motivational speakers to infuse the culture with laughter and positivity. Today, I'm one of those speakers hired to rev up the crowd and remind people how to implement humor in their day-to-day lives. And I see results. People come to me weeks or months later and tell me how the positive message helped them be more productive and see more possibilities. Why? Because I got them laughing and learning at work.

Many of these pro-humor companies also offer learning libraries where employees can check out books, DVDs, and other resources to enhance their skills and enrich their souls. Why? That's the topic we explore throughout this chapter. You'll learn that positive material feeds us in the same way that good food does. It goes to the part of the brain and heart that helps us see possibilities and act on them. And it fosters relationships.

People Don't Quit Jobs That Provide Well-Being— Promoting Happiness at Work

Do you remember from Chapter 1 that disengaged employees cost American companies $350 billion each year? Some of these folks steal from you—tangible items as well as time. Why do they do these things, acting like they've been personally offended and hurt? Because often employees feel punished or ignored. When employees feel as though they're treated like machines, even criticized for taking bathroom breaks, it becomes personal, and they act out.

So what's your job as a manager? At the hygiene level, don't treat your employees poorly.

Do you remember the four behavioral consequences? Minimize using these three: punishment, extinction, and negative reinforcement.

But when you're ready to maximize performance and engagement levels of those around you, strive for something greater: well-being—or happiness—at work. Happiness at work is all the rage right now, with books like *Delivering Happiness* by Zappos founder and CEO Tony Hsieh (New York: Business Plus, 2010) making the rounds, and the growing popularity of positive psychology. And it should be. Why? People don't quit jobs that provide well-being, enjoyment, and pleasure—or what we might call happiness. Actually, people are willing to *pay* for activities that provide those experiences!

How do you provide happiness? The quickest way is through positive reinforcement, as we discussed in Chapter 3. And humor and fun happen to be among the most incredible, accessible, and instant positive reinforcers! In this chapter, I lay out a case for humor and fun, and how to implement laughter, and thus, promote well-being into your workplace culture—thereby activating their *minds, memories, relationships*, and *activity levels*.

As you can see from the sidebar, humor and fun go hand in hand, and both promote well-being—or happiness.

> **KEY TERMS**
>
> **Happiness** A mental state of well-being characterized by positive or pleasant emotions ranging from contentment to intense joy.
>
> **Fun** 1. What provides amusement or enjoyment; *specifically*: playful often boisterous action or speech (full of *fun*) 2. A mood for finding or making amusement (all in *fun*)
>
> **Well-being** Defined by the dictionary as "the state of being happy, healthy, or prosperous." This is a fairly broad definition, but it really encompasses the gestalt of engagement. In fact, studies suggest that engaged employees report higher levels of well-being.

If engagement is like a dance, the excitement and fun you create not only make people want to show up; they want to stay and stay.

Are You Serious? A Scientific Case for Humor

Let's start by discussing humor. Just as "breaking bread" with and telling stories to your employees can build an environment of engagement, the same applies to sharing humor with others. Humor spreads instant positive endorphins while shrinking the world, promoting a common language, and building memories for people to pass on to others.

In case you're the type who likes statistics, let me lay out the case for humor and fun in the workplace. According to studies, engaging in activities that promote humor and fun not only foster well-being, but also help us in:

- Living not only longer lives, but happier lives, too
- Unleashing more creativity and productivity
- Igniting energy
- Reducing physical discomfort and pain
- Decreasing stress, fear, intimidation, embarrassment, and anger

Here are a few studies that back up those stats, in case you're nerdy like me and want to check them out:

- R. Robinson, D. N. Khansari, A. J. Murgo, & R. E. Faith. "How Laughter Affects Your Health: Effects of Stress on the Immune System," *Immunology Today 11* (5), 1990.
- W. S. Hamerslough. "Laughter and Wellness," Paper presented to *Southwest District of AAHPERD*, Kahuka, Hawaii, 1995.

Laughter as Medicine

Let's talk specifically about laughter for a moment. It's a cliché to say that laughter is the best medicine, but for the purposes of engagement, I need to state as much. Laughter has healing power because it:

- Decreases blood pressure
- Increases heart rate and respiration
- Releases endorphins (happiness-producing chemicals)
- Decreases depression

(L. S. Berk. "Neuroendocrine and Stress Hormone Changes during

Mirthful Laughter," *American Journal of the Medical Sciences*, 296(7), 1989.)

Even more amazing is that the health benefits from laughter extend as long as the next day (K. S. Peterson. "A Chuckle a Day Does Indeed Help Keep Ills at Bay," *USA Today*, October 31, 1986). I would say that benefit trumps the few minutes of chemically induced, toxic euphoria created by nicotine from a cigarette or even the few hours of benign happiness found in the caffeine from a cup of coffee.

Humor and the Mind: A Natural Brain Stimulant

Laughter, like exercise, produces endorphins. In 2005, the University of Maryland School of Medicine conducted a study on the effect of laughter on one's circulatory system. A selection of volunteers was shown both a scene from a movie that would cause mental distress and a scene from a humorous film. The study showed a marked correlation between the subjects' arterial flow and the type of movie watched. According to a March 7, 2005 press release on the university's website (www.umm.ed news/releases/laughter2.htm), "Overall, average blood flow increased 22 percent during laughter, and decreased 35 percent during mental stress." The press release goes on to say:

> "The endothelium is the first line in the development of atherosclerosis or hardening of the arteries, so, given the results of our study, it is conceivable that laughing may be important to maintain a healthy endothelium, and reduce the risk of cardiovascular disease," says principal investigator Michael Miller, M.D., director of preventive cardiology at the University of Maryland Medical Center and associate professor of medicine at the University of Maryland School of Medicine. "At the very least, laughter offsets the impact of mental stress, which is harmful to the endothelium."

Proper blood flow helps the brain function optimally. A blockage in the cerebral arteries can trigger a stroke—often destroying memory and cognitive ability.

If humor increases blood flow, and circulation promotes brain function, wouldn't it make sense that humor could also improve thinking? Let's explore this idea.

Humor and Memory: Laugh and Learn

Another study conducted by Valparaiso University psychology professor Dr. Keith Carlson in 2008 showed that humor can actually boost memory. Dr. Carlson created posters to mimic the inspirational ones that hang in offices worldwide. Except on his posters, while the image and keyword remained identical, he replaced half the motivational phrases with humorous anecdotes. Subjects were asked to recall the image and keyword. The subjects who viewed the posters with the humorous anecdotes were significantly more apt to remember the content than those who viewed the traditional inspirational phrases. According to a January 18, 2008 press release on the university's website (www.valpo.edu/news/news.php?releaseId=3358):

> In all cases, the humorous posters were more easily recalled than the inspirational posters and, more importantly, Dr. Carlson says that after controlling for photographic image, keyword, order of presentation, length of phrases, and the mental incongruity created by the inspirational and humorous phrases, subjects' ratings of humor explained an additional 50 percent of the variance in recall performance.

FUNNY TRAINING STICKS

In one of my corporate roles, I served as speechwriter for several members of senior leadership. Additionally, my department created, compiled, and crunched audience feedback from all leadership presentations—those I supported as well as those I did not directly support. Training professionals know these as training evaluations—sometimes derisively referred to as *smile sheets*. Without going into the details of a Level 1 evaluation as opposed to a Level 2, 3, or 4 evaluation, let me just say that the senior leaders who delivered speeches that incorporated humor saw better outcomes than those who didn't use humor. From surveys completed immediately after the session as well as retention results months later, the numbers demonstrated a statistically significant correlation between speakers' use of humor and audience level engagement/information retention:

- Higher audience participation during the sessions
- More responses on the open-ended survey questions at the end of the session
- Higher retention of key facts as measured after the session
- Higher team and departmental employee engagement scores

Managers and training professionals, make a note of this: Integrating humor into your workplace and learning may actually increase retention.

The Scottster

Do you remember Richard, aka "The Richmeister," played by Rob Schneider on *Saturday Night Live*? Richard sat by the copy machine and engaged anyone who came nearby with a salvo of wordplay on the person's name. For example, he might call a colleague named Tim "The Timinator" or Cindy "The Sin-stress."

If you saw it, you remember that character. Whenever I'd travel to different parts of the country when that particular sketch was popular, I could count on hearing someone call me something like "The Scottster" or "The Scottman" whenever I would walk past a copier. Why? It's catchy! And it's pretty funny. And it built an instant rapport and relationship. We feel more connected to others when we share a laugh or a common experience. With something as silly as being called "Scott-i-ramma," I had an "in" with an employee, and that shrunk our geographic and cultural distance as well as erased any barriers of title and role. A simple shared joke between two insiders made us equals.

Humor increases blood flow, it makes people more alert and able to concentrate. Want people to engage with you *and* remember more of what you say to them? Use more humor.

Humor and the Engagement Tie

Since this book isn't designed as a medical textbook or a research paper, let me tie it more directly to the topic at hand: employee engagement. Which of these employees has the best chance to become engaged, giving you discretionary effort and serving you with loyalty and outstanding performance?

- A living one or a dead one
- A healthy one or a sick one
- A happy one or a depressed one
- An energized one or a pained one

Of course I'm asking these questions facetiously, but the core of my question underlies the obvious reality that positive, healthy, energized employees are happier and more engaged, and produce better results than their sickly, sleepy, and sad counterparts. And humor promotes such positive, happy feelings.

Come to think of it, there might be a reason why more people suffer heart attacks Monday morning than any other day of the week. In fact, most of these attacks occur from 4 a.m. to 10 a.m. (health.msn.com/health-topics/monday-morning-heart-attacks-and-other-health-risks-by-the-day-of-the-week). Perhaps after a weekend of relative inactivity, the scramble to get out of bed and head to work is to blame for the trend. But it might also have something to do with the stress and dread some employees associate with starting another workweek at a job they dislike. We can turn that around on a daily basis, using W.H.I.P. (What we Have In our Possession)—to promote laughter.

Good Humor Index as a Performance Indicator

In one of the first departments in which I was asked to consult, I used my most potent counseling tools: my eyes and ears. I couldn't pretend to understand the business context in which these people operated. The department was called Medical Services Advisory, and every employee in the room with me was either an R.N. or M.D.

On a sheet of paper, I sketched the table and placed each team member's initials to mark where they were seated at the table. Next, I listened to their interaction. Each time a team member contributed, I placed a hash mark next to their initials. Each time an employee smiled, I drew a smiley face. Then I drew arrows to show the interaction level of the people in the room, and I noted who smiled, nodded, or agreed by using an exclamation point; conversely, I placed a question mark next to anyone who shook their head, rolled their eyes, or grimaced.

Remember that I had no idea what they were talking about, and with the exception of the director named Mary Beth, I had never so much as laid eyes on these people before.

After the meeting, I debriefed with Mary Beth. I shared some observations with her about the people I'd observed. To describe her people, I used words like "involved" and "invested" for those employees who seemed engaged, and I used words like "distant" and "frustrated" to classify those who seemed disengaged.

Mary Beth was amazed at how my 30-minute observation mirrored her own beliefs and opinions about the team.

Next, I suggested that she look at the "good humor" of each of her team leads, and evaluate them with these questions using 5 for the lowest level and 1 for the highest level:

Good Humor Index

____ Laughs at himself/herself

____ Uses humor to get a point across

____ Demonstrates warmth

____ Uses eye contact with others

____ Smiles regularly

I asked her to rank her team leaders by placing them in order for overall effectiveness and performance. Finally, I asked her for her observations about the ratings and rankings she just completed. Here's what she found: *The team leaders with the most 1s on the Good Humor Index were also the most effective leaders.*

But Does Good Humor Pay Off?

Let's take this a bit further to quantify the performance effect of humor. During a short workweek around a holiday weekend, the company I worked for showed a one-hour humorous/business motivation video to nearly 7,000 employees. Many managers balked at the idea, already missing eight hours out of the workweek due to the holiday and because it was a busy time of year. When we were done, we measured performance results based on production and quality from the same calendar period the previous year.

What happens when you carve an additional 7,000 production hours out of the 224,000 hours available during a compressed workweek? Maybe production levels sink or stay the same, depending on what you do with those 7,000 hours. But as a result of showing a business motivation video to our employees, both production and quality had increased. The only explanation is that people felt valued, appreciated, and motivated, and they unleashed their discretionary effort as a way of saying thank you.

Leaders, does this entice you?

If you need more evidence, look at companies like Google, which keeps scooters in the hallways and video games in the break room, and Zappos, which integrates fun at work policies and procedures. Both companies are consistently listed among *Forbes* and other top-100 lists for fastest growing, best places to work, etc.

I can't find research that indicates that corporate financial success drives higher engagement levels. In fact, it often happens the other way around: Engagement drives corporate financial success. Consider the Zappos engagement culture, which started well before they had the revenue to back it up. Tony Hsieh consistently demanded that they hire only people whom they would want to hang out with after work, and he implemented a culture that fostered friendship and camaraderie in all settings. It's no wonder that when the company struggled, employees were willing to cut their salaries and come up with solutions to help Zappos get over the next hurdles before true success awaited them. Some of those same employees are now in top leadership positions in the company.

When Happiness Doesn't Come Naturally— Using Humor and Fun as Survival Tools

Before I go any further, you should know something personal about me. I wasn't born a positive person or a comic. For me, these traits evolved in me as primitive survival skills. When I served as a crisis counselor in the worst of situations, I found myself heavy-hearted seeing the despair and suffering around me. I experienced moments of joy when I helped people overcome dire circumstances. At times I reaped exponential rewards when I reunited runaways with their parents, helped addicts find recovery, or kept struggling juveniles from spiraling from delinquency to prison. But I was also in proximity to suicides, accidental deaths stemming from addictions, and countless acts of unspeakable abuse and

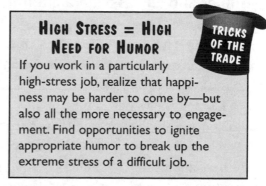

HIGH STRESS = HIGH NEED FOR HUMOR

TRICKS OF THE TRADE

If you work in a particularly high-stress job, realize that happiness may be harder to come by—but also all the more necessary to engagement. Find opportunities to ignite appropriate humor to break up the extreme stress of a difficult job.

neglect. These aren't the situations most people would innately label as fun or funny.

When my work gave me little to laugh at, however, humor was sometimes my survival. I kept a stack of Gary Larson's *Far Side* books along with a few volumes of Bill Watterson's *Calvin and Hobbes* in my car. I would keep in touch with my lifelong friends, Bryan and Jeff, whose stories would make me laugh until I cried. I recorded and watched (and rewatched) *Saturday Night Live* and any other program that tickled my funny bone. And at work, I would spend time with my colleague, Steve, whose twisted way of looking at the world never ceased to make me laugh out loud.

GALLOWS HUMOR

FOR EXAMPLE A family member of mine worked as the third-shift charge nurse in the emergency room in a small-town hospital. She once admitted to me that the overnight hours created far less strain on new R.N.s than did the constant tension of dealing with gunshot wounds, car accidents, burn victims, and other traumas. Beyond her role as more than making the E.R. run smoothly, she saw that her job included keeping morale high. She made it her job to exercise her funny bone in between crises by doing things to engage her team with using humor. For example, she ...

- Organized wheelchair relay races
- Served hot fudge ice cream sundaes in bed pans
- Used pre-formed leg casts and wads of gauze for batting practice in the hallways
- Played volleyball games with blown-up latex gloves as the ball

---

Humor and Fun as a Morale Builder in Hard Times

According to Steve Lipman, who studied the use of humor on morale during the Holocaust, "Wit produced on the precipice of hell was not frivolity but psychological necessity. Humor is one of the greatest gifts God gave mankind to pull itself out of despair."

Lipman shows how some Auschwitz inmates conducted vaudeville shows to boost the morale of fellow prisoners. One inmate said, "We had to make jokes to save ourselves from deep depression" (http://humanre sources.about.com/od/employeeretention/a/humorretention.htm). It could be said that humor helped Holocaust prisoners stay engaged in their sole purpose: remaining alive.

If humor could be used by concentration camp prisoners to stave off depression and boost morale, it seems fair to say that no work environment exists today that is so dire that the humor cannot be found and used. And if humor could help these prisoners survive amid a constant threat of death, surely it could improve the morale levels of employees affected by a foul economy, difficult or dirty tasks, unwanted change, or a Negative Nancy. In my days working in a group home and as a crisis counselor, I in fact noticed that humor and fun—or the lack of it—were a way to gauge morale and engagement.

It's been said that the couple that plays together stays together. Couples that don't laugh together are often ones who have gotten caught up in a downward spiral of negativity. Over time, they have a hard time remembering the enjoyable times they've shared. I found the same to be true in my corporate experience. Teams, departments, and companies who play together stay together.

TOM SAWYER AND HIS FENCE

Do you remember the story in Mark Twain's book *Tom Sawyer* where Tom's Aunt Polly forced him to whitewash the old fence? Instead of doing the work himself, Tom pretended that whitewashing the fence was exciting and he enticed others to want to do it. In the end, friends traded their treasures with Tom for the privilege of doing the work for him! Why? The work provided them with positive reinforcement once they believed it was fun to whitewash a fence. Tom didn't have to pay them to do the work for him; instead, they paid *him*!

Yes, Tom Sawyer was a manipulator, but that's not what I'm advocating. I'm suggesting that you take away this moral of the story: Leaders find a way to make work fun, rewarding, and engaging.

Strengthening Relationships Through Humor

We've explored the importance of relationships in engagement. How then do we strengthen relationships while fostering humor?

Laugh at Yourself First

You can always laugh at yourself. As a leader, this makes you more human and it makes you approachable. Also, by laughing at yourself first, you take away the opportunity for others to take something light

TEST THIS OBSERVATION

Children laugh a lot. In fact, children average 400 laughs per day, whereas adults average only 15 times. What's behind a laugh? The next time you have the opportunity to watch a group of children who are engrossed at play, notice the role of laughter. You'll hear it when they're carefree—experiencing well-being and camaraderie. You'll hear it as a sign of excitement, when they're engrossed in an activity. You'll hear it when they're hatching a plan with a cohort and fellow-conspirator.

Don't excitement, being engrossed, and "hatching a plan" with another sound like something you'd like to see employees doing at work? I think you do. And when you see it at work, you don't call it kids at play but rather engaged employees.

and turn it into a personal attack or insult. Finally, laughing at yourself gives you an endless and safe source of humorous material.

For years, my boss kept a picture on his desk of himself and a few colleagues from 20 years earlier where they were singing and dancing on stage … wearing elf costumes! Whenever anyone would ask him about it, he would say with a twinkle in his eye, "The things we do for the greater good!"

For my part, I have dressed up as a milk carton and danced live on stage in front of 600 leaders before that video got shared with 13,000 employees. That I'm no dancer is painfully obvious. I've been the subject of good-natured roasts and impersonations and I've been the target of more than one practical joke. In short, I've been unafraid to embarrass myself for the purpose of making employees laugh. How much more do you think I would be willing to make a fool of myself if I could not only share humor with others but also foster trust, build relationships, and increase engagement?

If you can laugh at yourself, others are more apt to laugh at themselves. If you can make light of the pure and the positive in a way that also "makes fun" of your own weaknesses and quirks, you're more apt to foster the type of culture in which employees can come to you openly with their struggles. By being willing to subject yourself to jokes and good-natured ribbing, you tear down the veil of secrecy and supremacy that often exists between leadership and employees.

You might say, "But leaders need to keep an air of respect! I can't act like a weirdo in front of my employees." It's possible to foster respect for

---

WHAT'S AN OP GOD?

FOR EXAMPLE

I hired a humorous speaker named Joe Marlotti from Times-Four (www.times-four.com) to teach 500 supervisors how to maximize the four generations that show up at work each day. Before the meeting, Joe asked me if I would help him by shouting out my job title when he asked for volunteers during his show.

"Op God!" I yelled out when he asked for a volunteer, as a tongue-in-cheek acknowledgment that, while I worked in the operations division, I never considered myself an operational guru. "That's short for Operations God," I added.

"Oooh, I love it!" Marlotti's character yelled back from the stage. "*Op God!* That has such a nice ring. Hey! Did you know backwards that spells *Dog Po?*"

No one laughed louder or longer than I!

---

your skills and position while also having a light-hearted approach. If your leadership is characterized by a culture of camaraderie and fun, your employees will be more apt to follow you.

BY REPUTATION

FOR EXAMPLE

In my early days as a leader, I would fill open positions in my department the way most managers do. I'd contact human resources, fill out a job requisition, post ads in newspapers and online job boards, and then cull through reams of résumés. It didn't take long before I didn't need to go looking to find qualified applicants. In fact, I didn't even need an opening before I'd receive résumés.

Why? Reputation. Happy, engaged employees on my team wanted to attract other likeminded, fun-loving, high-performing individuals. They talked up the department, the work we accomplished, and the exciting culture we created together. People wanted in. At times, I'd have 20 qualified applicants vying for a position that didn't yet exist!

Using Humor Rather Than Correction

I've mentioned a team member named Tara. One time she filled in for a coworker to plan some meeting details involving menu selection for an upcoming leadership meeting. Tara had a delicious sense of humor and playfulness about her. So I wasn't surprised that, since she was a vegetarian, the family-style meal she ordered included salad, vegetable soup, bread, pasta, potatoes, and steamed, mixed vegetables. And of course, no meat.

How could I be playful yet still command respect? After seeing the menu she planned, I sent Tara an e-mail saying, "Nice try, Tara, but my boss is a card-carrying carnivore. Please order chicken. The neck you save may be mine. Thanks."

The fix required no issuing of stern commands or directives—just a little bantering and clarifying expectations with a light touch.

Before ruling out the possibility that leaders can foster both humor and respect, consider many prominent politicians, including Abraham Lincoln, who used humor in their leadership. Or see the sidebar about Ronald Reagan for examples.

Quotes from The Gipper

FOR EXAMPLE

Ronald Reagan was known for integrating humor into his job. Below are a few of his quotes.

- My fellow Americans. I'm pleased to announce that I've signed legislation outlawing the Soviet Union. We begin bombing in five minutes. —joking during a mike check before his Saturday radio broadcast
- It's true hard work never killed anybody, but I figure, why take the chance?
- I hope you're all Republicans. —speaking to surgeons as he was wheeled into the operating room following a 1981 assassination attempt
- Honey, I forgot to duck. —to his wife, Nancy, after surviving the assassination attempt
- I'm not worried about the deficit. It's big enough to take care of itself.
- I did turn 75 today, but remember, that's only 24 Celsius.

Why Managers Might Avoid Humor

If fun and humor are effective tools in increasing employee engagement, why don't more managers use them? Let's look at the three biggest reasons that managers give.

Reason #1: "I Don't Have a Sense of Humor"

It's true that some personalities are a little more reserved than others, but you don't have to take improv classes or have aspirations for stand-up comedy to practice a good sense of humor or create an environment of fun. Remember my short Good Humor Index shared earlier? Good humor is more than being a joke machine; it's about fostering an envi-

GOOD HUMOR INDEX

Look at the Good Humor Index again, but this time rate yourself on the five statements using the following scale: 5–Almost never; 4–Rarely; 3–Occasionally; 2–Often; 1–Almost always

Good Humor Index

TOOLS

_____ Laugh at yourself
_____ Use humor to get a point across
_____ Demonstrate warmth
_____ Use eye contact with others
_____ Smile

You can up your level of good humor by increasing small things like the amount of time you smile or have eye contact with others. Those convey warmth to others, and that's all it takes to create an environment of humor and fun.

"Every time you smile at someone, it is an action of love, a gift to that person, a beautiful thing" —Mother Teresa

ronment where humor creates energy for employees to accomplish more or to push past setbacks.

Reason #2: "I Don't Want to Look Unprofessional"

Some managers erroneously believe that being personable and good-natured aren't leadership traits. Researcher Geert Hofstede developed a Cultural Dimensions Theory that demonstrates how some cultures or professions naturally encourage or discourage certain traits. In cultures defined as paternalistic and masculine, some leaders would consider using humor and having fun with subordinates as taboo.

But the world is getting smaller. More companies are becoming global or at the very least multicultural. Leaders can't afford to hold a narrow world view or a limited set of tools to reach a broader population.

Salute when you say that! Management consultant and speaker Ken Grant understands that serving as an engaging leader isn't only about issuing orders and cracking whips. Ken spent over 20 years in the Army and was assigned to the Pentagon in the Office of the Secretary of the Army, retiring as a Lt. Colonel, and then spent the next 20-plus years as a senior project manager. Today, he runs his own company, Insight Solutions Consulting. Along the way, Ken learned that engaging leaders are responsible for maintaining the morale of the team.

While serving in Germany as the operations officer, Ken's battalion was responsible for making and keeping current the war plans for the missile unit. During a time of particular stress and tension, little things began to grate on nerves. Ken heard tempers rising in the meeting room next door. Knowing that tempers and distraction didn't mix well with precision technology and explosives, Ken intervened by walking into the next room, climbing up on a desk, standing at attention, and then reciting the Marc Antony soliloquy from Shakespeare's *Julius Caesar*: "Friends, Romans, countrymen, lend me your ears," he began.

In Ken's words, "The astonished looks on everyone's faces soon turned to smiles as they looked at the crazy major standing on the desk. Without a word, I returned to my office. There were some murmurs in the next room, but I had accomplished what I intended. The tension was broken and work continued."

I know what you're thinking: The United States military complex and project management leaders are known worldwide for producing some of the best comic minds! No, that's not the point. The point is that any leader in any industry and in any culture must be willing to step out of his or her comfort zone to give the team the kind of leadership it needs and deserves: engaging leadership.

Using and encouraging good humor and fun at work isn't about what you're comfortable doing; it's about what your employees need to give you their focus, their discretionary effort, and their engagement.

Reason #3: "I Don't Work for a Company That Encourages Humor and Fun"

Some companies, like Southwest Airlines, were founded by leaders renowned for possessing a fun-at-work management style. If you work for that sort of company, you likely not only have permission but also a prerogative to lead using similar traits. But what about the top-down, white-collar companies that seem to pride themselves on stuffiness and decorum?

What does your boss care about? Chances are your boss wants you to get results. Even if your boss is stuffy and gray and covered in frown-lines from his receding hairline down to his wrinkled toes, what likely matters most to him is that you get results. And what have you read so far? Engaging bosses get better results. Engaging bosses maximize results because they bring out the best in others. If your company or boss doesn't take a shine to a light-hearted approach at work, you don't have to wear a clown nose to a board meeting. But use your humor with your team, because they're the ones who'll get you positive results.

Ignite a Culture of Humor and Fun by Minding Your P's

Many managers who are afraid of getting sued might shy away from humor in the workplace, thinking it's too dangerous to mix laughter and fun amid policies and HR regulations. But clear guidelines exist to make applying humor simpler than nuclear science.

Use humor in the workplace in the same way you'd use a pat on the back ... making sure that both are of the nonsexual harassment variety. My buddy Sam Glenn further clarifies that humor should spotlight "the pure and the positive ... or get a good lawyer." I like that. If you aren't sure whether to crack a joke, run it by Sam's litmus test. Is it pure? Is it positive?

Let's first define what is *not* pure and positive. Your humor is likely ranging on inappropriate if it doesn't pass the Three P Test:

Mind Your P #1: Too Personal

For obvious reasons, humor that makes fun of an individual's appearance or ability is obviously off limits unless you know each other extremely well. I got away with pushing the envelope with my employees because I knew them so well, *and* they knew me well—including knowing that I would never honestly intend to offend them or do anything but esteem them. I showed this not only by respecting them in my interactions, but also by being willing to be the brunt of their jokes. But in most cases when implementing humor in the workplace—especially in a culture that's not yet fully engaged—getting too personal too soon is not only risky to the company, but also risky to your relationship with the employee. Avoid attempts at humor that could be taken as harassment or discrimination. In other words, avoid topics like race, color, religion, creed, sex, national origin, age, disability, and sexual orientation.

Mind Your P #2: Too Profane

Swearing, cursing, sexual jokes, or anything that would be considered lewd or obscene will do more harm than help. And yes, lawsuits abound when company leaders repeat at work comic routines that aired on prime-time television! Just because something illicit garnered a laugh on TV doesn't make it pure and positive. Ask yourself what kind of culture you want to promote. And then use this as a test before risking going too far: When it doubt, leave it out!

Mind Your P #3: Too Political

Yeah, this kind of fits in with personal, and it should be avoided. Unless you're all working for a political party, your funny crack at the opposing politician might cut to the heart of someone else's values.

AVOID OBSCENITY

Something that's not pure and positive is often obscene. *Obscene* is defined by Webster's dictionary as:

CAUTION

- Disgusting to the senses
- Repulsive to morality or virtue
- Designed to incite to lust or depravity
- Containing or being language regarded as taboo in polite society
- Repulsive by reason of crass disregard of moral or ethical principles

When fostering a culture of fun and humor, avoid obscenity. Even if it makes your employees laugh, it's not right. You are their leader. Ask yourself what would happen if others followed your lead and, say, added just one more line-crossing twist ... in the presence of the company president? Better safe than sorry.

Tricks and Tips for Promoting Fun

Here are some ideas I've gathered or used in my work. Determine which might be appropriate to customize and use in your office.

Pajama day. My doctor's office used to hold pajama day once a month. On that day, they would post a sign on the front desk announcing "Pajama Day!" All employees (front desk, nurses, and even a few of the doctors) wore PJs and robes in the office. When I joked with the receptionist about it on my way out of the office, she said, "It's perfect on days when I oversleep but still want to be on time for work!"

Share your photos. My department developed presentations for many of the senior leaders in the company. Instead of using stock images off the

Internet, I would encourage my employees to send me any photos they'd taken that they'd be willing to share should they be needed. This not only saved us money paying for royalties for using pictures, it also allowed them to showcase their talent. Remember my former colleague, Chris, with the graphic design company? He took a photo inside St. Peter's Cathedral in Rome that I've used so many times that I used to joke with him that I believed I'd taken it myself!

Name that tune. One supervisor sent out clues on e-mail to her employees about a song. Usually the clues weren't enough to provide an answer. As a twist, she began tying in her Name That Tune game with performance improvement. After setting a team productivity goal, she told them she would act out the song if the team reached its goal. Her team met and exceeded the goal. True to her word, on the next Friday near closing time, she cranked the Ray Stevens' song *The Streak* while riding a scooter around the office wearing sunglasses and a raincoat (I should add that she remained *fully clothed* under that raincoat!).

Photo scavenger hunt. I've used photo scavenger hunts with groups of employees. Most phones have cameras, and the games can be played over lunch hour. All you need to do is create a list of possible photos to collect along with point values. Create teams, and send them off. Not only does this get employees active and moving, it develops an environment for teamwork and a "best friend at work."

Silly e-mails. After making an offhand comment about my dislike of cats (which isn't true, by the way), a group of employees started sending me cat pictures from those e-mails you likely have coming through your e-mail. Instead of discouraging that or saying, "Please remember that e-mail is a corporate resource that should not be used in any way for fun, enjoyment, or other pleasurable purposes," I used the pictures to create a presentation to kick off a new program my department was launching. The presentation went over so well, it got shared across the entire organization. For years afterward, I was known as the Cat Man, and employees would send me cat pictures they came across.

Model a sense of humor. If you as a leader set the stage for positivity, your employees are more apt to follow. If you aren't comfortable with initiating humor yourself, promote it in others. When you hear someone say something that promotes good humor, ask that person if he or she would mind sharing it with others in the office.

Create a humor bulletin board. Let employees post jokes, quotes, funny pictures, or whatever suits them. Post it in the break room or a prominent place where it'll be noticed.

Hire people with a sense of humor. As Southwest Airlines CEO Herb Kelleher says, "What we are looking for, first and foremost, is a sense of humor … We hire attitudes."

Highlight humor. Hire a motivational speaker who incorporates humor, or purchase humorous DVDs to use during meetings to cement your learning points. Or, go a cheaper route. I used to show humorous YouTube or movie clips as part of my meetings to home in on particular points, such as showing customer service gaffes. Many employees would circulate the current page from a humorous desk calendar that featured one-liners or cartoons.

THE SHINY OFFICE

FOR EXAMPLE

Practical jokes can provide a way to engage others. One time I took off a couple of weeks around the end of the year because I had to use up my vacation days before the New Year. While I was out of the office, my manager, Amy, had an idea: Let's cover Scott's office in aluminum foil! An invite went out to the whole team asking for volunteers to bring in foil. Teams were assembled that came in early or spent their lunch hours in my office wrapping *everything*—down to the two pennies on my desk—in foil!

I returned to work early on a day I had scheduled an interview with a potential job candidate, and I was surprised to find that my managers had called a team meeting before 8 a.m. The employees were gathered in the hallway and aisles when I turned the key in my office door. My office faced east, and the glare off that aluminum foil–covered office was blinding once I opened the door! The office floor erupted in laughter and applause as I turned around with my mouth wide open.

And here's an interesting side note. I ended up hiring the woman I interviewed a short time later. After her first week, she told a coworker that she had been entertaining a job offer that paid a little more money, but once she saw the foil in my office and way the employees got along, she knew she preferred the job with our company.

Mr. Potato Head, Part 2

I mentioned in Chapter 3 about the Mr. Potato Head stickers and how an enterprising, positive leader used something so silly to make great improvements in performance. In one unionized company, I shared this story with a team of leaders as a way of getting them to think about how they could build some fun into their own units.

One manager sat back with his arms folded the whole time and occasionally shook his head and even grunted as a way of saying he thought the topic of conversation was beneath him. Since I'd been asked to work with his team and was getting paid to produce results, I couldn't sit back and let this guy spread his negativity to others in the room.

"I see you shaking your head about the Mr. Potato Head sticker idea," I challenged him. "Does that strike you as a little kindergarten?" I offered him an out.

"Yeah," he answered. "That might work with some country bumpkins out in the sticks. But this is Chicago, and this is a union shop. My people are more sophisticated and jaded than that."

Perhaps I should have paused a moment longer before responding, but I didn't. Instead, I said, "Okay, Mr. Potato Head stickers won't work here. Then think more sophisticated. What would it take to turn them on? Firearms and cocaine? You tell me what will work."

Sniggers spread across the classroom. I later learned that this man's coworkers were tired of listening to his negativity and nay-saying. I hadn't meant to put this man in his place, but I hoped to get his mind involved by engaging him with my attempt at ironic humor. After what seemed like a long pause, a big smile crossed the manager's face.

"You're all right," he snorted. "Yeah, maybe I'm the one who's jaded."

The manager did two positive things in that moment. One, he smiled, demonstrating the first sign of good humor. Two, he acknowledged that perhaps he was the person who was jaded, and perhaps he needed to look at his team and his positive reinforcement with fresh eyes.

Laughter Strengthens Relationships

According to speaker and author Tim Gabrielson, who combines magic, comedy, and inspiration at his presentations, "It should be no surprise that in addition to good health and mental well-being, humor lends itself to a certain level of popularity. Laughter builds unity and companionship, so it should be no surprise that people flock to those with a strong sense of self as well as those who make them laugh" (*Lemons to Laughter*, Magic Man Inc., 2008, p. 25). Tim's book includes clean tips for spreading humor and also for having fun "despite yourself." If you can learn to laugh without the help of anyone else, you'll be well on your way to finding humor in the workplace. Here are a few highlights you can practice if you are brave or simply laugh at these suggestions:

- Fill your umbrella with confetti; in case of rain, always offer yours.
- One day prior to a gathering at your home, fill some wine glasses with Jell-O. After the first glass or two of real wine, substitute the Jell-O for the next glass and watch the faces as the confusion occurs; very funny!
- Walk into a store with a sign that says, "Have a penny? Give a penny! Need a penny? Take a penny!" with a *huge* jar of pennies. Take a penny out of the cup, put it into your jar, and walk out.

Exercise as a Means of Fun and Relationship Building

More and more companies include fitness facilities as part of their workplace. Companies like SAS, RedHat, Google—all of which are regularly ranked as best places to work by independent sources—promote wellness.

Why? Besides the physical effect that exercise has on the body—releasing endorphins that promote happy feelings—these facilities also offer the benefit of fostering relationships between employees with like-minded interests. What better way to build best friendships at work than by playing a game of racquetball during lunch? Even if you don't like exercise, you can't argue with the chemical benefits or the relationship-building opportunities it brings.

In fact, according to the U.S. Office of Personnel Management,

[I]n 2002, The Surgeon General's Call to Action to Prevent and Decrease Overweight and Obesity called on all sectors of society, including worksites, to take part in the call to action. The Surgeon General's Report on Physical Activity and Health, July 1996, states that a moderate amount of physical activity on a regular basis can improve health, and asks employers to provide supportive workplace environments and policies that help employees become more

> ### THE WELLNESS–WELL-BEING LINK
>
> Coors Brewing Company leadership reported that for each dollar spent on their wellness program, they saw a $5.50 return—and staff members who participated reduced their absentee rate by 18 percent.
>
> Toronto municipal employees missed 3.35 fewer days per person in the first six months of their wellness program than their non-enrolled coworkers.
>
> British Columbia Hydro employees taking part in an internal wellness program had 7 percent less turnover than non-enrolled coworkers.
>
> With only 60 percent staff participation, Coca-Cola Company reported a $500 per employee annual savings as a result of their worksite program.
>
> Companies that invest in the wellness and well-being of their employees save money, retain employees, and reduce absenteeism. It's like hiring extra employees without spending additional money (http://worksite-wellness programs.com/tag/roi)!

physically active. (www.opm.gov/employment_and_benefits/work-life/officialdocuments/handbooksguides/employeehandbook/Chapter2/index.asp)

As a result, government agencies were encouraged to support the implementation of physical exercise in the workplace, including flex time for employees who wanted to participate.

Tying It All Together

My boss of many years kicked off a meeting with frontline employees using a light-hearted, effective presentation. As he segued from humor into the business at hand, he asked a series of questions before telling the employees why he was excited about pulling the group together:

"Did Scott assemble this team together here because we're nice people? No. I mean, I'm a nice person. I can't speak for Scott. But either way, that's not why we're pulling you together.

"Did we create this team because we had some extra money lying around and thought we'd show a small group of employees from regional offices the big city of Chicago? No. Hopefully, you'll take some time to see the city, but that's not why we're here, either.

"No, the reason we want you here is because we've discovered the power of harnessing and implementing your thoughts on making this company the best place to work."

GET MOVING!

Engage in physical activities with your employees. Encourage exercise programs that get the endorphins going and foster relationships. Exercise also gets the blood moving to and from the brain. One supervisor offered to any of her employees who were interested to join her at lunchtime for a brisk walk. It started off with the supervisor and two of her employees. Within a few months, other supervisors and employees joined, too, and before long, it looked like an unbroken circle of employees surrounding the office in a march! In addition to the health and happiness benefits, this got employees talking with each other and building stronger social relationships.

This team went on to create ideas that saved our company money at the same time it accelerated buy-in from others on the frontline. Two of the frontline employees in that meeting became my employees—one of them I mentioned in the opener to this chapter.

Where did it start? We engaged them, we educated them, and we pulled them in using humor along the way as a relationship-building tool. Where did it end? It hasn't ended. Several members of that initial team have since assumed leadership roles in the organization where they keep alive the engagement practices they experienced years before with their own teams today.

Whether you have a million-dollar budget to spend on increasing motivation or none at all, you can implement actions that evoke humor and fun in the workplace. And it will pay off! It's impossible to keep your eyes open when you sneeze. Even more relevant to this chapter is that it's impossible to complain, bad-mouth, or spread a disease of disengagement when you're in good humor. Having fun and humor at work doesn't undermine performance, but rather, deals a blow to disengagement.

Manager's Checklist for Chapter 9

- ☑ Humor has healing power because it promotes laughter, which decreases blood pressure, increases heart rate and respiration, releases endorphins (happiness-producing chemicals), and decreases depression.
- ☑ Happiness and humor build engagement through sharing positive emotions and building relationships.

☑ Humor increases productivity and results.

☑ We are often our best source of humor.

☑ Avoid humor that's profane, too personal, or political.

☑ Practice developing your "humor muscle" so you can engage it at work to get your team through hard times and foster more creativity and camaraderie.

☑ Exercise gets the blood going and stimulates happiness and relationships.

Chapter
10

Tackling Barriers to Engagement

While writing this book, I talked to several colleagues about their experiences and challenges in engaging their teams. While the techniques I've introduced form the basis of solid engagement-building efforts, some situations require a refined approach to unleash the potential within your employees. You may be gliding smoothly in your engagement dance until a new emcee takes over, you encounter someone who hates dancing, or you find the doors are locked and the dance floor will also become your sleeping quarters. Or, put in manager-speak, you encounter changes or an environment that make engagement seem like a distant hope or lost priority.

What's In It For Me (WIIFM)?

In reality, all work environments are "special"—requiring a slightly customized engagement approach. Each of these special circumstances can be seen as barriers to engagement if not managed properly. When I conduct coaching workshops, I emphasize the What's In It For Me?

Change is constant, and that means leaders must become change agents instead of change phobic. WIIFM? Managers will be in demand until success can be automated and the need for change eliminated. Until then, *what's in it for managers* is the opportunity to leave a mark by creating success with others.

ARE YOUR CIRCUMSTANCES SPECIAL?

Place a checkmark next to any situation that could be said of your work environment for the period covering the last 12 months:

TOOLS

_____ You have a new boss.

_____ Your boss doesn't seem to value engagement or care about your personal engagement.

_____ Your company has changed ownership (e.g., merger, acquisition, hostile take-over, buy-out, etc.).

_____ You're new in your management role or new within your current team.

_____ Your employee base has experienced downsizing or outsourcing involving displacement of more than 10 percent of the organization's employees.

_____ You've experienced significant change in the nature of your work, business processes, or performance criteria.

_____ You work in a union environment, public sector, or military (environments where employees do not readily leave voluntarily and, therefore, often feel "stuck" in their positions regardless of how much they enjoy them).

The conditions above fit loosely into three groups: (1) bad boss, (2) business changes, and (3) backdrop. If you lead others, it's your role to manage your boss, business changes, and the backdrop of where business occurs. At any given time, most leaders will experience one or two checkmarks on the list above. The more checkmarks you make, the more your engagement activities need to be your priority!

The Goal: To Flourish

I want to address some of the most common changes/challenges you may face as a leader wanting to build an engaged workforce. But first, I want to take a moment to refine the engagement goal, so that in spite of any difficulties or changes, you're still focusing on the positive outcome you want to achieve—much like a downhill skier is taught to focus down the hill on her destination so she can smoothly traverse the moguls right beneath her.

Good vs. Happy

A friend of mine asked his three-year-old son, "Do you know what Mommy and Daddy want most for you?"

The boy shrugged at first and then asked, "To be good?"

The dad was dismayed to hear that his son believed that "being good" trumped everything else. Those words probably were being uttered with regularity to the boy. Certainly, he and his wife wanted their children to behave and function well in society, but they also talked about having fun, finding their passions, and exploring their worlds. When my friend told me this story, he concluded, "I still have to remind my son to be good, but now I ask him all the time to tell me what makes him happy and what excites him." Do you see the difference between *good* and *happy*? It's similar to the difference between *satisfied* and *fulfilled*. One suggests a state wherein nothing is out of line; the other suggests a state of *flourishing*.

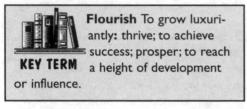

Flourish To grow luxuriantly: thrive; to achieve success; prosper; to reach a height of development or influence.

KEY TERM

If we think of engagement goals in terms of flourishing, we know what we're aiming for when we institute the practices in this book. Now, let's visit our special circumstances or barriers to our goal of flourishing in our engagement culture.

Special Circumstance #1: My Boss Is a Barrier to Engagement

This is a complaint I hear regularly in my consulting. It comes across like this: "My boss doesn't care about our culture" or "My boss is the problem."

If this is the case, what do you do? First, you need to know your boss, just as we suggested you should know your people. To engage your boss, you have to "engage up," which means putting the same practices into place that you put into place with your employees.

Start simply with this question: What does your boss care about? Since people do what they do to get what they want, your boss, too, is driven by something. Without knowing your boss, I would say that the one factor all bosses have in common is that they want results. Maybe it's "less stress" or "more money" or "higher customer satisfaction" or "lower costs."

When it comes to your boss, know what he or she considers good. Likely, your boss views getting results as good. Manager, you need to know your boss's priorities and goals.

Urgent vs. Important

In the 1960s book *Freedom from Tyranny of the Urgent*, author Charles Hummel (Downers Grove, IL: InterVarsity Press, 1997) suggests that too often we spend our time on urgent tasks. How often do you sit down to spend time with your family and then get caught up in a phone call that zaps an hour, an e-mail request that becomes a full-blown exchange, an angry boss who needs to be calmed, a last-minute work request caused by someone's lack of planning? While urgent tasks need attention, they should never come at the expense of what's most important.

Important things are those that matter most in the long haul, and they might include preserving quality time with your family, building more meaningful relationships with others, or pursuing a deeper relationship with God.

At work, it's possible that your boss gets so caught up in urgent tasks that he or she fails to take the time to share with you what's most important: priorities and goals. Manager, make it your job to find out your boss's priorities and goals.

Discover the Boss's Priorities and Goals

Most companies have performance appraisals, and a component of those appraisals involves writing out personal and departmental goals. If your boss doesn't share his or her goals with you, take advantage of the performance appraisal goal-writing session to ask to see them. Here are some ways to have that conversation:

- While I'm writing my goals, I want to make sure I include everything that's important to you.
- Are there some goals you have this period that I can help you accomplish?
- I want to make sure that I'm giving you everything you need to keep your boss happy. Is there something I should pay particular attention to as I write my own goals?

I've never worked with a boss who didn't gladly share his or her goals

KEY TERMS

Manage up This involves assessing your boss's weaknesses and coming up with a strategy for dealing with them. At the very least, managing up includes the art of paying attention to the management and communication style of your boss, and changing your style to be an asset instead of a liability.

Suck-up A person one who ingratiates himself or herself, often using insincere behavior. A suck-up may be said to "cozy up with the boss." In more erudite circles, a suck-up may be referred to as a sycophant. But a suck-up is best known for "brown-nosing" those who may help him or her.

Engaging up This means providing positive reinforcement to your boss on the things your boss most values, while simultaneously letting your boss help engage your employees. It's not manipulation; rather, it's bringing out the best side of your boss. Your goal in engaging up is to link what your boss wants with what you and your team deliver.

with me. And do you know what I did with my goals as soon as they were written and approved? I made sure all my employees got a copy! Goal-sharing promotes the concept of "We're in this together."

You can take this step to the next level by asking your boss this: Do you have a pet project that you'd love to see some research on, or do you have an idea that you'd love to see implemented outside of the goals you have on your plate?" Now you're speaking to what really energizes your boss's passion.

Once you know what's driving your boss, you can *engage up*. No doubt you've heard the concept *manage up* and probably even *suck up*. But to *engage up* is different. When you engage up, you're giving your boss reasons to become engaged with you.

Look at Table 10-1, Engaging up. In the left column are a couple examples that your boss might consider a priority or goal. In the center column is an accomplishment or result that a member of your team accomplished. Finally, in the right column is a list of possible ways you can engage up with your boss. Fill in the blanks with information about your boss's goals, team accomplishments that might align with those goals, and ideas about getting your boss to recognize your team for their results.

Align your objectives and concerns with language that speaks to your boss's needs. In the case of engagement, illustrate how a lack of it is hurting your business's profits—if that's what he or she is concerned with—

and ask for his or her support as you seek solutions.

Finally, take it a step further. Once you have basic agreement on your boss's main objectives and how to tie them into engagement goals, try to find out what brings out the passion and excitement of your boss at work. That will tell you what makes your boss truly happy. Feed into happiness, you'll unleash your boss's engagement and create an environment wherein he or she flourishes.

Boss's Priority/Goal	Accomplishment/ Result	Engaging Up Action Ideas
Customer satisfaction	Improved customer satisfaction based on survey results Thank-you note/e-mail from a satisfied customer	Give a thank-you note to your boss to sign that's addressed to your team for the improved score. Give a thank-you note for your boss to sign to the customer who expressed appreciation. Post the satisfaction scores or note/e-mail in a common area so all employees can see it.
Sales	Selling a new account Reaching a sales quota	Invite your boss to a brown-bag lunch to speak to your team. Inform your boss of the accomplishment in writing, spelling out team members' names and efforts. Ask your boss if he or she could stop by to personally thank your team or the individual who made the accomplishment. Pass on to your team any positive feedback your boss shares with you.

Table 10-1. Engaging up

What If My Boss Still Doesn't Engage?

What if you're doing everything in your power to engage your boss and get your boss to engage in the results you're achieving, but you're still not seeing positive results for your efforts? Here are a couple of additional thoughts:

- You're receiving extinction when your boss gives you no acknowledgment, praise, or attention for the good work you accomplish. *Remember that feeling of frustration and make sure your employees never feel that way as a result of your treatment.* Frustration and lack of appreciation are engagement busters. By investing more in your people, they'll engage you back.

- While you don't have to share every criticism you hear from your boss, *make certain your employees hear every favorable word* or at least *how proud you are of them* for doing

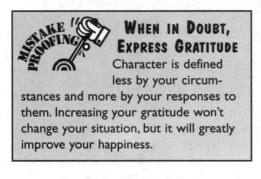

WHEN IN DOUBT, EXPRESS GRATITUDE
Character is defined less by your circumstances and more by your responses to them. Increasing your gratitude won't change your situation, but it will greatly improve your happiness.

things that your own boss loves to see! Does it sound like I'm suggesting that you compensate for your boss's interpersonal weaknesses? Good. Because that's exactly what I'm suggesting. A boss who focuses on the negative is on par with one who ignores the positives. Break the cycle. Focus your attention by ensuring that your employees hear about all the things that are going right.

Special Circumstance #2: Change Is Hindering Employee Engagement

Given that change is such a part of life, it would be nice if change were easier to face. It's been said that the only one who likes change is a wet baby. And it's certainly true that some changes make it difficult for employees to remain engaged at work.

As a leader, understand what makes changes so hard on your employees. Let's explore a few common changes that can disrupt engagement.

> ### NEED ENGAGEMENT? GIVE AWAY SOME PRAISE
>
>
>
> **SMART MANAGING**
>
> Sitting around talking with my leaders, I asked each of them to tell me something they had learned during the last year. One manager told me something like this:
>
> "One time I felt like I wasn't making progress engaging [a certain company leader]. You told me to 'control the controllables.' So instead of worrying about [the leader], I focused on what my people were doing well and I let them know how much I appreciated them. My employees responded so well to my praise and encouragement that they actually re-engaged me to stay upbeat and positive."
>
> When you're feeling down, you can pull yourself out of it by thanking or praising someone else.

Common Change #1: Change in Leadership

Let's say you're the new boss. Employees have to start from scratch learning your preferences, policies, priorities, etc. For the employees who loved the former boss, you might have big shoes to fill. And you might be dealing with their feelings of loss and separation, especially based on the circumstances around the boss's departure (e.g., illness or death, termination as opposed to retirement or taking a better position). Employees who loved the former boss don't immediately get credit for all that they've accomplished in the past.

And it's no better with the employees who didn't care for the old boss. While they might be glad to get a fresh start, the old boss was a known factor. You're an unknown. They have to put in the work to get to know you so their new start isn't just another bad beginning.

Here are some tips if you're a new boss:

Tip #1: Get PSST—Especially get personal and get strengths-based. Don't feel pressured to fill the old shoes or become best friends. Get to know your employees personally and tap into their unique strengths. Soon there will be no comparisons between you and the former boss, and over time you might become the standard by which other bosses are measured.

Tip #2: Provide a way for employees to share their emotions and transition in the change. Most emotionally healthy individuals would prefer conversations that include positive emotions instead of negative ones. As a leader, it's not imperative that you excel in confrontation or dealing with negative emotions. But as a leader, you can't shy away from it, either.

However, there's a benefit in letting people complain for a bit. My friend, Marlene Chism, suggests in her book *Stop Workplace Drama* and in her coaching that employees be allowed to vent for a designated period, but that they also be required to come to meetings armed with ideas for solutions. She suggests setting a stopwatch to gauge time for a complaining session, and then moving on quickly to finding answers.

Tip #3: Open a two-way conversation. When I assumed responsibility for several new employees, their former boss wanted to meet with me to give me the details on each person. I declined that offer until I had first met with each employee one-on-one to gain firsthand experience. Why? It's hard to shake a first impression, so I wanted to give each employee the courtesy of making his or her own impression on me, not taking the word of a former boss. Ask your new employees to prepare a list of Five Things You Want Me to Know About You, and a list of Five Things You Want to Know About Me. This transparency allows employees maximum freedom to spotlight their personal and professional preferences, and lets your employees know about what drives you.

Tip #4: Clarify your expectations. No doubt your predecessor valued and demonstrated a certain communication and work style, established policies and procedures that worked at the time they were set up, and made the team function in a way that made sense for that particular leader. Pretend your new employees can remember only two things. When you're the "new boss," what two things do your employees need to know about your expectations? Make sure they know them.

The Funeral: Making Change Formal. Early in my consulting career, I worked with a company that had seen four CEOs in as many years. Each leader brought in cronies who funded pet projects or developed completely new policies, work streams, etc. Employee emotions were high. They were angry and hostile; many of them openly criticized the company for its string of business losses and leadership failures.

The new CEO, Jim, contacted me a month after the board hired him as the successor. In our first meeting, Jim told me that he'd met with every employee and found the level of resentment about the losses second only to fear about the future of their jobs.

MAKING THE "WHY" OF CHANGE PERSONAL

SMART

MANAGING

Lawrence Polsky, whom I've mentioned, is founding partner of PeopleNRG, a firm specializing in optimizing corporate change efforts. PeopleNRG exists because companies and people alike change continually. According to a recent interview I had with Lawrence, people are most likely to embrace change when they experience the reason for change as something:

- Selfish
- Emotional
- Huge

For example, one might choose to adopt a healthier lifestyle after being diagnosed with heart disease, because of a "selfish" desire to live longer. This change has huge personal ramifications, and thus becomes emotionally driven.

Here's another way to look at change: You can change who you are, but you must first want to change. And as Polsky suggests, if the reason for change is big enough and personal enough, people will want to change.

Keep this concept in mind if your company is going through major change. Make it personal by showing how the change affects them, and how engaging through it will increase their chances to flourish.

I suggested we hold a funeral for the old company—the company the employees hated and feared. We'd have a service where employees could talk about the things they would miss as well as the things they hoped would change in the new organization.

We rented a casket (yes, a real casket) and one leader dressed in black led the service in the office building. Employees came up to the front and talked openly and at times emotionally about things that were on their minds and hearts. Others wrote their thoughts on pieces of paper and deposited them in the casket as they walked past to share their last respects.

We held the funeral on a Friday; on Monday, the office was decorated with birth announcements and congratulation banners! The new CEO spent a weekend outlining what he heard at the funeral and what he committed to change based on what he'd heard.

Common Change #2: Change in the Business, Processes, or Performance Standards

In my change workshops, I often start with a statement written on the screen that says, "I'm okay with change. Change doesn't bother me." I then ask participants to stand up, read aloud from a statement on the screen, write that statement down, and then stand up with their arms crossed. I time how long it takes the group to accomplish this simple task from the moment I say, "Go!" The average group completes this exercise in about 15 to 20 seconds.

Next I ask the group to do the same exercise, but I change two of the instructions. I ask them to write the same statement with their *opposite hand*, and I ask them to cross their arms the *opposite way* than they did the first time.

The second time through can take 45 seconds or longer! The best group managed to accomplish this "simple" feat by merely doubling their time.

The point is obvious: It's easier to do the things we know automatically and fluently than to unlearn and relearn those same things with a twist. When we have to think and intentionally perform in a new, different way, we get frustrated because we don't achieve success for our efforts. We get used to performing well, and when our process for doing things changes, we're no longer able to be successful ... at first.

So what can you do if you find yourself leading in a time of change? Here are some tips to guide you if your business, processes, or standards are undergoing significant change:

Tip #1: Be honest about the change. When I led an internal communications effort around a merger, I met regularly with groups of managers to explain the whys and wherefores of the merger. Often I would hear questions like "Will jobs be cut?" Think about that for a moment. What is that questioner really asking? Isn't he or she asking "Will *my* job be cut?" Yes, the question comes from a place of fear, and the questioner wants reassurance of hope.

Earlier I spelled out the difference between being pragmatic versus being pragmatic yet positive. The pragmatic answer to this question would be: "Duh! We aren't merging to *lose* money! It makes sense that jobs will be cut!" The purely Pollyanna answer—in this case one that involves making a promise one can't keep—would be to say, "No! Of course not. I can promise you that no jobs will be cut. In fact, we'll probably create new jobs."

The pragmatic yet positive answer that I gave sounded something like this:

I don't know how to answer your question. Perhaps our company can stay independent and strong for another few years without changing anything. But the best way to assure the future of our company is to grow customers, market share, and revenue. If we don't accomplish that, instead of being in a position to go through a merger of equals, we'll more likely be acquired by a more powerful company. Given what happens in cases like that, odds are that few of us will have jobs.

Leaders, your employees aren't kids who need to be protected from the truth. Tell your employees as much as you can tell them, neither selling despair nor promising salvation. Just tell them the truth.

Tip #2: Understand that all change is emotional. Another post-merger project I supported involved consolidating and standardizing job titles. Until that project, I had no idea that people felt such an emotional connection to the title of assistant manager as opposed to senior supervisor. The job function remained identical; the pay and benefits, unchanged.

My initial efforts to help people embrace this change failed. Why? I had approached it with logic instead of understanding the underlying emotion. People didn't give two spits that the only thing changing was the words entered into the human resources and payroll databases. No, they felt as though they had earned the title assistant manager (emotionally, only one small step below a full-fledged manager), and they were now being demoted to senior supervisor (emotionally, only one small step above a frontline supervisor).

I had to allow employees to vent, to tell me their emotions about the change, even when their emotions were heated.

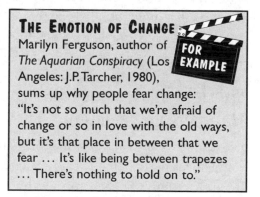

THE EMOTION OF CHANGE Marilyn Ferguson, author of *The Aquarian Conspiracy* (Los Angeles: J.P. Tarcher, 1980), sums up why people fear change: "It's not so much that we're afraid of change or so in love with the old ways, but it's that place in between that we fear ... It's like being between trapezes ... There's nothing to hold on to."

No, I couldn't change things, but until I demonstrated a willingness to absorb their frustration by listening and drawing them into authentic dialogue, they had no reason to listen to me.

Tip #3: Focus on what's not changing. Sometimes it helps to reassure employees that the most important things aren't changing. Think of Tom and Tina, the proud parents of four-year-old Tracy, who bring home their new baby, Tony. What question pops into Tracy's mind and out of her mouth? "Do you love Tony more than you love me?" What do Tracy's parents tell her? "No, Honey! Just because we brought your brother, Tony, home doesn't mean that we love you any less. Tony needs our help more right now because he's so little. But now I want to spend time with you, my precious *big girl*!"

Tip #4: Remember that *hope* is a leader's essential commodity. Sell the hope that some things will remain the same, and the hope that some things may even be an improvement. And no matter how difficult things may be at the hardest moment, they will get better.

Tip #5: Increase your positive reinforcement. While the Losada Ratio demonstrates an almost 3-to-1 positive-to-negative ratio helps a team flourish, that ratio was developed in a relatively static environment—not one undergoing significant change. In situations of great change, a leader needs to increase that ratio to nearly 12-to-1 to counteract the negative impact of the emotional drain change can create. It's hard to dislike or disengage from someone who's telling you that you're doing great!

Tip #6: Communicate, communicate, communicate. Don't worry about repeating yourself. In fact, I'm not worried that I've already used a point that says, "Communicate, communicate, communicate," earlier in the book. It's *that important*. Tell your employees what's changing, give them an opportunity to express their emotions, and reinforce them when they start making steps to engage you and engage in the new world.

Special Circumstance #3: The Business Backdrop Hampers Engagement

I've heard several managers who work in the public sector or a union environment tell me that "the rules of engagement" are different in their world, because the business backdrop rewards mediocrity and doing just enough to get by. I've spent a little time waiting in line at the Illinois Department of Motor Vehicles in Naperville. If you've seen *The Simpsons* on TV, you might recall that the chain-smoking, toxic-attitude twins Selma and Patty Bouvier work at the DMV. They epitomize what it looks like to be disengaged at work. They hate what they do and they hate the people they're employed to serve. So when I went to the Illinois DMV to renew my driver's license, I will admit that I held very low expectations about the experience.

Are you waiting for the punch line? There isn't one. The experience was great. Why? The people working there knew their jobs, performed efficiently, seemed to care about serving customers, and a few had a gleam in their eye as opposed to the vacuous, thousand-yard stare I anticipated. In fact, when I left I asked the person who directed customers at the center desk if I could speak to the manager. He smiled and said, "Sure. Can I tell him what it's about?" Moments later, the manager of the facility came around to the front and listened to me gush about what a nice experience I'd had at the DMV. He smiled and said, "I hear that a lot. Thanks for letting me know. I'm going to make sure the people working here today hear what you had to say, too."

Here's my point: I believe that the business backdrop is far less important than the business leader when it comes to shaping and promoting an environment of engagement. I've witnessed union shops work hard and with passion, giving that little extra that differentiates something done well and something done great. In talking with union workers, I've heard the same things that I hear in nonunion environments: It's all about the boss. Do you remember the Pygmalion Effect? When employees are treated as if they're superstars and they're expected to perform well, they do. Conversely, when employees are expected to be lazy and do as little as possible (as some extreme Theory X leaders believe), employees don't give more than is expected, and sometimes less.

Manager, can you imagine leading a team of employees whose job required them to stand on three-inch-wide beams at a dangerous height while facing bitter cold and severe winds? What sounds like a situation where engagement is challenging might not be the case. Perhaps some leaders might find engaging a team of union welders responsible for securing the skeleton structure of a skyscraper difficult. But a wise leader would remember that every year people stand on narrow beams at a similarly dangerous height for the pleasure of facing the bitter cold and severe winds. These people have no problem engaging, because they love what they do. In fact, they talk about it all the time and join groups of others who share their passion. On top of that, these people pay a hefty sum for that privilege, too. But for them, it's called skiing.

If you believe that you work in a unique business backdrop that makes engagement more challenging, here's something to keep in mind: People do what they do because they get what they want when they do it. What do your people want? As we discussed earlier, most people want the same things at work. Take a look at the list below for some additional examples. Don't you want these things?

- An opportunity to do what you do best at work, the ability to apply your strengths
- Recognition when you do a nice job
- Being able to share your opinion and having your opinion matter
- To be treated with respect, kindness, and decency
- Ownership over some part of your work
- A belief that what you do makes a difference to someone
- Some positive correlation between your efforts and rewards
- An environment that makes you happy and feel valued

If that's what you want, doesn't it stand to reason that your employees want some of the same things? This isn't like music or food where everyone has a personal favorite. These are about feeling respected and valued. When you value and respect your employees, those employees will want to be on your team because they'll know that you're on their side.

Servant Leadership: A Lesson from the Army

A powerful way to get employees on your side is to literally be on their side, by practicing servant leadership. I mentioned Ken Grant earlier, who spent more than 20 years in the U.S. military before retiring at the rank of Lt. colonel. I once asked Ken how the military engages "employees" given that soldiers can't quit and go home if they don't like it. Ken laughingly acknowledged that in the military, unlike in civilian life, you can make people do whatever you ask them to do because you have the nearly infinite power to punish them until they submit.

But the most effective way to get and keep the respect of your troops, Ken pointed out, was by being a servant leader.

"When we were in the field, I used to make sure I was the last to eat," Ken offered as an example. "Doing this served several purposes. First, I could stand as the line passed and chat with the soldiers. Second, it gave me an opportunity to observe their morale firsthand. Third, by eating last, I assured myself and the troops at the end of the line that all the good food wouldn't be gone before we got there."

Ken summed up the spirit of servant leadership this way: "Engaged leaders show their people that their welfare is of vital importance." Whether or not your employees are bound to stay with your company, much can be learned from Ken's servant leadership style. If you treat your team as if their welfare matters as much as yours, you not only build their trust, but also their engagement.

There are two additional special circumstances that I believe merit consideration: engaging remote employees and "engaging" the unengageable.

Special Circumstance #4: Engaging Remote Employees

In any relationship involving geographical distance, there's a tendency for the phrase "out of sight, out of mind" to apply. In a work relationship, as in a marriage, spending time apart doesn't have to spell disaster, but both situations require more attention for that physical distance not to create an emotional divide. You have to find creative ways to communicate, know your employees, and engage them.

Four Tips to Keep Remote Employees Engaged

Tip #1: Lock in regular times to connect. This is especially true when you work in different time zones. When a New York acquaintance of mine assumed responsibility for employees in New Delhi, he had difficulty holding real-time conversations at first. E-mail worked well for simple transactional exchanges, but he struggled to build a relationship with his employees and even the manager in that New Delhi office. Together they settled on holding a conference call from 4 p.m. to 6 p.m. New Delhi time every Thursday. That meant he connected to the call from home each Thursday since it was 5:30 a.m. in his time zone.

To maximize these pre-scheduled calls, have a business agenda. For example, review progress on goals, milestones, or accomplishments. But also allow time for some small talk, for getting to know each other on a more personal level. And in the case of a 10½-hour time zone difference, you might find that you share one thing in common immediately: Neither of you know what day it is in the other country!

Tip #2: Connect *just because* and not *because I need you to* ... Since it often takes more effort to get in touch with someone by phone or video conference, don't make it even harder by conditioning your employee that the only reason you reach out is to deliver another work assignment. Last year, I sat in the office of a manager when the phone rang. The manager looked at her caller ID, shook her head, and continued talking. When I offered that she could take the call if she needed to, she declined, saying, "No, it's fine. It's my boss. He only calls when he has something he needs done yesterday." Talk about conditioning! Don't let yourself fall into that same, predictable pattern. Call, e-mail, or IM your employees "just because," to say hello, to let them know you were thinking about them, to see if they need anything from you.

Tip #3: Find creative ways to deliver positivity. It might involve sending a hand-written thank-you card periodically for a job well done. One of our long-distance clients at Spiritus Communications sends a thank-you card along with each check she delivers to us for our services, *and* writes "thank you" on the back of the checks—reminding us of her gratitude even up to the point when we endorse her checks! And guess what? This engages us to answer the phone even at 11 p.m. if she needs us for an emergency conference. You can also send e-mails of praise, share humor via e-mail, and ensure that

THE POWER OF TONE

CAUTION As I've mentioned, as much as 93 percent of communication is nonverbal. Much of it is picked up in body language, which can't be read over the phone or e-mail. So, for virtual communications, try smiling before you get on a call, so your words come across with a positive tone. And double-check your e-mails before you hit Send to ensure they come across with the intended emotion.

your tone on the phone and in e-mail is always positive. If you're connected on Facebook or LinkedIn, check in and "like" or comment on their status updates, or their fan pages if they're contractors promoting themselves.

Tip #4: Communicate and involve long-distance employees in values, mission, and goals. Just because your employee works across the country or the globe doesn't mean he or she is any less apt to be more engaged by knowing what's going on with the company and knowing how he or she fits into the bigger picture. Provide regular briefings on important company changes and plans, and ask for their feedback.

Special Circumstance #5: Engaging the Unengageable

"Do you think every employee wants to be engaged?" I hear that question all the time.

The answer is complicated. As a way of answering, let me pose a few questions:

- Does every person like positive reinforcement? The answer is *yes.* Positive reinforcement makes people happy by giving them what they want, and it releases their discretionary effort to give a repeat performance.

- Does every person like the same type of positive reinforcement? The answer is *no.* We all like different things.

- Does everyone want to be engaged? Let's review the definition: the level of dedication, commitment, passion, innovation, and emotional energy a person is willing to expend. A highly engaged person tends to demonstrate what subjectively might be called happiness.

No, not everyone is willing to expend dedication, commitment, passion, innovation, and emotional energy at work. I'm not being Theory X, but I am telling you what you already know. Not everyone wants to be engaged, much the same way that not every person you know could be defined as happy or knows how to find happiness.

The real issue for each manager who comes across an unengageable employee is this: How do I deal with a strongly disengaged employee?

The reason this section isn't in the front of the book is because I believe that most employees want to be engaged. And I believe that by following the tips and tools in this book, you can engage them. But if you find yourself with a truly disengaged employee, it's time to apply a consequence I mentioned in Chapter 3 that I told you to not get good at using: punishment. But first, let's discuss how to use feedback to improve behavior.

Do you remember that consequences follow behaviors? If you have to deal with a disengaged employee, don't talk in terms of attitudes—or labels. Refer to behaviors.

Now it's time to deliver some employee feedback in Table 10-3. I want to use the behavior of a disengaged employee for this example, but the steps are equally effective when dealing with problem or poor performance. But do you remember the importance of focusing on the positive? Even if you strongly believe your employee is hopelessly disengaged, give

---

CONVERTING LABELS INTO BEHAVIORS

Effective feedback is based on observable and objective data, not opinions and interpretations. Look at the Label column in Table 10-2 that reflects comments people frequently make about poor performers at work. Then find the corresponding "Behavior" to get an idea of how to find the best descriptive phrase to use when delivering feedback.

TOOLS

Label	Behavior
Lazy	Takes longer to perform a similar task or assignment; Accomplishes less than others in similar roles
Disorganized	Prioritizes insignificant tasks at the expense of accomplishing most urgent tasks; Delivers past the due date
Disrespectful	Continues talking to others even after the start of meetings; Interrupts others when they are speaking
Unmotivated	Comes in late and leaves early even during crunch time; Delivers subpar quality on projects requiring a high attention to detail
Bad attitude	Frowns when given an assignment; complains to coworkers; talks about the company, the leaders, and coworkers in a way that could harm the business; rolls eyes; shrugs when asked questions; glares at coworkers or boss; initiates conversations on how "broken" or "flawed" the company or its employees are

Table 10-2. Converting labels into behaviors

Feedback Step	Sample Conversation
Offer sincere empathy (Demonstrate that you understand what might be causing the behavior)	I know our team is smaller than it was a year ago, and we all miss our friends who were let go. And I know quite well that we are all being asked to do more work than ever …
Description of problem (Instead of blaming or labeling, describe the situation as you see it)	I couldn't help overhear you at the staff meeting this week say "good luck" under your breath when I asked for a volunteer to head up this new project.
Description of positive (Describe what you want to see in the future)	Next time I update the team on the direction and work ahead of us as a division, I would appreciate it if you can keep any negative comments to yourself. But more than that—let me ask you as someone who's been here for as long as you have—what can you say to demonstrate your support?
Rationale of positive (Describe how making that positive change will give some WIIFM for your employee)	When you do that, you show me and others that you're excited to be here and part of the team. Your positive statements in our public meetings and even your private conversations demonstrate that you want to be here.
Provide a practice (Whenever possible, set the employees up to do better during the near future)	I have another meeting next Tuesday. And as you might guess, I have another new project that I'd like someone to head. Let's pretend we're in the meeting now. And I'm saying, "I have another project that needs a volunteer. Any takers?" Okay, what are you going to say? What are you going to do?

Table 10-3. Employee feedback

it one more chance. Look at the feedback steps and the feedback conversation below. Note that this is designed to be a dialogue, not a management monologue.

Theory X managers believe their employees will perpetually choose wrong when given an option. Theory Y managers believe that employees want to do their best. Split the difference. When an employee demonstrates a poor attitude by practicing disengaged behaviors, you have to step in.

- It lays out your expectations and calls the employee on unacceptable behavior.
- It suggests some sort of consequence for future unacceptable behavior.
- If unacceptable behavior stops, you have an opportunity to provide positive reinforcement to that employee—a consequence that produces happiness.
- If the unacceptable behavior stops, your team will be happier.

TRICKS OF THE TRADE

A Lesson from Parenting

In the often-referred-to book, *Parenting the Strong Willed Child*, the authors Rex Forehand, Ph.D., and Nicholas Long, Ph.D., state that when you want to eliminate negative behavior in a "difficult" child, you often start from a place of complete exasperation wherein it's difficult to find the positive. They suggest a method that involves observing a child's actions and commenting on them neutrally—a process they call "attending"—as a means of showing that you're paying attention to something other than the child's negative behaviors. Then, replace this language over time with praise when he or she is caught in the act of behaving well. By focusing on the positive, the child's behavior improves (New York: McGraw-Hill, 2002).

As adults, we can learn from this simple behavioral lesson. When dealing with a difficult employee, focus on your employee's positive actions whenever possible. If you find you're spending more time and energy on corrective action, shift the balance of your communications so that you can issue more praise when things go well. Issue punishment as a last resort.

What if that approach doesn't work and the negative behavior continues? Now it's time for stronger feedback that involves giving your employee something he or she doesn't want: the promise of future punishment. This is why I call this *the feedback of last resort*. Think of your role like a surgeon who removes cancerous cells. You have the responsibility to the rest of your employees to keep the toxin of disengagement from spreading throughout your unit.

Unlike the other feedback conversation that's intended to be a dialogue, the feedback conversation in Table 10-4 is more in line with a monologue where you clearly lay out your case.

Ironically, even though this is a tough conversation, the power remains with the employee. Your currently disengaged employee gets to

Feedback Step	Sample Conversation
Description of problem (Instead of blaming or labeling, describe the situation as you see it)	We've talked about the comments you made at the last meeting. Since that time, it's continued. At the last meeting, you rolled your eyes several times while I was talking and you grunted when Bill offered to head up the research for the new project.
Consequence (Describe why this behavior is a problem)	That kind of behavior does not show respect to members of the team, and it tears down morale.
Specific consequence (Describe how this behavior is a problem for the employee)	At this point, I'm at a loss. Your behavior creates a problem for me, the team, and now for you, too. I've talked to you about it, and it hasn't improved. I'm not able to partner you with other team members because I don't want your attitude to rub off on them. And since we function as a team and not a group of individuals, I don't know that you fit on this team any longer.
Description of positive (Describe what you want to see in the future)	I need your commitment to this team and every member on it. I need the negative comments to stop. I need your face to remain neutral at least instead of shrugging and rolling your eyes.
Rationale of positive (Describe how making that positive change will give some WIIFM for your employee)	If those behaviors stop, you'll be showing me that you might be able to make it on this team. If you build up the team by making positive comments and contributions, or offer some encouragement, you show me that you want to be here.
Determine employee's commitment (Ask the employee to tell you how it's going to play out)	The ball is in your court. If you value this job, I've laid out what needs to stop and what needs to start. If you don't want to be here, let's talk about that, too. I need to hear from you. What are you going to do?

Table 10-4. Last-resort feedback

CAUTION

BUILD TRUST EVEN NOW!

Trust is built when you pair an antecedent (what you say will happen) with a consequence (making sure what you say will happen *will happen*). For that reason, I strongly advise you to talk with your human resource department or senior leadership before entering into this conversation. Since it involves a threat you intend to follow through with if necessary, it's essential that you have corporate backing. Otherwise, you lose credibility by looking powerless.

tell you what he or she is willing to say, willing to do, and willing to change.

Does it work? Yes. I've had to use this kind of feedback with a couple of disengaged employees before. In one case, the employee flat-out told me that she didn't want to be in her role, and she wanted to leave my department. I helped her find another job more suited to her skills and interests, while I cautioned her that it was her disengagement behaviors and not her work results that would be her undoing.

I have to say that I didn't feel good about that outcome. Why? I believed that I practiced *ownership* at work, and I felt like I had done the company—my company—no favors by passing that employee on within the same company. I felt like if the company were my horse barn, all I had done was shoveled crap out of one stall and threw it over the wall to the next. I didn't remove the problem, I just moved it. It would still be there later, and my horse barn would still contain the same amount of crap it did when I started.

The next time I had to have that conversation, I did better. The employee answered my question of "What are you going to do?" by responding that she wanted to take another job at the same level but in another department within the company. In fact, she had seen this coming, so she had already found the job and applied for it. She told me that the job was hers if I would sign off on it.

I declined. And here's the gist of what I told her:

I believe in you. I've seen you at your best, and you're as good or better than anyone else. But you've gotten yourself in a place of poor performance. And that can't fly. I won't sign your transfer. I'm sure you'd be successful and maybe even feel happier in that job. And I'm not going to lie; it would make my job easier if I didn't have to have

---

ARE YOU WILLING?

TRICKS OF THE TRADE

My friend Marlene Chism, speaker and author of *Stop Workplace Drama*, suggests through her "release resistance" coaching for eliminating workplace drama that you ask, "Are you willing …?" in regard to a desired change. It may be a question you first ask yourself, such as, "Are you willing to confront the employee (or even boss) you struggle to communicate with?" Or it may be a question you ask of your employee, such as "Are you willing to do what it takes to make this job work for you?" or "Are you willing to communicate more positively in meetings?" This question cuts to the chase and requires a commitment from the other person (or yourself) to follow through.

---

another meeting like this with you ever again. But I'm afraid that if you don't resolve this issue now, it's going to follow you wherever you go, and you're going to do the same thing when you get unhappy in that job. So stay here and fix it first. Once you do, I'll sign off on your transfer. I don't ever want you to look back with regret that your solution to a bad situation was to run away instead of fixing it.

I had a great relationship with this employee, and what I told her was true. I did believe in her, and I didn't want her to run away from her problem. And if she couldn't fix it, I didn't want the cancer to spread elsewhere in the company. So I held her hostage by letting her know that she could keep going and change nothing—until I had to fire her, or she could improve her performance.

She fixed the problem. She ended up staying with me for another 18 months, during which time she found reasons to engage and recommit, and she delivered her best, most consistent performance ever. When she did finally leave to take another job, it was a promotion, one that she had earned.

Years later, she told me something that made my day—maybe my whole month. She said, "Thanks for not giving up on me."

Not all employees have that same level of awareness. And not all of them can tell you with any sort of certainty what they want and what they're willing to do when they're on the spot. But do you know how you can find out their answer? Watch their behavior. People do what they do because they get what they want when they do it. If your employee wants to stay, you'll see performance levels transform. And then you should see engagement levels increase, too. On the other hand, if the behavior doesn't change, the employee has just told you that he or she wants to leave.

Do you know one way to tell that you care about your employees? When you have to discipline one of them, perhaps even fire one, it grieves you. It's a similar feeling you get when you have to chastise your child by taking away something she wants or giving him something he doesn't want, like a time-out. When an employee needs to go, it should feel like a personal failure on your part. It means that you failed to make a difference. Now I don't say this so you'll beat yourself up or feel bad; but I want you to understand that the only reason you would go through such a process is that you care about the whole of your team more than you can care for any single employee.

When you've tried coaching, multiple feedback sessions, training, retraining, and mentoring, yet see no improvement, you have no choice but to follow the path of corrected action until the disengaged employee improves or is no longer able to tear down the engagement of others. Leaders, you have the power to engage 99 percent of your employees; but you can't save them all. Some don't want to be saved. So remove those who are unable to become anything other than disengaged and focus your energy on those who are the most engaged. After all, they are the ones who keep your business afloat.

In Conclusion: Starting the Dance

The world has changed, and whereas satisfaction used to suffice at work, it's no longer enough. I started the book with the metaphor of the steam engine that ran on shovels full of employees to pick up steam. Those days are gone. Employees remain the source of fuel, but they aren't a limitless resource. And they can't be flung on the fire and consumed, used like a tissue, and then discarded.

Engagement is a dance. Employees want to attend, and they want to be part of something special. So what's your role, leader? You have to set the environment. Maybe you have to convert the gym into a dance hall. Yes, it's still a gym, but you have the power to transform the environment, just like the sun and the rain have the power to convert dried up twigs into a garden exploding with life each spring. And you have to learn to dance. Engaged leaders can't point others to where they themselves are unwilling or unable to go. You have to invite others to the dance. Great food and music won't matter if you're the only one in the room. Finally, once others show up, you have to make them glad they came.

When you make employee engagement a priority, the first employees to benefit are those who were already engaged. For them, it's like "Hey, I was already at the dance. But it's nice to see a new face. You're my manager, right? I've seen you before."

Others will soon follow. Fun generates fun. There's an adage in sales that says, "The best time to make your next sale is right after you close your last sale." Excitement creates excitement, and confidence creates more confidence. We all want to be insiders. Even those employees who are currently disengaged or not actively engaged want to be part of a winning team. When they feel the engagement rising, they will want it for themselves, too. Many of them will show up at the dance, maybe just to check things out. They may sit in the shadows, maybe even making fun of those who are lost in the music. It doesn't happen with everyone, but over time, most will start to tap their feet in tune with the rhythm. And do you know what's the best feeling? When you see the last person you ever expected to show up not only attend the dance, but finally join the dance floor and start swaying with the music.

Are you ready to dance?

Manager's Checklist for Chapter 10

☑ All work environments are "special"—requiring a slightly customized engagement approach.

☑ Make it your job to find out your boss's priorities and goals.

☑ When you're the "new boss," let your employees know two things that you expect.

☑ Change can frustrate employees because they don't immediately know how to be successful in their new world.

☑ When you value and respect your employees, they'll want to be on your team because they know that you're on their side.

☑ While not every employee is able or willing to be engaged, 99 percent of your employees are just waiting for you to ask them to the dance!

Index

A

ABC model
   antecedents in, 58–62, 63
   consequences in, 63–72
   fostering trust with, 72–73
   overview, 57–58
Absenteeism, 15
Action orientation, 129–130
Active extinction, 68
Active listening, 200–201
Actively disengaged employees, 12,
   13. *See also* Disengaged
   employees
Affirmation, 102–103
Alexander, Scott, 128
Aluminum foil joke, 228
Amygdala, 106
Anger, 70–71
Antecedents, 58–62, 63, 72
Anthrax scare, 147
Attorneys, 93
Attrition. *See* Turnover
Authentic communication, 129, 130
Authoritarian managers, 31–32, 34
Autonomy, 123–124, 130–131

B

Baby picture guessing game, 175
Bad bosses, 29–30
Behavior modification
   antecedents in, 58–62, 63
   consequences in, 63–72

fostering trust with, 72–73
negative reinforcement, 76–77
overview, 57–58
positive reinforcement, 74–76,
   78–84, 246
Behaviors, labeling, 252
Best friends at workplace, 173–177
Bezos, Jeff, 118, 121
Blood flow, humor and, 212
Body language, 183
Book exchanges, 176
Brain function, humor and, 212–214
Brainstorming sessions, 176
Branding values, 141–144
British Columbia Hydro, 231
Brown-bag lunches, 175
Bruce, Anne, 105, 123
Bruno effect, 8–10
Bulletin boards, humorous, 228
Bureaucracy, 113–114

C

Can-do words, 102
Caring managers, 39, 258
Carlson, Keith, 213
Carrot and stick metaphor, 57
Catch Phrase game, 176
Certainty of consequences, 66
Change
   as engagement barrier, 240–246
   explaining, 199–200
Charitable services, 152–155

Checklists, 62, 82
Children, correcting, 254
Chism, Marlene, 95, 242, 257
Chouinard, Yvon, 116, 141, 143
Circulation, humor and, 212
Clay alligator example, 176–177
Clinton, Bill, 47, 183–184
C.O.A.C.H. Guidelines, 74–76
Coca-Cola Company, 231
Commitment, 127–128
Communication
   authentic, 129, 130
   costs to firms, 193–195
   effective, 181–185
   engagement-building tips,
     195–203
   importance, 181
   improving, 203–204
   obstacles, 187–193
   with remote workers, 249–251
   in response to change, 246
   three I's, 185–187
Companies, benefits of engagement
   to, 14–17
Compensation, 21–22, 192–193
Complaints, 104, 241–242
Complexity, providing for employees, 131
Concentration camps, humor in,
   218–219
Consequences
   in behavior modification, 59
   carrot and stick metaphor, 57
   for disengaged employees,
     252–258
   effectiveness, 64–67
   examples, 63–64, 72–73
   harmful to engagement, 67–71
   negative reinforcement, 76–77
   positive reinforcement, 74–76,
     78–84
Consistent reinforcement, 75
Control, granting to employees,
   123–124

Convergent thinking, 115–116
Coors Brewing Company, 231
Core values. *See* Values
Corporate politics, 113–114
Corporations, early metaphors, 2
Correction. *See also* Consequences
   administering, 38, 75
   humor versus, 221–222
Cortisol, 91
Counseling experiences of author,
   54–55
C.O.U.R.S.E. model, 115–123
Creativity
   in communications, 250
   of entrepreneurs, 115–117
   fostering, 129
Crisis intervention counseling,
   54–55
Criticism, 186. *See also* Complaints;
   Consequences
Cross-department training, 48–49
Csikszentmihalyi, Mihaly, 158
Cultural Dimensions Theory, 223
Culver's restaurants, 140
Customer loyalty, 15, 17
Customer retention, 19

D
Dance metaphor, 51–52, 258–259
Deming, W. Edwards, 60
Dialogs, 61
Discretionary effort
   Bruno effect, 8–10
   hiring for, 35
   positive reinforcement, 78–84
Disengaged employees. *See also*
   Engagement
   costs to firms, 15–16, 24–25
   identifying, 12, 13
   obstacles to engaging, 251–258
   reasons for, 22–23
Divergent thinking, 116
Do-It-yourself training, 48
Dole, Bob, 183

E

Economic downturn, 5–6

E-mail communications

  costs to firms, 194

  errors, 187–188

  fun with, 227

Emergency room humor, 218

Emotions with change, 244–245

Employee Bingo, 176, 177

Employee loyalty, 43–44, 134

Employee satisfaction, 2–6

Employee turnover. *See* Turnover

Empowerment, 37, 124, 126–129

Endorphins, 212

Engagement. *See also* Disengaged

  employees

  benefits to firms, 14–17, 24

  elements of, 7–8

  goals of, 235–236

  harmful consequences for, 67–71

  hiring for, 35

  humor and, 214–217

  importance of training to, 48–49

  leadership tips, 37–41

  myths, 17–22, 24

  positive reinforcement and, 78,
    82, 83

  as relationship building, 39,
    49–52

  relation to mission, 146

  of remote workers, 249–251

  research findings, 10–13

  satisfaction versus, 6

  through social service, 152–155

  understanding employee motiva-
    tions, 55–57

  W.H.I.P. model, 42

Engagement barriers

  bosses as, 236–240

  change, 240–246

  for remote workers, 249–251

  strongly disengaged workers,
    251–258

  unique business environments,
    246–249

Engagement Wheel, 36

Engaging up, 238–239

Entertainment, negative influences

  in, 104

Entrepreneurs

  advantages, 115

  engagement of, 124–125

  fostering in workplace, 129–134

  traits, 115–123

Exercise

  for positive thinking, 100–101

  for relationship building,
    230–231, 232

Expectations, defining, 60–62, 242

Extinction, 67–70, 240

F

Facial expressions, 192

Favoritism, avoiding, 200

Favors, asking others for, 204

Fear of change, 244–245

FedEx, 152

Feedback

  for disengaged employees,
    252–258

  facilitating, 62

  seeking from others, 51, 203–204

Ferguson, Marilyn, 245

Fight-Flight Reflex, 91, 106–107

Firms, benefits of engagement to,
  14–17

First, Break All the Rules (Buckingham and Coffman), 11

First impressions of employees, 242

Fitness, 100–101, 230–231, 232

Flexibility, 133–134

Flooding, 106

Flourishing, 235–236

Flow, 158, 159, 160

Franklin, Benjamin, 204

Frankl, Viktor, 119

Fredrickson, Barbara, 92

Friendships at workplace, 173–177
Friends, optimistic, 101–102, 104
Frustration, 62, 69
Fulfillment, as management goal, 5
Fun, 210. *See also* Humor
Funeral illustration, 242–243

G

Gallup survey on employee
    engagement, 10–13
Games, 176
Ghoshal, Sumantra, 38
Gino's East, 85–87
Glenn, Sam, 36, 102, 225
Goals
    aligning personal with organiza-
        tional, 136–137, 177–179
    aligning with values, 145–147
    communicating, 199
    employees aligned with, 151–152,
        237–238
    of engagement, 235–236
    universal, 140–141
Godfrey, Jocelyn, 95, 179
Good Humor Index, 215–216,
    222–223
Google, 117, 129, 217
Gossip, 38
Grant, Ken, 223–224, 248–249
Gratitude, practicing, 99–100, 240
Group home experiences, 54–55
Guyer, Britt, 112–113

H

Habitual reinforcement, 75–76
Happiness, 83, 209–210. *See also*
    Humor
Harassment, avoiding, 225
Health
    fitness promotion, 230–231, 232
    humor and, 211–214
    optimism and, 91, 100–101
Heart attacks, 215
Help, asking others for, 204
Hipps, Patricia, 26

Hiring for attitude, 35, 228
Holocaust, humor in, 218–219
Honesty about change, 244–245
Hope, fostering, 46–48, 246
Hsieh, Tony, 217
The Human Side of Enterprise
    (McGregor), 30–31
Humor
    in difficult times, 217–219
    engagement and, 214–217
    importance, 208–209
    inappropriate, 225–226
    positive thinking through, 101,
        102
    promoting in workplace, 226–230
    reasons given for avoiding,
        222–225
    research findings, 211–214
    to strengthen relationships,
        219–222

I

Immediacy of consequences, 66
Important versus urgent tasks, 237
Inappropriate humor, 225–226
Influence, communicating for, 186
Information, communicating for, 185
Innovation, 15
Insiders, creating, 198
Inspirational communication,
    186–187
Intensity of consequences, 65–66
Interest, demonstrating, 201
Interest inventories, 164, 165
Internal experts, 48–49
Internal locus of control, 122–123
Internal training, 49
Interviewing for engagement, 35
Intrapreneurs, 115, 124
Investment in employees, 50

J

Jacobellis v. Ohio decision, 14
Japanese soap company example,
    117

Jelly bean jar, 83
Job-hopping, 20–21
Job title changes, 245
Jokes, 228
Journaling, 95

K
Kindle, 121

L
Labeling behaviors, 252
Laughter, 211–212, 219–220,
    229–230
Lawyers, 93
Layoffs, 5–6. *See also* Change;
    Turnover
Leadership
    engagement tips, 37–41
    fostering trust, loyalty, and hope,
        42–48
    handling changes in, 241–243
    management versus, 27–28, 29
    modeling engagement in, 36, 40,
        42, 89
    negative examples, 29–30
    relationship building in, 34, 39,
        49–52, 157, 161–166
    servant approach, 248–249
    shortcomings leading to
        turnover, 22–23
    Theory X and Theory Y, 30–34
Learned helplessness, 69
Learners, managers as, 41
Learning libraries, 49
Learning Management Systems, 49
Learning maps, 144
Let My People Go Surfing
    (Chouinard), 143
Life Board of Directors, 105–106
Listening, 200–201
Locus of control, 122–123
Long-term relationships, 127–129
Losada, Marcial, 78
Losada Line, 78–79, 81–82, 171–172,
    246

Loyalty
    customer, 15, 17
    employee, 43–44, 134

M
Management
    engagement tips, 37–41
    importance of training to, 48–49
    leadership versus, 27–28, 29
    negative examples, 29–30
    outdated models, 27–28, 29
    relationship building in, 34, 39,
        49–52
    shortcomings leading to
        turnover, 22–23
    Theory X and Theory Y, 30–34
Managing up, 238
Mantras, 102–103
Marathon Margin, 95
Marlotti, Joe, 221
McGregor, Douglas, 30
McKinley, Doug, 36
Mehrabian, Albert, 183
Mementos, 105, 160
Memory, humor and, 213–214
Mentoring for communications, 189
MetLife 9th Annual Study of
    Employee Benefits Trends, 5, 6
Meville, 191–192
Military leadership, 248–249
Mission statements
    defined, 139
    effective, 139, 140
    employees aligned with, 148–149
    employees out of alignment with,
        150–151
    universal principles in, 140–141
Mistakes, correcting, 38
Money, engagement and, 21–22
Motivation, 54–57
Mr. Potato Head stickers, 83, 229
Music, negative influences in, 104

N
Name That Tune game, 227

Negative campaigning, 46
Negative reinforcement, 76–77
Negativity, avoiding, 103–108
News stories, negative, 104–105
Nondisclosure agreements, 198–199
Nonverbal communication, 182,
    183–184, 192, 250
Not engaged employees, 12, 13. *See
    also* Disengaged employees

O
Obama, Barack, 47
Objective reinforcement, 75
Objectives. *See* Goals
Obscenity, avoiding, 225–226
Observing employees, 163
Occupy Wall Street, 45
The Office, 166
Office politics, 113–114
Open-ended questions, 201
Openness in communication,
    198–200
Optimism and health, 91
Optimism of entrepreneurs, 117–119
Optimistic leaders, 42–43. *See also*
    Positive workplace cultures
Options defined, 119
Ownership attitude, 114, 126–129

P
Pajama days, 226
Parenting the Strong Willed Child
    (Forehand and Long), 254
Participative managers, 31, 32–33,
    34
Passion
    assessing, 161, 163–166
    entrepreneurial, 121–122
    impact on performance, 158–160
    tapping into, 162–163, 168–171
Passive extinction, 68
Patagonia, 116, 143
PeopleNRG, 243
Performance appraisals, 167, 237
Personal humor, 225

Personal Interest Inventory, 164, 165
Photo scavenger hunts, 227
Photos, sharing, 226–227
Physical activity, 230–231, 232
Playing favorites, 200
Political campaigns, 46–47
Politics, avoiding, 226
Polsky, Lawrence, 130, 243
Polyannas, 91
Pornography, 14
Positive affirmations, 102–103
Positive psychology, 167
Positive reinforcement
    basic principles, 74–76
    ideas for using, 78–84
    in response to change, 246
Positive thinking
    activities to develop, 99–103
    benefits to firms, 91–93
    defined, 90
    demonstrating, 96–98
    developing habit of, 93–96
    impact on workplace environ-
        ments, 108–110
    promoting, 129
    protecting habit of, 104–108
    self-assessment, 98–99
Positive workplace cultures
    achieving, 108–110
    impact on outcomes, 90–93
    importance, 88–89
Positivity
    acquiring, 93–96
    creative approaches, 250
    responding to change with,
        244–245
Potlucks, 175
Practical jokes, 228
Pragmatism, 91
Praise
    building trust with, 73
    facilitating, 62
    promoting engagement with,
        37–38, 84, 172, 241

Preferences, 161–166
Processes, changes in, 243–246
Productivity
impact of employee engagement, 15
impact of employee turnover, 19
impact of positivity, 92–93
Profanity, avoiding, 225–226
Professional Preference and Passion Inventory, 161
Profits, engagement and, 15
Progress, recognizing, 132–133
PSST acronym, 157, 158
Public sector workplaces, 246–247
Punishment
appropriate uses, 71–72, 254–256
defined, 69
impact on engagement, 67, 69–71
negative reinforcement from, 77
timing, 75
Pygmalion Effect, 108–110, 247

Q
Q12 Index, 10, 11, 173

R
Reagan, Ronald, 46–47, 222
Realism of entrepreneurs, 120–121
Recognition, 39–40, 132–133. *See also* Praise
Reinforcement
negative, 76–77
positive, 74–76, 78–84, 246
Relationships
building with employees, 34, 39, 49–52, 157, 161–166
communication in, 184–185
fostering long-term, 127–129
friendships at workplace, 173–177
negative influences in, 104, 105
strengthening through humor, 219–222
Remote workers, 249–251

Renting versus owning, 126
Replacement costs, 19
Reponsibility, modeling acceptance, 39
Reputation, 221
Resilience, 119–120
Rewards, training as, 49
Roadblocks to communication, 187–193
Role models, managers as, 36, 40, 42, 89
Roles, assigning in communications, 202–203
Root Learning, 144
R.O.T.E. jobs, 132

S
Sales, 118, 121–122
Sanders, L. H., 28
Sarcasm, 104
Satiation, 81
Satisfaction, shortcomings of, 2–6
Scavenger hunts, 227
Scheduled communications, 249–250
Scripting, 100
Self-assessment, 98–99
Self-centered communications, 191–192
Self-fulfilling prophecy, 94–95, 118
Seligman, Martin, 167
Sense of humor, modeling, 101, 222–223, 227–228
Servant leadership, 248–249
Sick time, impact of engagement on, 15
Smile sheets, 213
Smith, Greg, 23
Snooze buttons, 10
Soap company example, 117
Social media, 16, 24
Social reinforcement, 81
Social relationships. *See* Relationships

Social service, 152–155
Southwest Airlines, 224
Special business environments, 246–249
Spectator-free workplaces, 50
Speeches, humor in, 213
Spiritus Communications, 142
Staff cuts, 5–6. *See also* Change; Turnover
Standards, changes in, 243–246
Stanley Cup, 81
Starbucks, 145
St. Baldrick's Foundation, 153
Steam locomotive illustration, 1–2
Stewart, Potter, 14
S.T.O.P. method, 106–107
Stop signs, 63
Storytelling, 142–144, 165, 195–198
Strengths (employee)
    assessing, 169, 170, 174
    focus on building, 171–173
    tapping into, 167–171
Strengths Questionnaire, 169, 170
Stress, humor and, 217–219
Strong-willed children, 254
Success, visualizing, 100
Suck-ups, 238
Supreme Court pornography ruling, 14
Survey data on employee engagement, 10–13
Survival skills, humor as, 217–219
Sustainability of employee satisfaction, 4–6

T
Tangible reinforcements, 79–81
Taylor, Stephen, 37
Teaching-Family Homes of Upper Michigan, 54
Television programs, 104
Terrorism scare, 147
Testing employees, 163–164
Testing for understanding, 61

Theory X and Theory Y management, 30–34
Threats, 70, 256
Three I's of communication, 185–187
Tom Sawyer, 219
Toronto wellness program, 231
Training benefits, 48–49
Training evaluations, 213
Transference, 201
Transparent communications, 198–200
Trust, fostering, 44–46, 72–73, 256
Turnover
    costs to firms, 19–20
    fear of, 134
    impact of engagement, 14–15, 18
    myths, 20–22
    reasons for, 22–23, 29–30
Two-way communication, 201–203, 242

U
Understanding, testing for, 61
Unengageable workers, 251–258. *See also* Disengaged employees
Unintentional communication, 182–183
Union shops, 246–247
Unique business environments, 246–249
Urgent versus important tasks, 237

V
Values
    adopting from employees, 152–155
    aligning personal with organizational, 136–137
    aligning with goals, 145–147
    branding, 141–144
    employees aligned with, 148–149
    employees out of alignment with, 150–151
    importance, 137–140

universal, 140–141
Video production example, 206–209
Visualizing success, 100

W
Walmart mission statement, 142
"We are the 99%," 45
Well-being defined, 210
Wellness promotion, 230–231, 232
W.H.I.P. model, 42

Whiteboards, 175
White elephant gift exchanges, 176
Why Am I Here? questions, 151
Willingness to change, 257
Work hours, flexible, 133–134
Wortmann, Craig, 101–102, 165
Wrzesniewski, Amy, 158

Z
Zappos, 141–142, 217

About the Author

As a corporate leader, Scott Carbonara guided a staff of 13,000+ through extensive changes and mergers and solved complex employee engagement issues that resulted in converting a dismal attrition rate of 38 percent, to a phenomenal 6.5 percent. He also launched internal communications campaigns that not only dramatically improved the corporate culture but were also used with external customers to foster greater loyalty. He has served as executive director of strategic communications, chief of staff of internal operations, and key liaison for stakeholders in the largest non-investor-owned health insurance company in the world—overseeing Blue Cross Blue Shield of Illinois, Texas, Oklahoma, and New Mexico.

Prior to that, as a therapist, Scott directed a group home for at-risk youth, and later served as a crisis intervention counselor for their families. In that role, through often traumatic circumstances, he learned how to listen authentically, think on his feet, and find and apply simple solutions to complex human problems. His unique approach in this role resulted in a Family Therapist of the Year award from the State of Michigan.

Today as The Leadership Therapist, Scott Carbonara combines his dual background in working with people and applies it as a keynote speaker, trainer, consultant, and executive coach. He seeks to "bring authentic leadership to life, from the boardroom to the family room," as he nurtures, inspires, and trains leaders of all types, including C-suite executives, leaders, managers, employees, and individuals seeking to lead more authentically and effectively. Scott's presentation and coaching style is dynamic, humorous, skills-based, approachable, and highly effective—covering positive and practical leadership topics that lead to a more inspired workforce and bottom-line results. He specializes in leadership topics pertaining to employee and customer engagement, change management, and creating positive cultures.

Scott is also the author of several other leadership books and training programs including *Go Positive: Lead to Engage* (Pfeiffer), *Firsthand Lessons, Secondhand Dogs*, and *Don't Throw Underwear on the Table and Other Lessons Learned at Work*. He has also written into several best-selling HR and inspirational books. Scott serves as CEO of Spiritus Communications Inc., a management and marketing consulting firm for leaders and entrepreneurs (www.spirituscommunications.com).

You can learn about Scott's topics and read his blog at www.Leader shipTherapist.com or connect with him at the following sources: www.Twitter.com/ScottCarbonara and www.Facebook.com/Leader shipTherapist. To contact Scott directly, e-mail him at Scott@Leader shipTherapist.com. In his spare time, he enjoys hiking, biking, and spending time with his wife, four kids, four cats, and one lone dog.